A NATURALIST'S GUIDE TO THE

BIRDS
OF
BORNEO

Sabah, Sarawak, Brunei and Kalimantan

Wong Tsu Shi

JOHN BEAUFOY PUBLISHING

This edition published in the United Kingdom in 2023 by John Beaufoy Publishing Ltd
11 Blenheim Court, 316 Woodstock Road, Oxford OX2 7NS, England
www.johnbeaufoy.com

10 9 8 7 6 5 4 3 2 1

Photo Captions
Front Cover: *Main image* Blue-banded Pitta; *bottom left* Bornean Banded Pitta, *bottom centre* Chestnut-hooded
Laughingthrush, *bottom right* Bristlehead. **Back cover:** Sabah Partridge. **Title page:** Blue-headed Pitta, female.
Contents: Scarlet-breasted Flowerpecker.

ISBN 978-1-913679-44-6

Designed by Gulmohur

Printed and bound in Malaysia by Times Offset (M) Sdn. Bhd.

·CONTENTS·

■ Geography and Climate ■

Acknowledgements

My thanks to Clive Mann, who generously allowed me to quote, extract and refer to his *The Birds of Borneo: An Annotated Checklist* (2008); to Quentin Phillipps, for his guidance and unselfish share of knowledge; to John Beaufoy, my publisher; to Rosemary Wilkinson, for coordinating; and to Kong Ket Leong, Ku Kok On and Stanley T Shao, who accompanied me on numerous expeditions to capture bird images that are included in this book.

Geography and Climate

Borneo is the third largest island in the world (approximately 743,380sq km), and lies on the Sunda Shelf between 108°00'E and 119°00'E, and 07°40'N and 05°50'S. It is occupied by three different countries: the states of Sabah and Sarawak of Malaysia; the state of Kalimantan of Indonesia, itself divided into four provinces named Kalimantan Barat (West Kalimantan), Kalimantan Tengah (Central Kalimantan), Kalimantan Selatan (South Kalimantan) and Kalimantan Timur (East Kalimantan); and Negara Brunei Darussalam, the smallest of the three and the only country located entirely within Borneo.

Most of the coastal areas of Borneo are low-lying and relatively flat, with mountainous areas confined to the interior regions. The major mountains are concentrated in a central chain running down the middle of the island, from Gunung Kinabalu in Sabah in the northeast to Gunung Batu Tibang in Kalimantan in the southweswt, and throwing out several long spurs in all directions like the legs of a starfish along the way. Much of this chain is significantly higher than 1,500m above sea-level. The frequency of cloud cover above this altitude, and consequently the rainfall patterns, soil composition, temperature range and forest composition, have resulted in a significantly distinct avifauna composition in the highlands.

In Sabah in northern Borneo, the mountain chain is known as the Crocker Range, with Gunung Kinabalu (4,095m) forming a part of it. The western chain runs from Gunung Batu Tibang to Gunung Pueh in Sarawak, the eastern chain runs from Gunung Batu Tibang to the Sangkulirang Peninsula, the southwestern chain runs from the Kapuas–Mahakam divide to the Madi sandstone plateau, and the southeastern chain runs discontinuously from where the three great rivers of Kapuas, Barito and Mahakam diverge towards the Meratus Mountains.

Borneo's climate is equatorial, with high temperatures, humidity and rainfall. However, daily variations are the norm, with afternoon showers common. There is no distinct dry spell – rain is recorded in every month of the year, although certain months are wetter than others due to effects of the monsoons. Generally, the wettest months are during the northeast monsoon from October to March, with the heaviest rainfall between November and February. The southwest monsoon, from May to September, does not bring as much rain. However, the rainfall of a particular area is very much affected by local conditions, altitudes, windward or leeward location, and other factors, with some areas having their own characteristic microclimates. The annual rainfall pattern is becoming more unpredictable and is further compounded by the El Niño phenomenon, which affects the rainfall of Borneo cyclically approximately once every five years.

The central highland area around Kapit in Sarawak and adjacent areas in Kalimantan receive the island's highest annual rainfall and form its watershed, as almost all the major rivers in Borneo originate from here. Coastal Kalimantan Timur and Kalimantan Selatan, on the other hand, receive the least annual rainfall, but as with many other parts of the world, climate has become much more unpredictable.

VEGETATION

The plant life in Borneo is characterised by high species diversity and low endemism. The natural vegetation over most of the island consists of evergreen rainforest of various types. The forest type of a place is determined by its soil characteristics and rainfall.

Generally, most of the coast is fringed by swamps of mangrove and Nipah *Nypa fruticans*. Lowland and hill forests up to about 1,200m in altitude are dominated by trees of the family Dipterocarpaceae. This family includes the most commercially valuable timber species. Many other types of tree also grow in this zone, as well as numerous woody climbing plants, flowering plants, and ferns that grow as epiphytes on the larger trees. Vegetation above 1,200m gradually transforms into montane forest.

The following classification, based on Mann (2008), concentrates on major vegetation types as habitat for birds:

Primary (Natural) Vegetation
- **Mangrove forests and swamps** – in estuaries, lagoons and other low-wave-energy coasts on most islands. Typical trees are those with breathing roots and a tolerance to salt water.
- **Beach/coastal vegetation** – on high-wave-energy coasts on most islands, where trees are not dominant but *Casuarina equisetifolia* occurs commonly with the screw pine *Pandanus odoratissimus*, palm *Oncosperma* and terrestrial creepers.
- **Coastal scrub forest** – on most islands, with *Casuarina* and palms, and dense undergrowth at the edge.
- **Kerangas** (an Iban word meaning an area where hill rice cannot grow) – a well-drained heath forest on coarse sandy podzolic soils. Usually comprises three storeys of trees, up to 10–25m tall, has a dense undergrowth and many climbers, but tree ferns and bamboos are absent.
- **Peat-swamp forest** – usually found in river valleys and estuaries, on completely waterlogged peaty soils. Comprises two to three storeys of trees up to 20–60m tall, plenty of undergrowth and many epiphytes, but no lianas, tree ferns or bamboos.
- **Riparian forest** – includes brackish-water forest, freshwater tidal forest, riverine forest and alluvial forest. These forests are usually flooded, seasonally or permanently. It comprises several storeys of trees reaching 30–50m in height, with poor undergrowth and no tree ferns or bamboo.
- **Lowland dipterocarp forest (rainforest)** – on well-drained loam at 0–50m above sea-level, dominated by members of the family Dipterocarpaceae. Consists of a ground layer and three storeys of trees, the highest at 30–50m.

- **Hill or upper dipterocarp/submontane forest** – usually at 500–1,200m above sea-level; similar in structure to lowland dipterocarp forest, but with trees reaching 20–30m.
- **Lower montane forest** – at 700–2,400m above sea-level, consisting of a ground layer with two storeys of trees reaching 20m.
- **Montane forest/moss forest** – at 1,300–4,000m above sea-level, consisting of a ground layer and one storey of trees reaching 10–15m. Rhododendrons, heathers, shrubs, hanging mosses and lichens are characteristic plant types.
- **Tropical alpine** – above 4,000m on Gunung Kinabalu only.
- **Grassland** – created mostly by repeated fire trauma of lowland forest and usually dominated by lalang (*Imperata cylindrica*); similar to the next category, but predominantly resulting from natural causes.

Secondary (Human-influenced) Vegetation
- **Grassland** – predominantly lalang (*Imperata cylindrica*), and the first succession stage resulting from swidden agriculture before secondary forests develops.
- **Grassland savannah** – may form on drier areas of low fertility after primary vegetation has been removed by man.
- **Secondary forest** – regenerates after swidden agriculture or logging have removed primary forest. Older forest trees may grow up to 20m, and some primary forest trees may remain, as after selective logging.
- **Agricultural land** – mostly paddy (rice) fields on alluvial and submontane land.
- **Plantation forests** – include *Albizia*, *Eucalyptus*, *Acacia* and old rubber (*Hevea brasiliensis*) trees, but exclude oil palms (*Elaeis guineensis*).

Brackish water swamp: habitat for rails, herons, egrets and wintering waders.

Vegetation on offshore islands: habitat for island specialists like some fruit doves and imperial pigeons.

Opportunities for Naturalists

Borneo is a large island whose vast tracts of wilderness are still relatively underbirded. Visiting and local birders tend to frequent a few well-known locations for exotics and endemics, and so many of the lesser known areas could harbour plenty of hidden jewels. The lack of visitor facilities in the remote interior compared to established locations means it is not particularly travel-friendly. Because of this, however, it could prove rewarding for endemics that are otherwise difficult to locate owing to habitat loss, for documenting new information regarding distribution of species that has not been noted previously, and for documenting local migration of species to a different altitude or forest type owing to changing circumstances.

Knowledge of bird species is still at its infancy in Borneo, and most ordinary folks will not pay much attention to any bird unless it is really exceptional looking or colourful. The Aleutian Tern *Sterna aleutica*, for example, must have been wintering in waters off the Greater Sundas for quite some time, and spotted regularly by fishermen during the winter months, but until recently remained undocumented.

As islands act as stop-overs for migratory birds, they can tell us a lot about the migration patterns of these species, as the timing of sightings could be used to determine the routes taken. Records from islands could also indicate any possible spread of new species, as any new birds that reach Bornean shores must have arrived by hopping from island to island.

With the increased interest in birdwatching in recent years, greater publicity has been accorded to birding island-wide as a step towards enhanced awareness of conservation efforts. The Sandakan Borneo Bird Club has run the annual Borneo Bird Festival in Sabah since 2008 and the Malaysian Nature Society organizes the Sarawak Bird Race.

The increasing population of local birdwatchers and photographers means there are more eyes looking at the birds, this has resulted in more observation and rare sighting reports which have tremendously augmented the local bird information database. The Sunda Teal *Anas gibberifrons*, for example, which previously had an uncertain status due to infrequent records, was photographed with ducklings in a disused prawn farming pond in Tawau, Sabah in early 2016, an area that is not a traditional birding site; the occurrence of Buff-banded Rail *Gallirallus philippensis* all over Borneo was also reported with digital images from S Sabah and Sarawak. Rainbow Bee-eater *Merops ornatus*, an Austral migrant, was first reported in 2010 from P. Maratua in E Kalimantan; the next sighting of this species from mainland Borneo should logically come from Kalimantan, but instead it came from the E coast of Sabah in 2016 and again in 2017.

Offshore islands are the front line for recording new species reaching Borneo, and rare migrants stopping over these islands are much easier to spot due to limited land area. One such recent record was a Willow Warbler *Phylloscopus trochilus* in Matananni island, a bird hitherto unknown in Borneo.

There is still much to record and document on Bornean avifauna. Information on distribution limits in relation to altitude and forest type, foraging behaviours, nesting habits and dates, migration dates and population size in specific locations are all valuable data that will aid future study and conservation.

PLACES TO GO

The major birding locations in Borneo are listed below with a brief description of selected sites, which are also shown on the map on the inside front cover. Further information on a particular location can be readily researched from the Internet.

Birding Sites in Sabah

Kinabalu Park Headquarters (06°09'N, 116°39'E) is the main birding site for montane birds in Borneo, with easy access by regular transport, and excellent trails and facilities. Since most Bornean endemic birds are montane, a visit to this park is a must. Target birds are Everett's Thrush, Bornean Partridge, Bloodhead and Whitehead's Trogon. **Mesilau Nature Resort** (05°59'N, 116°35'E) is a part of Kinabalu Park and, though lacking in good trails, is also good for montane endemics.

Danum Valley Conservation Area (04°49'N, 117°28'E–05°04'N, 117°49'E) has 438sq km of undisturbed, virgin lowland rainforest surrounded by 2,400sq km of logged forests, and has a canopy walkway at the luxurious lodge within. It is the place to see some of Borneo's most elusive birds, most of the pittas, pheasants and firebacks. The newest Bornean bird, Spectacled Flowerpecker, was photographed here on the canopy walkway.

Rain Forest Discovery Centre and forests around Sepilok (05°47'N, 117°55'E) has convenient transport and visitor facilities; it has a world-class canopy walkway to observe canopy birds at eye level. This is a good place for Bristlehead, pittas, kingfishers and trogons.

ABOVE: *Mount Kinabalu: World Heritage Site and a must-visit birding destination in Sabah.*
RIGHT: *The canopy bridge at Rain Forest Discovery Centre, Sepilok, is a rigid steel structure that is perfect for bird photography and digiscoping.*

Poring Hotspring (06°03'N, 116°42'E) is not far from Kinabalu Park, has a canopy walkway, and is a good spot for submontane birds, especially when the cinnamon trees in the park are fruiting. It is also the spot to look for Orange-breasted Trogon and the elusive, endemic Hose's Broadbill.

Rafflesia Forest Reserve (05°40'N, 116°20'E) is a highland forest reserve along the Kota Kinabalu–Tambunan road; it is good for montane endemics. When the trees are fruiting, birds like Whitehead's Broadbill, Fruit-hunter, Mountain Barbet and Bornean Barbet are easy targets.

Rafflesia Forest Reserve as viewed from Gunung Alab power station.

Areas along the **lower Kinabatangan River**, near the village of Sukau (5°30'N, 118°16'E). Many birds and mammals can be observed by cruising on the river, its tributaries and on the many nearby ox-bow lakes. Storm's Stork, Bornean Ground Cuckoo and all eight species of hornbill that occur in Borneo can be found here.

Tabin Wildlife Reserve (05°10'N, 118°30'E–05°15'N, 118°45'E) is an area twice the size of the Republic of Singapore comprising mostly secondary forests, which are not as dense as virgin forests; it is a good place for lowland forest birds including hornbills and pittas.

Tempasuk Plain (06°21'N, 116°27'E) and **Penampang Plain** (05°55'N, 116°07'E) are the rice bowl of Sabah. Low-lying and flat, their freshly ploughed fields during the northern winter months provide enormous foraging wetlands for migrating waders and waterbirds. Most of the waders that favour freshwater habitats during migration can be found here.

Tawau Hills Park (04°22'N, 117°47'E–04°31'N, 118°04'E) is an unlogged water catchment for the surrounding areas. G. Magdalena within the park reaches over 1,000m above sea level. Most of Borneo's lowland birds have been recorded here, but the thick forest cover and dense undergrowth do not make observation easy.

Maliau Basin Conservation Area (4°50'N 117°18'E) consists of both regenerating and unlogged lowland to sub-montane forests, with accommodation facilities and forest trails; has

An early morning cruise along Kinabatangan River near Sukau is usually the most rewarding excursion in terms of birds and mammals.

many rare birds including Bulwer's Pheasants, Bornean Crested Fireback, Bornean Ground Cuckoo, Bornean Banded Pitta, Blue-banded Pitta, Bristlehead, Blue-winged Leafbirds and Spectacled Flowerpecker.

Other Birding Sites in Sabah
Crocker Range National Park, Pulau Tiga National Park, Pulau Layang-Layang, Klias Wetlands, Mantanani Islands, Likas Bay and Likas Swamp, Tunku Abdul Rahman Marine Park, Tun Sakaran Marine Park and Gomantong Caves.

Birding Sites in Sarawak
Gunung Mulu National Park (04°02'N, 114°54'E) is the second largest park in Sarawak. Its famous caves almost guarantee the presence of Bat Hawk. Its bird list includes the elusive Hose's Broadbill, Bornean Oriole, Bulwer's Pheasant, all eight species of hornbill that occur in Borneo, plus most of the Bornean montane endemics at higher altitude.

Borneo Highlands Resort is located 850–1,300m above sea level on the Penrissen Range (01°20'N, 110°13'E), bordering Kalimantan. It is about an hour's drive from Kuching. It offers a mixture of submontane and montane species, and is one of the best places to see Blue-banded Pitta and Pygmy Heleia.

Buntal Bay (01°41'N, 110°22'E) is part of Bako-Buntal Bay IBA, and is located at the estuary of Sarawak River. It is a place for wintering waders and a breeding ground for Malaysian Plover. The first Bornean records of Pied Avocet, Eurasian Oystercatcher and White-faced Plover were from here.

Kubah National Park (01°35'N, 110°07'E) is 20km west of Kuching, and is easily accessible by road. It is made up of lowland rainforests and is a place for Rufous-backed Kingfisher, Blue-banded Pitta, Bornean Blue-flycatcher and Great Argus.

Chupak (01°14'N, 110°26'E) is an area of paddy fields, very much like Penampang and Tempasuk Plains in Sabah. It harbours waterbirds and waders that favour freshwater habitats during migration.

Semenggoh Nature Reserve (01°24'N, 110°18'E) is 30 minutes' drive from Kuching; it is an excellent location for lowland forest birds.

Maludam National Park (01°39'N, 111°02'E) is an area of logged peat-swamp forest that contains the largest single patch of peat-swamp forest remaining in Sarawak. Hook-billed Bulbul, Scarlet-breasted Flowerpecker and Brown-backed Flowerpecker can be found here.

Longan Bunut National Park (03°45'N, 114°16'E) contains Sarawak's largest freshwater lake, and is surrounded by peat-swamp and dipterocarp forests, suitable habitats for birds like Oriental Darter, Grey-headed Fish-eagle, Lesser Fish-eagle and Osprey. Roulroul, Great Argus and Hook-billed Bulbul have also been recorded in the Park.

Niah National Park (03°54'N, 113°41'E) consists of lowland dipterocarp forests. Its Niah limestone caves complex harbours swiftlets in the tens of thousands, the flocks made up of Edible-nest Swiftlet, Uniform Swiftlet and Black-nest Swiftlet.

Pulong Tau National Park (03°35'N, 115°22'E) is the largest park in Sarawak, and is located in Bario and the Kelabit Highlands. It has a wide altitude range and its bird list includes Bulwer's Pheasant, Black Partridge and most of the montane endemics of Borneo.

Other Birding Sites in Sarawak
Lambir Hill National Park, Similajau National Park, Bako National Park, Kuching Wetlands National Park, Ba' Kelalan, Long Banga and Long Lamai, Long Lellang and Talang-Satang National Park.

Birding Sites in Brunei Darussalam
Peradayan Forest Reserve (04°45'N, 115°09'E) is the most accessible rainforest in Brunei Darussalam. Most lowland species including hornbills can be found there.

Ulu Temburong National Park (04°27'N, 115°11'E) is regarded by many as the best preserved tropical rainforest in Borneo. It has 7km of elevated boardwalks, a canopy walkway and an observation tower. It is a good place for most primary lowland forest birds including seven species of Bornean hornbills.

Tasek Merimbun National Park (04°35'N, 114°41'E) contains the largest freshwater lake in the Sultanate; it is surrounded by peat-swamp forest. It is good for herons, Darter and lowland forest birds.

Wasan ricefields and swamps (04°47'N, 114°48'E), 45 minutes' drive from Bandar Seri Bagawan, has congregations of wintering waders and resident waterbirds. Lesser Adjutant and Straw-headed Bulbul can be found here.

Kuala Balai Road (04°27'N, 114°19'E) is flanked by forests that are populated with many lowland bird species, including woodpeckers, raptors, bulbuls, pigeons, hornbills and nightjars.

Other Birding Sites in Brunei Darussalam
Tasek Lama Park, Pulau, Selirong, Tutong Beach and Tutong Sewage Works, Sungai Liang Forest Park, Penaga, Badas Road, Labi Road, Bukit Teraja and Pelong Rocks.

Birding Sites in Kalimantan
Kayan Mentarang National Park (02°40'N, 115°45'E) borders Sabah and Sarawak. It is difficult to access, but could be the best site for montane Bornean endemics in Kalimantan. Its long bird list includes Bulwer's Pheasant, Bornean Peacock-pheasant, Whitehead's Trogon, Whitehead's Spiderhunter and Whitehead's Broadbill.

Mahakam River and Mahakam Lakes (00°16'S, 116°23'E). Mahakam River is the major waterway into the interior of Kalimantan from Samarinda. There are extensive swamps and mudflats at the river's delta, which is one the richest locations for waterbirds and migrating waders in Borneo. Further upstream there are thousands of square kilometres of seasonally flooded swamp forests, marshes and freshwater lakes that attract large numbers of waterbirds, including both northern and Austral winter visitors.

Sungai Wain Protection Forest (01°15'S, 116°50'E) is a small patch of lowland forest under the administration of the local government that is easily accessible from Balikpapan. This may be the easiest location to view Bornean Peacock-pheasant in Borneo. Other endemics are Bornean Ground Cuckoo, Bristlehead and Yellow-rumped Flowerpecker.

Tanjung Puting National Park (02°44'S, 111°54'E) comprises 50% peat-swamp forests, which are seasonally flooded, 40% kerangas and 10% grassland. Its bird list has 218 species, including pittas, frogmouths and Bristlehead.

Betung Kerihun National Park (00°40'N, 112°15'E–01°35'N, 114°10'E) borders Sarawak's Lanjak Entimau. It is little explored, hilly and mountainous, and has 300 species of birds recorded.

Barito Ulu Project Research Area (00°23'N, 114°08'E), located within the Heart of Borneo World Heritage Park, is the longest running forestry research programme in central Borneo. It combines rainforest management with research into improving methods for regenerating forest destroyed by commercial logging and traditional slash and burn farming. It has a long bird list that includes Black Partridge, Crestless Fireback, Bulwer's Pheasant and Bristlehead.

Gunung Niut (00°58'N, 110°10'E) is a remote montane forest on the same mountain range as Gunung Penrissen in Sarawak. Most of the Bornean montane birds including endemics can be found here.

Gunung Palung (01°14'S, 110°14'E) consists of mangrove, lowland and lower montane forests. Its long bird list, comprising birds from the varied forest type, includes the endemic Bornean Ground Cuckoo.

Other Birding Sites in Kalimantan
Kutai National Park, Danau Sentarum and Kapuas Lakes, Bukit Baka and Bukit Raya, Karimata Islands, Natuna Islands and Anambas, Muara Kendawangan, Sebangau, Negara Lakes and Maratus Mountains.

Where to Submit Records and Information

Malaysian Nature Society encourages up-to-date observations at eBird for a host of benefits for the observers as well as the birding community at large.

For formal assessment of claims of rare and previously unrecorded species, please submit sightings to the following national Record Committees:

Malaysian rarities can be submitted to Malaysian Nature Society-Bird Conservation Council Records Committee at https://sites.google.com/site/mnsbccrecordscommittee/home/rare-and-new-record-submission-form

Indonesian rarities can be submitted to Burung Nusantara at http://burung-nusantara.org/birding-indonesia/submit-records

Glossary of Abbreviated Non-English Terms

G.   Gunung (mountain)
P.   Pulau (island)

BIRD TOPOGRAPHY

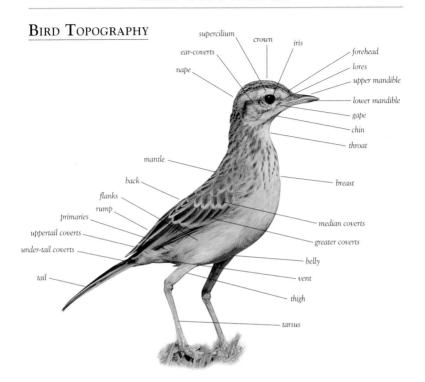

supercilium
crown
iris
forehead
ear-coverts
lores
nape
upper mandible
lower mandible
gape
chin
throat
mantle
breast
back
flanks
rump
primaries
median coverts
uppertail coverts
greater coverts
under-tail coverts
belly
tail
vent
thigh
tarsus

ABOUT THIS BOOK

There are 675 species of bird reliably recorded in Borneo, 71 of which are endemic. This book describes 280 species, including 46 that are endemic. As far as practicable, they are identified to subspecies based on current knowledge with occasional mention of other races occurring on nearby islands. Each species included has been illustrated with one or more colour photographs. All photographs are taken in Borneo, and so accurately illustrate the particular bird subspecies that occur there.

The common and scientific names, sequence of family and species used in this book, as well as in the checklist at the end of the book, follow Eaton, J. A., Van Balen, B., Brickle, N. W. & Rheindt, F. E. (2021). *Birds of the Indonesian Archipelago. Greater Sundas and Wallacea.* Lynx Edicions. Barcelona. Malay and Indonesian names are given in parenthesis.

A checklist of the birds of Borneo is included on p. 156. For each species this gives its common and scientific name, IUCN status as at 2022, and status in Sabah, Sarawak, Brunei Darussalam and Kalimantan.

Wandering Whistling-duck ■ *Dendrocygna arcuata* 45cm
(Malay: Belibis Merantau. Indonesian: Belibis Kembang)

DESCRIPTION A medium-sized reddish-brown duck. Adult has dark brown crown with prominent thick, dark line running down hind-neck. Side of neck and face paler brown; black speckles at lower neck and upper breast. Back feathers blackish brown, fringed chestnut-rufous. Flanks buffish, interrupted with dark and chestnut markings. Pale under-tail coverts; when in flight, shows prominent white 'U' on rump. Iris dark reddish brown, bill black, legs and feet dark bluish grey. **DISTRIBUTION** Greater Sundas, Philippines,

Wallacea, New Guinea, Australia, SW Pacific. Used to be scarce in Borneo but in recent years has become a locally common resident in some wetlands. Race: *D. a. arcuata*. **HABITS AND HABITAT** Usually seen in flocks at wetlands, marshes, swamps, freshwater and brackish-water ponds. Rests on bare and grassy margins. Quite shy but will stay put if not spooked. Dives to feed and when in flight will make a *fee, fee, fee* whistling sound.

Sunda Teal ■ *Anas gibberifrons* 42cm
(Malay: Itik Kecil Indonesia. Indonesian: Itik Benjut)

ABOVE: *Female*. BELOW: *Male*

DESCRIPTION A medium-sized, mottled brown duck. Adult male has a distinctive bulbous forehead and speckled dark-brown head, paler at nape. Throat pale brown without speckles. Body feathers blackish-brown, fringe pale-brown, displaying a scaly appearance. In flight, underwing shows broad grey axillaries and upper wing shows dark speculum with greenish sheen edged in front with broad white bar. Adult female shares same colour scheme but lacks the bulbous forehead. Bill, legs and feet dark grey. **DISTRIBUTION** Sumatra, Greater to Lesser Sundas, Sulawesi and Timor. Swamp forest, mangrove, lakes, prawn ponds, estuaries and flooded rice fields, often seen perching in trees. Earlier Bornean records were from Kalimantan, most recent record was from Tawau, Sabah in late 2014 and photographed with ducklings there in early 2016. Monotypic. **HABITS AND HABITAT** Shares habitat with other migratory and resident ducks, usually in pairs or small groups. It is a dabbling duck, feeding in freshwater lakes and mangrove swamps.

Tabon Scrubfowl ▪ *Megapodius cumingii* 35cm
(Malay: Tambun Biasa. Indonesian: Gosong Pilipina)

DESCRIPTION Sexes alike, forehead and crown grey; unfeathered red bare skin on lores, around eye to ear coverts; distinctive red face. Throat and neck sparsely feathered grey, revealing red skin underneath. Upperpart feathers including wings olive-brown, upper breast grey-brown with lower breast, flanks and vent much browner. Bill dull brown, iris brown. Massive legs and feet dark greyish black. **DISTRIBUTION** Philippines Sulawesi and Wallacea. Uncommon island resident off coast of Sabah and E Kalimantan; moves about between islands. Race: *M. c. cumingii*. **HABITS AND HABITAT** Mainly coastal scrub forests on islands, prefers loose sandy soil close to the sea, occasionally on mainland Borneo. Terrestrial insectivore and frugivore. Strong legs are used for running away from danger as well as for scratching up loose earth, sand and decaying vegetation into great heaps for female to lay her eggs, sometimes these nest mounds are located near coastal houses on islands.

Roulroul ▪ *Rollulus rouloul* 25cm
(Malay: Burung-siul Berjambul. Indonesian: Puyuh Sengayan)

DESCRIPTION Adult male has distinctive upright burgundy crest, bordered in front by broad contrasting white crown patch; broad red eye-ring with red triangle of bare skin tapering behind eye, rest of head and nape black. Upperparts dark bluish green, wings black. Underparts and short tail blackish blue. Bill black with red to basal half of lower mandible, legs and feet coral red. Other than its unmistakable crest and white crown patch, the male appears entirely black in dimly lit forest. Female has no crest, has grey forehead to crown, rest of head and neck black with grey ear patch and less pronounced red bare skin behind eye. Upperparts, tail, breast and flank feathers dull green; wings chestnut; belly and vent grey. Bill black without any red; legs and feet coral red. **DISTRIBUTION** Sumatra and Malay Peninsula. Widespread near threatened resident throughout Borneo from sea level to 1,300m. Relatively common in protected forests. Monotypic. **HABITS AND HABITAT** Lowland and hill primary and secondary forests, alluvial, riverine, peat-swamp and kerangas. Terrestrial feeder, usually forages in small party for fallen seeds and insects by raking leaf litter in dense forest undergrowth. Will forage within a short distance of stationary observers.

LEFT: *Female.* RIGHT: *Male*

Bornean Partridge ■ *Arborophila hyperythra* 25–28cm ⓔ
(Malay: Seruk-gunung Borneo. Indonesian: Puyuh-gonggong Kalimantan)

DESCRIPTION Adult male *A. h. erythrophrys* (shown) has brown spotted black crown, black nape, broad brown-chestnut supercilium from forehead to side of neck, black lores, grey ear with large dark patch below to side of neck. Mantle, back to rump feathers olive brown with dark fringe, making upperparts appear to be barred. Bold black bands on wings, broad white spots on black flanks and wing-coverts. Throat to breast rusty-brown, belly to vent white. Iris grey with red bare skin around eye, bill black, legs and feet salmon-pink. Supercillium of *A. h. hyperythra* is grey instead of brown-chestnut. **DISTRIBUTION** Uncommon endemic along the central Bornean mountain ranges, from 600 to 2,200m. *A. h. erythrophrys* in Sabah and *A. h. hyperythra* in Sarawak and Kalimantan. **HABITS AND HABITAT** Upper hill and montane forests, from 600 to 3,050m, overlaps extensively with Bloodhead (opposite). A terrestrial feeder, usually in small family group, often seen walking along edge of forest streams, feeding on berries, seeds, insects and grubs.

Sabah Partridge ■ *Tropicoperdix graydoni* 28–30cm ⓔ
(Malay: Seruk-bukit Sabah. Indonesian: Puyuh-kalung Sabah)

DESCRIPTION Adult has brown crown, black-flecked whitish lores and supercilium, and white chin and throat with pale buff ear-patch. Black neck mottled white with a broad chestnut neckband on lower neck and upper breast. Rest of upperparts mottled brown, buff and black. Breast broadly barred black and buff, lower breast and flanks chestnut with darker-fringed feathers. Belly and vent pale white with short tail. Iris brown, bill brownish grey with yellow tip, legs and feet greenish yellow. **DISTRIBUTION** Locally common lowland endemic in NE Borneo and northern Kalimantan Timur. Monotypic. **HABITS AND HABITAT** Prefers lowland primary and disturbed forests, often near rivers. Moves about on the dense forest floor, searching for seeds, berries, grubs, insects, etc. An extremely difficult bird to see as its plumage blends in well with the leaf litter and dense undergrowth.

Great Argus ▪ *Argusianus argus* Male 165cm; female 60cm
(Malay: Kuang-raya Biasa. Indonesian: Kuau Raja)

DESCRIPTION Unmistakable bird in the field. Adult male has narrow band of black hair running from forecrown to nape, forming a short black crest. Blue face and upper-neck skin sparsely feathered. Upperparts, wings and tail mostly dark grey and brown, densely dotted with small white spots and vermiculations. Secondaries are enormously elongated up to 120cm, with ocelli that are rarely visible in the field. Lower neck and upper breast chestnut. Iris pale yellowish, bill ivory, legs and feet pinkish red. Adult female is smaller and more rufous, and lacks the long tail. **DISTRIBUTION** Thai–Malay Peninsula, Sumatra. Locally common Bornean resident, 0–1,800m. Regularly heard in primary forests; population should be declining due to loss of habitat. Race: *A. a. grayi*. **HABITS AND HABITAT** Lowland and hill dipterocarp forests, tall kerangas. Prefers hilly primary forests. A ground-dwelling bird, feeding on ants, other small insects, molluscs, fallen fruits, berries and young leaves. Male clears a display ground in forest for performing his courtship dance to females.

Male

Bloodhead ▪ *Haematortyx sanguiniceps* 25cm ⓔ
(Malay: Seruk Kepala Merah. Indonesian: Puyuh Kepala-merah)

DESCRIPTION Unmistakable, this is a striking beauty in the field with contrasting brightly coloured head and dark body. Adult male has bright crimson head, neck and upper breast. Other than the equally crimson undertail feathers, rest of plumage is black with a slight tinge of brown. Bill bright orange, bare skin around yellow eye. Legs and feet dark greyish-black. Adult female is similar but has throat and upper breast reddish chestnut, has one spur on each leg instead of 2. **DISTRIBUTION** Locally common to uncommon endemic along the central Bornean mountain ranges, typically montane up to 3,050m, occasionally at low altitude. Monotypic. **HABITS AND HABITAT** Sandy forests of the valley bottoms within the montane zone, lower and upper montane forests. A terrestrial feeder, usually in pairs, feeding on berries and insects. It overlaps with Bornean Partridge (p. 18). Often heard in montane forests, on rare occasions walks on path of forest trails ahead of visitors in Kinabalu Park.

Male

Bornean Crested Fireback ■ *Lophura ignita* 65–67cm
(Malay: Pegar Tatera. Indonesian: Sempidan-merah Kalimantan)

DESCRIPTION Adult male has cobalt-blue bare facial skin covering the entire face. Narrow, dark median crown-stripe connects to dark blue crown with crest feathers. Upper back dark blue, lower back chestnut, primaries and secondaries bluish black. Tail dark blue with yellow central tail feathers. Neck and upper breast concolourous with upper back; lower breast

and belly chestnut. Iris red, bill yellow, legs and feet pinkish buff with long spur. Adult female has brown crest and upperparts, blackish flight and tail feathers, plain chestnut upper breast, and chestnut lower breast and belly feathers with white fringes; legs lack spur. **DISTRIBUTION** Borneo and Banka island. Used to be common in Borneo but now an uncommon resident up to 1,300m. Races: *L. i. ignita* in S Borneo and Bangka is larger than *L. i. nobilis* (shown) in N Borneo. **HABITS AND HABITAT** Lowland and hill dipterocarp forests, alluvial forests, kerangas; also oil-palm estates adjacent to forest. Often seen in small parties of 5–6 birds with a single male, preferring to stay in dark forests. Forages on the ground for grubs of all kinds, fallen berries, seeds, etc.

Male

Eastern Spotted Dove ■ *Spilopelia chinensis* 28–30cm
(Malay: Tekukur Jerum Timur. Indonesian: Tekukur Biasa)

DESCRIPTION Medium-sized dove. Adult has distinctive silver-spotted black nuchal collar, and grey head with dark loral line. Upperpart feathers brown, fringed buff, with broad, dark shaft streaks on mantle and wing coverts. Longish progressive tail is brown above when closed; often fanned out when bird alights, showing conspicuous white tips

to under-tail feathers. Neck, breast and belly pinkish brown; vent buff. Iris orange-yellow, bill black, legs and feet pinkish red. **DISTRIBUTION** Greater and Lesser Sundas, Southeast Asia and the Philippines. Introduced to many other areas, including Australia. Common and abundant resident throughout Borneo, including offshore islands, up to 1,000m. Race: *S. c. tigrina*. **HABITS AND HABITAT** Open country, woodlands, disturbed forests, agriculture areas, towns, villages, parks, urban and suburban areas, often near human dwellings; absent from remote forests. Often seen perching on high wires along roads, and foraging on open ground, roadsides and in open areas in housing estates.

Zebra Dove ■ *Geopelia striata* 18–21cm
(Malay: Merbuk Biasa. Indonesian: Perkutut Jawa)

DESCRIPTION A small ground dove. Adult has pale bluish-grey forehead, face and throat, and plain greyish-brown crown. Nape and mantle finely barred black; rest of upperpart feathers narrowly fringed black, creating narrow black lines. Side of breast and flanks finely barred grey and black. Centre of breast and belly to under-tail coverts unbarred rufous. Uppertail brown; white-tipped outer-tail feathers visible only in flight. Bluish-white eye-ring, 2-toned iris with dark outer ring and bluish-white inner ring. Bill bluish grey, legs dull greyish pink.

DISTRIBUTION Southeast Asia, Greater Sundas, Wallacea to Australia. Locally common and abundant lowland resident in Borneo; some populations are believed to be descendants of released cagebirds or escapees, and it is still a common cagebird. Monotypic. **HABITS AND HABITAT** Open woodlands, sandy shores, gardens, parks, cultivated areas, open country. Forages on the ground, especially on gritty substrates (often seen at roadsides).

Little Cuckoo-dove ■ *Macropygia ruficeps* 27–30cm
(Malay: Tekukur-api Biasa. Indonesian: Uncal Kouran)

DESCRIPTION A long-tailed reddish dove. Adult male (shown) has cinnamon head, face and neck, with green and lilac reflections on nape if light is right. Upperparts dark brown with cinnamon-fringed wing coverts. Throat and breast orange-buff, mottled black and rufous; belly and vent yellowish brown. Iris bluish/greyish white, bill brownish grey with dark tip, legs and feet coral-red. Adult female is similar but lacks green and lilac on nape, and has more heavily mottled blackish on breast. **DISTRIBUTION** SW China, Southeast Asia, Greater Sundas, Wallacea. Locally common resident throughout Borneo, chiefly sub-montane up to 2,945m, but also recorded in the lowlands. Race: M. r. nana. **HABITS AND HABITAT** Favours hill and montane forests, and is locally common in montane and sub-montane habitats in interior highlands of Borneo. Feeds on small seeds, berries and ripe paddy. Has a powerful flight, especially when riding the winds above montane forests.

Asian Emerald Dove ■ *Chalcophaps indica* 23–27cm
(Malay: Punai-tanah Biasa. Indonesian: Delimukan Zamrud)

DESCRIPTION A short-tailed terrestrial dove. Adult male has grey crown bordered below by white forehead and white stripe above eyes. Nape grey, lower back and rump blackish with 2 pale grey bars. Mantle and wing coverts iridescent green with whitish-grey shoulder-patch. Face, neck and breast pinkish vinous, fading to pinkish grey at belly. Iris brown, bill bright red, legs and feet pinkish red. Adult female is similar but lacks whitish shoulder-patch and grey crown. **DISTRIBUTION** Indian sub-continent to Southeast Asia, S China, Taiwan, Greater Sundas, Philippines, Wallacea, Melanesia, Australia. Common resident throughout Borneo, including some offshore islands, up

to 1,590m. Race: *C. i. indica*. **HABITS AND HABITAT** Lowland and hill dipterocarp and secondary forests, coastal scrub forests, plantation forests, mangroves, gardens. Usually seen walking on ground along jungle paths and trails, foraging for seeds, fallen fruits and small invertebrates. Not easy to notice in the dim forest light owing to its colour scheme.

LEFT: *Male*. RIGHT: *Female*

Little Green Pigeon ■ *Treron olax* 20–22cm
(Malay: Punai Kecil. Indonesian: Punai Kecil)

DESCRIPTION The smallest green pigeon. Adult male has grey face, head and nape. Mantle, back and wing coverts dark maroon; black flight feathers edged yellow. Rump and uppertail coverts dark grey. Orange upper breast, fading into greenish-yellow belly. Vent to under-tail coverts cinnamon. Adult female is greenish, lacking all maroon and orange of male, with grey forehead and crown, dark green wing coverts and rest of upperparts, and yellow-edged black flight feathers. Pale greyish chin, yellowish-green breast, pale green belly fading into buffish vent. Yellow eye-ring, 2-toned iris with maroon outer ring and white inner ring. Bill creamy with greenish base, legs and feet coral-red. **DISTRIBUTION** Thai–Malay Peninsula, Greater Sundas. Widespread and locally common resident throughout Borneo, including some islands, up to 1,220m on G. Dulit. Monotypic. **HABITS AND HABITAT** Lowland to sub-montane forests, peat-swamp forests, woodlands, gardens, parks, plantation forests. Usually seen in pairs or small groups. Will wait at trees near fruiting figs, flying in to feed after bigger birds like hornbills have departed.

ABOVE: *Male*. BELOW: *Female*

Pink-necked Green Pigeon ■ *Treron vernans* 23–28cm
(Malay: Punai Kocok. Indonesian: Punai Gading)

DESCRIPTION A medium-sized colourful green pigeon. Adult male has grey head and crown, pinkish-grey nape and neck. Mantle, back and wing coverts green; flight feathers black, edged yellow. Rump orange-green; uppertail grey with

black sub-terminal band. Orange breast, fading into green belly; vent mottled yellow and green; under-tail deep chestnut. Iris is 2-toned, with dark outer ring and broader pink inner ring. Bill grey, legs and feet coral-pink. Adult female is similar but greenish overall, with dull green replacing the grey, pink and orange, and a buffish under-tail. **DISTRIBUTION** Southeast Asia, Greater Sundas, Philippines, Wallacea. Common and abundant lowland resident throughout Borneo, including surrounding islands. Monotypic. **HABITS AND HABITAT** Woodlands, primary and secondary forests, kerangas, swamp and riverine forests, scrub, gardens. Usually feeds in small flocks, on soft fruits, berries, and the tips of shrubs and shoots.

Thick-billed Green Pigeon ■ *Treron curvirostra* 25–31cm
(Malay: Punai Ara Biasa. Indonesian: Punai Lengguak)

DESCRIPTION A medium-sized green pigeon with a distinctive bright apple-green eye-patch. Adult male has grey forehead and crown, and green neck and nape. Mantle and wing coverts maroon, black flight feathers edged yellow. Yellowish-green breast and belly;

inner thigh to vent mottled green and white; under-tail cinnamon, edged and tipped greyish white. Adult female is similar but mantle and wing coverts are olive-green, and thigh, vent and under-tail are mottled green and white. Iris dark brown, bill yellowish with bright red base, legs and feet coral-red. **DISTRIBUTION** India, Nepal to SW China, Southeast Asia, Greater Sundas, Philippines. Locally common lowland resident throughout Borneo and on some offshore islands, up to 1,525m. Race: *T. c. curvirosta*. **HABITS AND HABITAT** Lowland dipterocarp and secondary forests, peat-swamp and riverine forests, mangroves, plantation forests. Usually seen in pairs or small groups. Feeds on figs, fruits and berries in noisy flocks, thrashing about in the trees.

Jambu Fruit Dove ▪ *Ptilinopus jambu* 22–27cm
(Malay: Punai-gading Jambu. Indonesian: Walik Jambu)

DESCRIPTION Adult male is a beautiful dove, with a bright plum-red forehead, forecrown, face and throat side, and black chin and upper throat. Hind-crown, nape and rest of upperparts green. Primaries greenish black with pale edging. Side of neck and rest of underparts white with pink breast-patch. Under-tail coverts chestnut with whitish terminal band. Adult female (shown) is similar, but forehead and face purple instead of red, breast plain and belly whitish, and under-tail coverts light brown. Iris brown with broad white eye-ring, bill bright orange, legs and feet dull red. **DISTRIBUTION** Thai–Malay Peninsula, Sumatra, W Java. Uncommon but widely distributed resident throughout Borneo, with marked local movements, from lowlands to 1,600m. Monotypic. **HABITS AND HABITAT** Lowland dipterocarp to lower montane forests, including secondary, alluvial and swamp forests. A shy and quiet bird that feeds on fruits and berries in the lower to middle storeys. Best chance to observe it is when feeding at a fruiting tree.

Green Imperial Pigeon ▪ *Ducula aenea* 40–48cm
(Malay: Pergam Daun Biasa. Indonesian: Pergam Hijau)

DESCRIPTION A large green and grey pigeon. Adult *D. a. polia* has pale pinkish-grey

head, neck, breast and belly; mantle and rest of upperparts metallic, iridescent bronze-green. Flight feathers black. Under-tail coverts chestnut, under-tail brown. Iris brown with obvious thin white eye-ring, bill grey, legs and feet dull coral-red. Very similar to **Grey Imperial Pigeon** *D. pickeringii*, but that is smaller, has a greenish-mauve mantle and grey under-tail, and is a rare nomadic resident on offshore islands. **DISTRIBUTION** Indian sub-continent, Southeast Asia, S China, Greater Sundas, Philippines, Wallacea to New Guinea. Common resident throughout Borneo's lowlands and surrounding islands, up to 1,050m. Races: *D. a. palawanensis* on P. Banggi, *D. a. polia* (shown) elsewhere. **HABITS AND HABITAT** Primary and secondary forests, plantation forests, coastal scrub, mangroves, Nipah swamps, riverine forests. Usually seen singly or in small flocks descending on fruiting trees. Often seen in straight flight high above the canopy, holding on steadfastly to its chosen line of flight.

Mountain Imperial Pigeon ■ *Ducula badia* 40–51cm
(Malay: Pergam Bukit Biasa. Indonesian: Pergam Gunung)

DESCRIPTION A large grey and maroon imperial pigeon. Adult has light purplish-grey head, neck, breast and belly; chin and throat whitish. Mantle, back, rump and wing coverts maroon, with blackish flight feathers. Uppertail black with terminal half grey. Vent and under-tail coverts buff, under-tail darker grey with grey terminal half. Iris greyish white with obvious crimson eye-ring, bill dull purplish with whitish tip, legs and feet dull purplish to crimson. **DISTRIBUTION** Himalayas, India, Southeast Asia, SW China, Greater Sundas. Locally common Bornean resident, mostly in montane forests up to 2,500m, occasionally in lowlands and mangroves, including surrounding islands. Race: *D. b. badia*. **HABITS AND HABITAT** Hill dipterocarp and montane forests, mangroves, lowland dipterocarp forests. A shy bird, more reserved than the Green Imperial Pigeon (opposite), usually seen singly making powerful flights high above the canopy. Montane birds have been known to make daily flights to lowland feeding grounds and mangroves.

Pied Imperial Pigeon ■ *Ducula bicolor* 35–42cm
(Malay: Rawa Biasa. Indonesian: Pergam Laut)

DESCRIPTION Bird of the coast and islands. Adult overall white except for wings and tail, sometimes with white tinged yellowish. Primary and secondary wing feathers black. Terminal half of uppertail feathers black, showing black terminal band when viewed from above. Under-tail feathers variable: some birds have black-edged white feathers, others have black at terminal half. Iris black, bill and feet dark bluish-grey. **DISTRIBUTION** Coasts and islands from Andaman and Nicobar, Greater and Lesser Sundas, Philippines, New Guinea, Australia. Found on islands and occasionally coasts of mainland Borneo. Monotypic. **HABITS AND HABITAT** Black-and-white imperial pigeon that mainly feeds on fruits of the nutmeg family, *Myristicaceae*. Usually seen in flocks, flying across from island to island in search of fruiting trees. A large flock in flight is a spectacular sight to behold.

Rhinortha ■ *Rhinortha chlorophaea* 30cm
(Malay: Cenok Kerak. Indonesian: Kedalan Selaya)

DESCRIPTION Used to be Raffles' Malkoha; now known not to be closely related to malkoha. Adult male has rufous upperparts, dark-tipped primaries, dark tail with fine grey barrings and broad white tail tip; chin to lower breast rufous, grading to dark grey belly and under-tail. Adult female has bluish-grey head to mantle and chin to upper breast. Back

to tail rufous, with black sub-terminal band and white tip on tail. Belly dull rufous, vent and under-tail rufous. Both sexes have brown iris, pale bluish-green orbital skin and bill, and slaty-grey legs and feet. **DISTRIBUTION** Thai–Malay Peninsula, Sumatra. Common resident throughout lowland Borneo, up to 1,100m. Monotypic.

HABITS AND HABITAT Lowland dipterocarp and secondary forests, peat-swamp and riverine forests, plantation forests, forest edges, gardens. Usually seen in pairs. Forages for caterpillars and insects by creeping among thick foliage in middle and upper storeys, and makes short glides from tree to tree.

LEFT: *Male*. RIGHT: *Female*

Red-billed Malkoha ■ *Phaenicophaeus javanicus* 42–46cm
(Malay: Cenok Api. Indonesian: Kedalan Kembang)

DESCRIPTION The second rarest malkoha in Borneo (the rarest is the **Chestnut-bellied**

Malkoha *P. sumatranus*). Adult has grey forehead, crown and nape. Back to rump darker grey; wings and long tail dark bluish grey, tail with white tip. Lores, chin and throat to upper breast rufous, graduating into pale grey breast. Belly and vent rich rufous. Under-tail dark bluish grey, interspersed with white tips of graduated inner-tail feathers. Iris dark, bare skin around eyes blue, bill pinkish red, legs and feet dark grey. **DISTRIBUTION** Thai–Malay Peninsula, Greater Sundas. Uncommon resident sparsely distributed throughout Borneo's lowlands, up to 1,750m; commoner in sub-montane habitats. Race: *P. j. pallidus*. **HABITS AND HABITAT** Lowland and hill dipterocarp forests, peat-swamp, logged and secondary forests, forest edges, gardens, plantation forests. Feeds on caterpillars, other insects, spiders and small lizards. Usually seen in pairs, creeping around thick foliage in middle and upper storeys like a squirrel, and making short glides from tree to tree.

Black-bellied Malkoha ■ *Phaenicophaeus diardi* 38cm
(Malay: Cenok Perut Hitam. Indonesian: Kedalan Beruang)

DESCRIPTION A dark grey and green malkoha. Adult has dark grey head and neck, and glossy blue-green back, wings and tail. Tail feathers broadly tipped white. Grey throat and upper breast washed rufous, belly and under-tail coverts blackish grey. Iris pale blue, extensive crimson skin patch around eyes, bill light green, legs and feet dark grey.

DISTRIBUTION Thai–Malay Peninsula, Sumatra. Uncommon resident throughout Borneo's lowlands and lower montane forests, up to 915m. Race: *P. d. borneensis*. **HABITS AND HABITAT** Lowland dipterocarp, peat-swamp and secondary forests, mangroves, plantation forests. Secretive bird that forages for caterpillars and insects by creeping around thick foliage in middle and upper storeys like a squirrel, and makes short glides from tree to tree.

Chestnut-breasted Malkoha ■ *Phaenicophaeus curvirostris* 42–49cm
(Malay: Ceruk Dada Coklat. Indonesian: Kedalan Birah)

DESCRIPTION The largest malkoha in Borneo. Adult male has dark grey head, nape and mantle. Back, wings and tail glossy blue-green, with chestnut on terminal half of tail. Narrow band of grey from chin to ear-coverts. Throat and rest of underparts rich chestnut. Iris pale blue, extensive rich crimson patch of bare skin around eye, bill pale green with crimson to most of base of lower mandible, legs and feet dark grey. Adult female is similar but has red-orange iris and a broader grey band from chin to ear-coverts. **DISTRIBUTION**

Thai–Malay Peninsula, Greater Sundas, Palawan. Common lowland resident throughout Borneo, up to 1,220m. Race: *P. c. microrhinus*. **HABITS AND HABITAT** Lowland and hill dipterocarp forests, secondary forests, gardens, plantation forests, mangroves, peat swamps, coastal vegetation. Feeds on caterpillars, other insects and small lizards, creeping among thick foliage in middle and upper storeys like a squirrel, and making short glides from tree to tree.

LEFT: *Male.* RIGHT: *Female*

Drongo Cuckoo ■ *Surniculus lugubris* 24cm
(Malay: Sewah Sawai Biasa. Indonesian: Kedasi Hitam)

DESCRIPTION A cuckoo that resembles a small drongo. Adult is glossy dark blue and black with a square tail. White thigh, white barrings on under-tail coverts and underside of outer-tail feathers. Iris dark brown, bill black, legs and feet dark grey. Juvenile is duller and irregularly spotted with white. **DISTRIBUTION** SW coastal India, Sri Lanka, S China, Southeast Asia, Greater Sundas, Philippines, Sulawesi. Common resident throughout Borneo, from lowlands to 1,300m. Race: *S. l. lugubris*. **HABITS AND HABITAT** Lowland dipterocarp and peat-swamp forests, kerangas, plantation forests, forest clearings, gardens. Canopy feeder. Song of 5–7 ascending notes is commonly heard in forests. Breeds parasitically; hosts recorded include Bicoloured Babbler (p. 113).

Malaysian Hawk-cuckoo
■ *Hierococcyx fugax* 28–30cm
(Malay: Sewah-tekukur Melayu. Indonesian: Kangkok Melayu)

DESCRIPTION Adult has dark brownish-grey head and upperparts; face grey, throat white, rufous wash on sides of neck and breast. Underparts white, conspicuously streaked dark brown and rufous. Vent and under-tail coverts white. Tail grey with blackish bars and rufous tip. Iris grey-brown with yellow eye-ring, bill dark grey with yellow/pale green base, legs and feet yellow. Similar to **Whistling Hawk-cuckoo** *H. nisicolor*, which has more rufous underparts and is a scarce winter migrant to N Borneo. **DISTRIBUTION** Thai–Malay Peninsula, Sumatra, W Java. Uncommon Bornean resident, sparingly distributed in lowlands, up to 1,620m. Monotypic. **HABITS AND HABITAT** Lowland and hill dipterocarp forests, kerangas, peat-swamp forests, secondary and plantation forests. Arboreal foliage-gleaning insectivore; also feed on berries. Breeds parasitically by laying its eggs in nests of other birds, which than raise the chicks; recorded hosts include Grey-headed Canary-flycatcher (p. 102) and Black-throated Babbler (p. 115).

Bock's Hawk-cuckoo

■ *Hierococcyx bocki* 30–32cm
(Malay: Sewah-tekukur Gunung.
Indonesian: Kangkok Gelap)

DESCRIPTION Hawk-cuckoo of the montane forest. Adult has dark grey head and upperparts, and tail barred with pale tip. Throat dirty white, unstreaked rufous breast, belly and flanks white barred black, vent white. Iris rufous with yellow eye-ring, bill mostly black with faint greenish tinge at lower mandible, legs and feet yellow. Differentiated from other similar-size hawk-cuckoos in Borneo by mostly black bill. Immature bird has browner and faintly barred upperparts. **DISTRIBUTION** Malay peninsula, Sumatra, Greater Sundas. Uncommon resident throughout montane forest in Borneo. Monotypic. **HABITS AND HABITAT** Aboreal foliage-gleaning insectivore, feeding mainly on caterpillars and beetles; also on berries. Breeds parasitically – one host is thought to be Mountain Leaf Warbler (p. 123).

Banded Bay Cuckoo ■ *Cacomantis sonneratii* 22cm
(Malay: Matinak Takuwih. Indonesian: Wiwik Lurik)

DESCRIPTION A medium-sized cuckoo. Adult has forehead, crown and rest of upperparts barred chestnut-brown and black; barred whitish supercilium and distinctive broad dark eye-stripe, dark upper-tail feathers notched chestnut, with dark subterminal band. Chin, throat and rest of underparts dirty-white, finely barred black. Vent buff with coarse bars, undertail feathers buff broadly tipped white with dark subterminal band. Bill black, iris brown, legs and feet grey. Similar hepatic morphs, Plantive Cuckoo (p. 30) and Sunda Brush Cuckoo (p. 30), do not have contrasting whitish supercilium and broad dark eye-stripe. **DISTRIBUTION** Indian sub-continent, Sri Lanka, SW China, SE Asia, Greater Sunda and Philippines. Locally common to scarce resident from sea level to 500m, commoner in Sabah. Race: *C. s. fasciolatus*. **HABITS AND HABITAT** Lowland and hill dipterocarp forests, regenerating forests, forest plantations and gardens. Arboreal, foliage-gleaning insectivore; feeds on caterpillars, grasshoppers, crickets, etc. Often heard calling in forest but difficult to locate.

Plaintive Cuckoo ■ *Cacomantis merulinus* 18–23.5cm
(Malay: Matinak Biasa. Indonesian: Wiwik Kelabu)

DESCRIPTION A smallish cuckoo. Adult has grey head, neck, nape and upper breast. Mantle and rest of upperparts dark brownish grey; tail blackish with visible pale notches. Lower breast to under-tail coverts orange-rufous. Under-tail barred black and white. Iris reddish orange; bill black, sometimes with orange base; legs and feet orange-yellow. Hepatic

female has upperparts barred rufous and brown; underparts whitish rufous, barred brown; tail completely barred. **DISTRIBUTION** E Himalayas to S China, Southeast Asia, Greater Sundas, Philippines, Sulawesi. Abundant and common resident throughout Borneo, up to 1,220m. Race: *C. m. threnodes*. **HABITS AND HABITAT** Gardens, open woodlands, forest edges, plantation forests, kerangas, peat swamps,

secondary forests; sometimes seen in open spaces in housing estates. Its *wee wiwit…wee wiwit…wee wiwit* call, rising in pitch and speed, is the most commonly heard cuckoo call. Feeds on insects, especially caterpillars. Breeds parasitically; hosts recorded include Yellow-bellied Prinia (p. 128), Bornean Spiderhunter (p. 149) and tailorbirds.

LEFT: *Adult.* RIGHT: *Hepatic female*

Sunda Brush Cuckoo
■ *Cacomantis sepulcralis* 21–28cm
(Malay: Matinak Dada Jingga Biasa. Indonesian: Wiwik Uncuing)

DESCRIPTION A smallish cuckoo, similar to Plaintive Cuckoo (above) but darker and distinguished by orange-rufous throat and neck. Head and upperparts dark grey, underparts orange-rufous. Under-tail barred rufous and brown with white notches on inner web. Iris light brown with yellow eye-ring, bill black with yellow base at lower mandible, legs and feet bright yellow. Hepatic female is similar to its Plaintive counterpart, but larger, with broader dark barring on upperparts, throat and breast, and an obvious yellow eye-ring. **DISTRIBUTION** Thai–Malay Peninsula, S Indochina, Greater Sundas, Philippines. Uncommon and local resident in Borneo's lowlands and lower montane forests, up to 1,715m. Race: *C. s. sepulcralis*. **HABITS AND HABITAT** Lowland and hill dipterocarp forests, mangroves, forest edges, plantation forests. Has a *wee wiwit… wee wiwit…wee wiwit* call, rising in pitch and speed, and is almost identical to that of Plaintive. Breeds parasitically; hosts recorded include Chestnut-naped Forktail (p. 137).

Violet Cuckoo ■ *Chrysococcyx xanthorhynchus* 16cm
(Malay: Sewah-zamrud Ungu. Indonesian: Kedasi Ungu)

DESCRIPTION A small cuckoo. Adult male has glossy violet head, breast, neck and upperparts. Lower breast to vent white with dark purplish bandings. Under-tail dark purple. Iris brown with red eye-ring, bill orange-yellow with reddish base, legs and feet grey. Adult female has bronze-green crown, nape and upperparts. Face and throat white with fine bronze-green barrings, breast and underparts white with bolder and darker barrings. **DISTRIBUTION** Southeast Asia, Greater Sundas, Philippines. Relatively common and local resident throughout lowland Borneo, up to 1,300m. Race: *C. x. xanthorhynchus*. **HABITS AND HABITAT** Forest edges, gardens, scrub, woodland, lowland and hill forests, kerangas, secondary forests, plantation forests, grassland. Feeds on insects and fruits. Creeps quietly up and down branches, gleaning for caterpillars and insects from foliage, sometimes sallying out to catch flying insects. Breeds parasitically; hosts recorded include sunbirds and spiderhunters.

Male

Greater Coucal ■ *Centropus sinensis*
47–52cm
(Malay: Bubut Besar Asia. Indonesian: Bubut Besar)

DESCRIPTION A large blackish cuckoo with a long, graduated tail. Adult has glossy black head with bluish sheen. Wings rich chestnut, rest of body including tail entirely black. Underwing coverts black. Iris crimson; strong, slightly hooked bill black; legs and feet black. **DISTRIBUTION** Indian sub-continent to Southeast Asia, S China, Greater Sundas, Philippines. Common lowland resident throughout Borneo; up to 1,200m in Kelabit Highlands, Sarawak. Race: *C. s. bubutus*. **HABITS AND HABITAT** Open country, gardens, lowland dipterocarp forests, secondary forests, mangroves, plantation forests, forest edges. Feeds on lizards, frogs, snails, small animals and insects. Forages by creeping and clambering among thick foliage and secondary growth, occasionally feeding on the ground. Often seen perching in the open, spreading wings to dry after a rain shower. Usually makes short glides among thickets; slow flights made up of flapping interspersed with gliding.

Lesser Coucal ■ *Centropus bengalensis* 40cm
(Malay:Bubut Kecil Asia. Indonesian: Bubut Alang-alang)

DESCRIPTION The commonest coucal in Borneo. Very similar to Greater Coucal (p. 31) when breeding, but smaller with a shorter bill and tail, and chestnut underwing coverts.

Breeding adult (shown) has buff-streaked glossy black head, upper back and underparts. Lower back and rump dull brown, wings chestnut, tail black. Iris reddish brown; bill, legs and feet black. Non-breeding bird has brown head and upperparts with prominent buff and brown streakings, and brown wing feathers with buffish shaft streaks and edging. Underparts buff, spotted white; bill light brown with dark culmen. **DISTRIBUTION** Indian sub-continent to Southeast Asia, S China, Taiwan, Greater Sundas, Philippines, Wallacea. Common lowland resident throughout Borneo; up to 2,000m in Kelabit Highlands, Sarawak. Race: *C. b. javanensis*. **HABITS AND HABITAT** Open country, gardens, secondary forests, swamps, mangroves, plantation forests, forest edges; particularly favours secondary scrub. Feeds on lizards, small mammals and insects. Unlike Greater Coucal, it does not clamber about in trees but prefers to forage in scrub, marshes and open grassy areas.

Whiskered Treeswift ■ *Hemiprocne comata* 15–16.5cm
(Malay: Layang-layang Berjambul Kecil. Indonesian: Tepekong Rangkang)

DESCRIPTION A handsome swift with a beautiful face pattern. Adult male has a blue head with short, erect forecrown feathers; 2 prominent white lines across face, made up from long, thin white supercilium above and an equally long 'whisker' running from chin to nape below, and sandwiching chestnut-coloured ear-coverts. Mantle and back brown, long sickle-like

wings dark blue with visible white tertials. Throat blue, breast to belly brown, vent white. Adult female is similar but ear-coverts are concolourous with head. Differentiated from larger Grey-rumped Treeswift (opposite) by 2 white lines on face and brown breast and belly. **DISTRIBUTION** Thai–Malay Peninsula, Sumatra, Philippines. Common lowland resident throughout Borneo, up to 850m. Race: *H. c. comata*. **HABITS AND HABITAT** Lowland dipterocarp forests, peat swamps, mangroves, secondary forests, often over rivers and forest clearings. Usually seen in pairs, perching on bare twigs on treetops and sallying out to catch insects. Flight is highly manoeuvrable and close to forest canopy.

LEFT: *Male*. RIGHT: *Female*

Grey-rumped Treeswift ■ *Hemiprocne longipennis* 18–21cm
(Malay: Layang-layang Berjambul Pinggul Pudar. Indonesian: Tepekong Jambul)

DESCRIPTION A handsome swift with a forehead crest. Adult male has dark greyish-blue head with blackish eye-band extending from lores, and chestnut ear-coverts. Mantle bluish grey, back and rump grey. Wings darker with pale grey tertials visible when perched; long black primaries extend over tip of needle-like tail. Chin and throat grey, rest of underparts dirty white. Adult female is similar but lacks chestnut ear-coverts. **DISTRIBUTION** Thai–Malay Peninsula, Greater Sundas, Sulawesi, Philippines. Common lowland resident throughout Borneo, up to 1,050m. Race: *H. l.*

harterti. **HABITS AND HABITAT** Primary and secondary forests, mangroves, forest edges, plantation forests, open country, clearings. Often seen in small flocks perched on open twigs at treetops or on overhead power cables, sallying out to catch insects in flight.

ABOVE RIGHT: *Male*. LEFT: *Female*

Edible-nest Swiftlet ■ *Aerodramus fuciphagus* 12cm
(Malay: Layang-layang Gua Sarang Putih. Indonesian: Walet Sarang-putih)

DESCRIPTION A small brown-black swiftlet. Adult has dark brownish-black upperparts, with some populations having a paler rump. Underparts grey-brown. Legs, feet and bill very short. When held closed in flight, tail is slightly notched. Almost identical to the other 2 common swiftlets of Borneo, the **Uniform Swiftlet** *A. vanikorensi* and **Black-nest Swiftlet** *A. maximus*. Positive identification of these 3 species in the field is extremely difficult; they are best identified at their nests. **DISTRIBUTION** Andamans, Nicobars, Southeast Asia, Greater Sundas, Wallacea. Common resident throughout Borneo, including offshore islands. Race: *A. f. vestitus*. **HABITS AND HABITAT** Occurs over a variety of habitats, from coastal areas to forests, plantations and urban townships. Feeds on flying insects and often dips in freshwater ponds with a splash. Only perches at nest. Uses echolocation to navigate in dark cave systems. Breeds in caves, building nests made of hardened saliva that are considered a culinary delicacy. Because of this, harvesting of nests using purpose-built structures is widespread over the species' range.

Plume-toed Swiftlet ■ *Collocalia affinis* 9–10cm
(Malay: Layang-layang Kecil Biasa. Indonesian: Walet Bulu-kaki)

DESCRIPTION The smallest Bornean swiftlet. Adult has glossy bluish-black upperparts. Throat and upper breast dark grey, lower breast to belly dirty white. Feathers on lower flanks dark-centred, fringed white, appearing like scales. Under-tail coverts bluish black, tail dark greyish. **Bornean Swiftlet** *C. dodgei*, which is endemic to upper montane forests, is very similar in appearance and virtually indistinguishable in the field. **DISTRIBUTION** Thai–Malay Peninsula, Greater Sundas. Widespread and common lowland resident throughout Borneo, probably up to 4,120m in montane habitats. Race: *C. a. cyanoptila*. **HABITS AND HABITAT** Occurs in most habitats, from the coast to the mountains, and from residential areas to forested areas. Prefers to build nests on man-made structures and in cave mouths where there is sufficient light (does not echolocate and hence does not nest deep in caves). Feeds on small insects on the wing, usually flying fairly low.

Large Frogmouth ■ *Batrachostomus auritus* 39–42cm
(Malay: Cucur Besar. Indonesian: Paruh-kodok Besar)

DESCRIPTION Largest frogmouth in Borneo; may be confused only with **Dulit Frogmouth** *B. harterti*, which occurs in montane forests. Adult has cryptic plumage and very wide bill, hence its name. Overall colour scheme rufous-brown, darker on wings. Ends of wing-covert feathers white, forming large, white, droplet-like spots. Barred back, primaries and tail. Throat plain, breast sparsely spotted buff. Iris dark, bill dark brown with broad yellow edge on upper mandible, feet yellowish. **DISTRIBUTION** Thai-Malay peninsula, Sumatra, Greater Sundas. Scarce in all types of lowland forest. Monotypic. **HABITS AND HABITAT** Nocturnal, feeding mainly by picking insects off branches or off the ground. Unobtrusive and often stays motionless for long periods.

Buff-banded Rail ▪ *Gallirallus philippensis* 30cm
(Malay: Sintar Topeng Merah Biasa. Indonesian: Mandar-padi Kalung-kuning)

DESCRIPTION A rail with an unmistakable head pattern, adult has olive-brown forehead and crown, bold grey-white supercilium extending to nape, bordered below by broad olive-brown eye-stripe which connects to chestnut coloured nape. White spotted upperpart feathers, brown dark-centred. Throat, cheeks and neck grey. Breast, belly and flanks grey barred black and white, vent buff. Iris red, bill pink/red, legs and feet olive-brown. Similar to Slaty-breasted Rail (below) which lacks grey-white supercilium and has plain grey breast. **DISTRIBUTION** Philippines, Lesser Sundas, Sulawesi east to Australia, New Zealand and SW Pacific. First recorded in Borneo in 2004, expanding rapidly and is now widespread, uncommon to locally common lowland resident. Race: *G. p. philippensis*. **HABITS AND HABITAT** Paddy fields, mangroves, marshes, swamps, estuaries and wetlands. Forages in shallow water and muddy fields like other rails, and feeds on aquatic invertebrates, frogs and fish.

Slaty-breasted Rail ▪ *Lewinia striata* 22–30cm
(Malay: Sintar Biasa. Indonesian: Mandar-padi Sintar)

DESCRIPTION Adult *L. s. striatus* has chestnut head and nape with a weak dark patch from top of crown to nape. Face, throat, neck and breast grey. Upperparts dark olive, spotted black and finely barred white. Belly to vent and flanks barred black and white. Tail short. Iris yellow-brown, bill black with broad pink base, legs and feet grey. Adult *L. s. gularis* is paler overall and has a white throat. **DISTRIBUTION** Indian sub-continent, East and Southeast Asia, Taiwan, Greater Sundas, Philippines, Wallacea. Common resident throughout Borneo's lowlands, up to 1,200m. Races: *L. s. striata* (shown) in N Borneo, *L. s. gularis* in the S. **HABITS AND HABITAT** Mangroves, brackish reedbeds, freshwater swamps, wet grassland, paddy fields, drainage canals. Generally solitary, shy and partly nocturnal, coming out to open edges only when foraging at the muddy strips crisscrossing marshes. Hard to observe owing to its secretive habits.

White-browed Crake ▪ *Poliolimnas cinereus* 15–20cm
(Malay: Ruak-ruak Kening Putih. Indonesian: Tikusan Alis-putih)

DESCRIPTION A smallish grey and brown crake with a distinctive black eye-patch from bill base to just behind eye, bordered by a broad white supercilium above and a longer but thinner broad white stripe below. Adult has grey neck and breast, crown darker grey. Mantle and short tail light brown. Back and wing feathers dark brown, broadly fringed buff. Lower belly to vent light brown. Iris red, bill yellowish olive with orange base, legs and feet greenish yellow. **DISTRIBUTION** Central Thailand to Malay Peninsula, Philippines,

Greater Sundas, Wallacea, Melanesia, Micronesia, Australia. Locally common lowland resident throughout Borneo. Monotypic. **HABITS AND HABITAT** Lowland freshwater and brackish swamps, marshes, mangroves, paddy fields; also water hyacinth, water lily and other dense vegetation near water, especially favouring mats of floating vegetation. A secretive and timid bird that is easily concealed in long grass near water's edge.

White-breasted Waterhen ▪ *Amaurornis phoenicurus* 28–33cm
(Malay: Ruak-ruak Biasa. Indonesian: Kareo Padi)

DESCRIPTION A contrasting white and dark bird. Adult has dark slaty-grey crown, nape and rest of upperparts, browner at wings. Forehead, face and throat to belly white. Lower belly to under-tail coverts cinnamon. Tail short. Iris dark brown, bill green with bright red patch at base of upper mandible, legs and feet dull greenish yellow. **DISTRIBUTION**

Indian sub-continent to Southeast Asia, China, Greater Sundas, Philippines, Wallacea. Abundant and widespread resident throughout Borneo, including offshore islands, up to 750m. Race: *A. p. phoenicurus*. **HABITS AND HABITAT** Vegetation along ditches, irrigation canals, swamps, paddy fields, plantations, suburban gardens, grasslands and similar habitats. Often seen on roadsides adjacent to ditches, and possibly the most common roadkill victim in Borneo. Not shy and willing to come out to forage in the open, sometimes wandering far away from water. Feeds on fish, insects, and paddy and grass seeds.

Purple Swamphen ▪ *Porphyrio porphyrio* 28–32cm
(Malay: Pangling Biasa. Indonesian: Mandar Besar)

DESCRIPTION An unmistakable big blue and purple rail. Adult has black head, nape and back. Wings black with turquoise patch on wing coverts. Throat and upper breast blue-turquoise, graduating to darker turquoise on flanks and belly. Under-tail coverts white. Iris red, massive bill and frontal shield bright red, leg and feet pink. **DISTRIBUTION** Africa, S Europe, South and Southeast Asia, S China, Greater Sundas, Philippines, Wallacea, Australia, New Zealand, W Pacific. Common resident of S Kalimantan, and very local resident in suitable habitats in Sabah. Races: *P. p. indicus* (shown), and possibly the pale Philippines form *P. p. pulverulentus*. **HABITS AND HABITAT** Freshwater swamps, ponds, lakes, marshes, paddy fields, reedbeds. Walks among water hyacinth and water lilies, flicking tail constantly. Feeds on aquatic plants and small insects, snails, etc. When feeding on plants, will hold them in one foot like a parrot.

Common Moorhen ▪ *Gallinula chloropus* 30–38cm
(Malay: Tiong-air Biasa. Indonesian: Mandar Batu)

DESCRIPTION A medium-sized grey-black and white rail. Adult has red frontal shield and red bill with yellowish-green tip. Overall dark bluish black with darker wings and tail. Prominent broken white bars on flanks. Under-tail coverts white with a black central stripe. Iris reddish brown, legs and feet dull greenish yellow with red at top of tibia. **DISTRIBUTION** Almost worldwide in temperate and tropical regions, except Australia. Both resident and migrant birds locally common in suitable habitats throughout Borneo. Race: *G. c. orientalis*. **HABITS AND HABITAT** Freshwater swamps, ponds, lakes, marshes, paddy fields, reedbeds. Constantly flicks tail. Not particularly shy, often foraging in the open. Swims and walks leisurely while foraging, sometimes in family groups consisting of adult and immature birds.

Black-winged Stilt ▪ *Himantopus himantopus* 35–40cm
(Malay: Kedidi Kaki-Panjang Biasa. Indonesian: Gagang-bayam Timur)

DESCRIPTION A tall, elegant black and white wader, unmistakable in the field. Adult non-breeding male has varying amounts of grey on crown, nape and hind-neck. Grey band across mantle, back to rump white, wings black, tail tipped grey. Underparts plain white. Adult female is similar but black is duller. Breeding male has entire head and neck white. Iris reddish brown, needle-like bill black, legs and feet pink. **Pied Stilt** *H. leucocephalus* is similar, but has white crown with varying amount of black on nape and mane. **DISTRIBUTION** Africa, Europe, South, East and Southeast Asia. Increasing, locally common winter migrant to N and NW coasts of Borneo, including Tawau in the NE. Monotypic. **HABITS AND HABITAT** Coastal mudflats, wetlands, swamps, marshes, shallow aquaculture ponds, paddy fields, lake edges. Usually seen in scattered flocks, walking gracefully on long legs as it forages in shallow water.

Tibetan Plover ▪ *Anarhynchus atrifrons* 19–21cm
(Malay: Rapang-sisir Kecil. Indonesian: Cerek-pasir Tibet)

DESCRIPTION A smallish plain-looking plover. Non-breeding bird has white forehead and supercilium, greyish-brown upperpart feathers and no white collar. Underparts plain white with greyish-brown patches on breast side. Breeding male has white throat with rich chestnut side of neck and breast, and variable black mask extending from ear-coverts to lores and across the forehead in some races. In breeding female black is replaced by brown or rufous. Shortish bill black, legs brownish grey to dark grey. Almost unidentifiable from **Siberian Plover** *A. mongolus* when it is here in its winter plumage, but Siberian is believed to be rarer in Greater Sundas, more common towards the east. The very similar-looking and

equally common **Greater Sand Plover** *A. leschenaultii* is generally larger, with longer and paler legs and a thicker and longer bill. **DISTRIBUTION** Breeds in Central Asia, migrating to E coast of Africa, Arabian Peninsula, South, East and Southeast Asia, Sundas, Philippines, Wallacea, Australia. Widespread and common winter visitor and passage migrant to Borneo's coast and islands. Races: *A. a. atrifrons*, and, presumably, *A. a. schaeferi*. **HABITS AND HABITAT** Coastal mudflats, estuaries and sandy beaches. Mixes freely with other waders. Forages like other plovers by running, stopping and picking. Feeds on polychaete worms.

Malaysian Plover ▪ *Anarhynchus peronii* 14–16cm
(Malay: Rapang Pantai Melayu. Indonesian: Cerek Melayu)

DESCRIPTION Adult male has white forehead and supercilium, black eye-line from
lores to ear-coverts, and black frontal bar that does not connect to eye-line. Thin white
collar is bordered below by black collar-line that extends to side of breast. Dark-centred
olive-brown feathers make upperparts appear scaly. Underparts plain white. Adult female
resembles male but black is replaced by rufous. Bill black, legs and feet greenish grey.

DISTRIBUTION Indochina, Thai–Malay Peninsula, Sundas,
Philippines, Sulawesi. The
only resident wader in Borneo;
widely distributed along the
coastline but uncommon and
local. Monotypic. **HABITS
AND HABITAT** Mostly on
sandy beaches. Always seen
singly, in pairs or in 3s, and
usually very tame. Does not
form flocks and seldom mixes
with other waders.

LEFT: *Female* RIGHT: *Male*

Nordmann's Greenshank ▪ *Tringa guttifer* 29–32cm
(Malay: Kedidi Kali Hijau Berbintik. Indonesian: Trinil Nordmann)

DESCRIPTION In non-breeding winter plumage, adult resembles **Common Greenshank**
T. nebularia but with paler and plainer upperparts. It can be distinguished from that species
by its bicoloured, straighter and thicker-looking bill; shorter and yellower legs; hunched
appearance, produced by a heavy breast; pale ash-grey upperpart feathers, which are narrowly
fringed white; and tertials that are narrowly fringed white, not notched black and white.
Breeding bird has varying amounts of grey-black and deeply notched white scapulars, dark
grey or blackish tertials with deep
white notches, and black spots
across white breast and flanks.

DISTRIBUTION Very rare East
Asian endemic, breeding on W
shores of Sea of Okhotsk and N
Sakhalin, and migrating to Japan,
South Korea, Taiwan, SE China,
Southeast Asia, Philippines.
Rare visitor to Borneo's coasts.
Monotypic. **HABITS AND
HABITAT** Coastal mudflats and
lagoons. Prefers to feed along the
tideline, chasing for prey.

Red-necked Stint ■ *Calidris ruficollis* 13–16cm
(Malay: Kedidi-kerdil Leher Merah. Indonesian: Kedidi Leher-merah)

DESCRIPTION A small, dark-legged *Calidris* wader, about the size of a sparrow. Non-breeding adult has white forehead and supercilium with obvious dark lores, and finely streaked head and neck with faint grey-brown wash over breast sides. Upperpart feathers greyish brown with narrow shaft streaks at scapulars. Underparts plain white. Bill, legs and feet black. Breeding bird has chestnut crown with brown streaks, variable rufous-orange to brick-red wash over head and breast, and rufous and black mantle and scapular feathers.

Similar to the rare vagrant **Little Stint** C. *minuta*, but that bird has slightly longer legs and bill, and in non-breeding plumage more extensive dark-centred upperpart feathers. **DISTRIBUTION** N and NE Siberia, wintering to Andamans, South and Southeast Asia, Greater Sundas, Philippines, Wallacea, Melanesia, Australia, New Zealand. Common and abundant passage migrant and winter visitor to Borneo's coasts. Monotypic. **HABITS AND HABITAT** Tidal mudflats, estuaries, sandy beaches; occasionally inland marshes and paddy fields. Large flocks sometimes congregate on mudflats. Walks briskly and feeds with a rapid pecking action.

Great Knot ■ *Calidris tenuirostris* 26–28cm
(Malay: Kedidi-dian Besar. Indonesian: Kedidi Besar)

DESCRIPTION A largish wader. Non-breeding bird has whitish head, face and neck finely streaked grey-brown. Upperpart feathers have broad, dark shafts and pale fringes. Underparts white with grey-streaked breast-band and variably spotted breast and flanks. Bill black, legs and feet dark greenish grey. Breeding bird has dark-streaked grey head and neck. Mantle, wings and tertials black with white fringes. Scapulars rufous with white fringes and black sub-terminal anchors. Breast black with white-fringed feathers, belly and

flanks spotted black. Similar to **Red Knot** C. *canutus* in non-breeding plumage, but that bird has more uniform greyer upperparts and a shorter bill, and is rarer. **DISTRIBUTION** NE Siberia (Yakutia, Chukotka and Koryakia), wintering to South and Southeast Asia, Greater Sundas, Philippines, Wallacea, New Guinea, Australia. Passage migrant and winter visitor in low numbers in suitable Bornean localities. Monotypic. **HABITS AND HABITAT** Coastal mudflats, estuaries, mangroves, beaches. Forms large flocks on intertidal mudflats and feeds by probing.

Common Snipe ■ *Gallinago gallinago* 25–27cm
(Malay: Berkik Kipas Erasias. Indonesian: Berkik Ekor-kipas)

DESCRIPTION Cryptically plumaged as all snipes, adult has a buff median crown-stripe, bordered on both sides by dark, broad lateral crown-stripes. Buff supercilium with brown loral stripe that is broader at bill base. Upperparts richly patterned dark brown with 2 creamy-buff lines edging the mantle and upper-scapular feathers; scapular feathers have wider buff fringes on lower edges. Dark tertial bars are wider than pale bars. Breast mottled light and dark brown, flanks barred, belly whitish. Legs and feet greenish yellow; long, straight bill greenish yellow with dark tip. Very similar to, and difficult to differentiate from, **Pintail Snipe** G. *stenura* and **Swinhoe's Snipe** G. *megala*, which are also common in Borneo in winter. **DISTRIBUTION** Holarctic, migrating to South America, Africa, South, Southeast and East Asia, Greater Sundas, Philippines. Relatively common winter visitor and passage migrant to N parts of Borneo. Race: G. *g. gallinago*. **HABITS AND HABITAT** Paddy fields, wetlands and marshes at sea-level. Probes deeply into soft mud or half-sunken vegetable matter with its long bill; sometimes freezes when disturbed.

Far Eastern Curlew ■ *Numenius madagascariensis* 60–66cm
(Malay: Kendi Besar Timur. Indonesian: Gajahan Timur)

DESCRIPTION The largest curlew, with the longest bill of all waders. Non-breeding adult has buffish head and neck, faint supercilium and obvious white eye-ring. Upperpart feathers dark brown, notched and fringed buff. Underparts paler brown with extensive streaking on neck, breast and flanks. Bill black with pink lower base, legs and feet bluish grey. Female has longer bill than male. Breeding bird has upperpart feathers fringed and notched rich chestnut. The similar-looking **Eurasian Curlew** N. *arquata*, also a winter visitor and passage migrant, is smaller and less rufous overall, generally has a shorter bill and a diagnostic dark loral spot in front of the eye, and shows a white rump and paler underwings in flight. **DISTRIBUTION** Breeds in NE Asia, wintering to E and S China, Southeast Asia, Greater Sundas, Philippines, Wallacea, Australasia, Melanesia. Uncommon to locally common winter visitor and passage migrant to Borneo's coasts. Monotypic. **HABITS AND HABITAT** Coastal mudflats, estuaries, sandy beaches, mangroves. Usually seen on exposed mud, foraging for small fish, crabs and other crustaceans by picking and probing.

Oriental Pratincole ■ *Glareola maldivarum* 23–24cm
(Malay: Kedidi-padang Biasa. Indonesian: Terik Asia)

DESCRIPTION Non-breeding adult has olive-brown upperparts and paler brown crown, lores and throat. Long black primaries extend well beyond tail. Buff chin and throat demarcated by indistinct throat-band. Breast feathers have dark brown centre and buffy-grey fringe. Belly and under-tail white. Bill black, legs and feet grey. Breeding bird (shown) has bright red gape and dark lores. Black and white line from beneath eye encircles

warm buff chin and throat. Upper breast greyish brown, lower breast washed rufous. **DISTRIBUTION** Indian sub-continent, East and central Asia, Japan, wintering to South and Southeast Asia, Greater Sundas, Philippines, Wallacea, New Guinea to Australasia. Regular and widespread winter and passage migrant to Borneo; also a small resident population. Monotypic. **HABITS AND HABITAT** Wetlands, grassland, paddy fields, ploughed open ground. Gregarious, often forming large flocks. Agile flyer that catches insects on the wing, and by running and lunging after them on the ground.

Little Tern ■ *Sternula albifrons* 22–28cm
(Malay: Camar Kecil Biasa. Indonesian: Dara-laut Kecil)

DESCRIPTION A smallish tern. Non-breeding bird has white forehead and lores, and black with white streaks from crown to nape. Upperparts pale grey with 2–3 black outer

primaries. Tail and rump white. Underparts white, bill and legs black. Breeding bird (shown) has less extensive white forehead, which forms a wedge tapering towards nape. Broad black loral line connects to black crown and nape. Bill yellow with black tip, legs orange-yellow. **DISTRIBUTION** Palaearctic, Europe to Africa, Middle East, South, East and Southeast Asia to Australasia, North and South America. Chiefly passage migrant and winter visitor throughout Borneo's coasts; breeding has been recorded. Race: *S. a. sinensis*. **HABITS AND HABITAT** Sandy shores, beaches, coasts, mudflats; occasionally inland. Rests on beaches, and hovers and plunge-dives for prey.

Oriental Darter ■ *Anhinga melanogaster* 85–97cm
(Malay: Kosa-ular Asia. Indonesian: Pecuk-ular Asia)

DESCRIPTION A large waterbird with a long, slender neck, small head and sharp, spear-like bill. Adult head and hind-neck rufous brown with whitish chin and throat. Upperpart feathers blackish with bold silver streaks on wing coverts and scapulars. Breast and rest of underparts black. Iris greenish yellow, bill yellow. Webbed feet greyish yellow.

DISTRIBUTION India, Southeast Asia to Philippines, Sundas. Locally common resident throughout Borneo. Monotypic.
HABITS AND HABITAT Large rivers, oxbow lakes, swamps, wetlands, coasts, mangroves. Dives to spear fish with its sharp bill, and is able to stay underwater for several minutes. When in the water and not diving, usually seen with its head and neck above the surface and its body submerged, thus has to spend great effort running and flapping over water to get airborne. Regularly seen perched and spreading its wings to dry on exposed branches.

Lesser Frigatebird ■ *Fregata ariel* 71–81cm
(Malay: Simbang Kecil. Indonesian: Cikalang Kecil)

DESCRIPTION Largish oceanic bird with long forked tail and angular wings. Adult male is greenish, glossed black, with conspicuous white 'armpit' formed by white axillary patches extending to flanks. Adult female has black hood extending to form a black arrow at throat pointing to belly; white collar, breast, belly and axillaries; black on vent extends to centre of lower belly, forming a black forward-pointing belly-patch. Iris dark brown, bill grey, legs and feet black to reddish brown. **DISTRIBUTION** Widespread in tropical oceans from S Atlantic to Indian Ocean and W Pacific. Abundant non-breeding visitor to coasts and islands off Borneo. Race: *F. a. ariel*. **HABITS AND HABITAT** Oceans, islands. Dives over small fry from shoals that have been driven to the surface by larger fish; also harries other seabirds to seize disgorged food. Usually seen at coastal areas in large flocks, dotting the sky in a graceful spiral flight.

Adult male

Storm's Stork ■ *Ciconia stormi* 85cm
(Malay: Upih Rimba. Indonesian: Bangau Storm)

DESCRIPTION A beautiful blackish stork. Adult has greenish-black crown, white throat and hind-neck; rest of upperparts and wings dark greenish black. Lower neck, breast and flanks black with a metallic sheen. Belly and vent white. Under-tail white with black edge feathers. Iris red, prominent broad yellow orbital ring, bill reddish orange, legs and feet pale pinkish. **DISTRIBUTION** Peninsular Malaysia, Sumatra. Almost extinct in Peninsular Malaysia; remaining small population in Borneo, where it is a scarce resident in suitable habitats. Monotypic. **HABITS AND HABITAT** Lowland dipterocarp forests, oxbow lakes and floodplains of large rivers, riverine swamps; occasionally paddy fields and marshes. Most often seen either in soaring flight above riverine forests or perched in twos or threes on trees along riverbanks.

Yellow Bittern ■ *Ixobrychus sinensis* 30–40cm
(Malay: Gelam Kuning. Indonesian: Bambangan Kuning)

Immature

DESCRIPTION A yellowish-brown bittern, adult male with dark crown and plain, light tawny-brown upperparts. In flight, black flight feathers and tail are diagnostic. Underparts pale creamy white, boldly streaked light rufous. Iris and facial skin yellow, bill yellow-horn with a dark culmen, legs and feet greenish yellow. Adult female has a browner crown and more prominent streaking on foreneck. Immature bird (shown) has heavier streaking above and below. **DISTRIBUTION** SE Siberia to South Asia, Southeast Asia, Taiwan, Greater Sundas, Philippines, Wallacea, New Guinea, Micronesia. Used to be scarce but now an increasingly common resident in N Borneo. Monotypic. **HABITS AND HABITAT** Reedbeds, grassy edges of freshwater wetlands, paddy fields, drains and canals. Always single; stay stationary in tall reeds when stalking prey, blending in well with its surroundings. Normally goes unnoticed until it takes flight when flushed, but will drop back to cover again after a short flight. Also seen clambering about reeds near water bodies in search of food.

Cinnamon Bittern ■ *Ixobrychus cinnamomeus* 40cm
(Malay: Gelam Bendang. Indonesian: Bambangan Merah)

DESCRIPTION Adult male has rich cinnamon upperparts, including wings, buffish throat with prominent white malar stripe and dark brown gular stripe, and almost light, uniform tawny underparts. Adult female is duller with some white streaks on upperparts, and buffish underparts with broad cinnamon streaks. Facial skin greenish yellow, turning red in breeding birds. Iris yellow with a black dot behind pupil resembling 'C'. Bill yellow with dark culmen, legs and feet greenish yellow. In flight, wings and tail are uniform cinnamon with no black. **DISTRIBUTION** China and India to Taiwan, Southeast Asia, Sundas, Philippines. Used to be the commonest bittern in Borneo, but now not as commonly seen as the Yellow Bittern (above). Monotypic. **HABITS AND HABITAT** Usually seen singly in wetlands, paddy fields, ponds and reedbeds. Shy and secretive; blends in well with the surrounding tall reeds, and is difficult to spot if it stays motionless. When flushed, will fly for a short distance then drop back to cover again.

LEFT: *Breeding male*. RIGHT: *Female*

Striated Heron ■ *Butorides striata* 35–48cm
(Malay: Pucung-bakau Biasa. Indonesian: Kokokan Laut)

DESCRIPTION The most common heron in Borneo. Adult has blackish crown and nape with long, dark neck plumes, mantle to rump dark grey, wings darker with prominent pale-fringed feathers, wing coverts washed brownish. Pale ear-covert patch bordered below by broad, dark streaks. Chin and throat whitish with broad whitish streak on centre of breast, rest of underparts plain dark greyish. Iris yellow, bill black with greenish yellow to base of lower mandible, legs and feet yellowish green. Female is a browner version of male. **DISTRIBUTION** Africa, South America, Middle East, South Asia, Greater Sundas, Australia, W Pacific islands. Common and widespread resident throughout Borneo. Race: *B. s. javanica*. **HABITS AND HABITAT** Coastal mudflats and lagoons, reefs, swamps, marshes, mangroves, rivers, ditches and drains. Not shy and will often feed out in the open. Usually solitary, often feeding by standing motionless in shallow water and striking with tremendous speed at passing small fish, which it swallows in an instant, or larger catches, which take longer to swallow.

Black-crowned Night Heron ■ *Nycticorax nycticorax* 58–65cm
(Malay: Pucung-kuak Biasa. Indonesian: Kowak-malam Abu)

DESCRIPTION A plump-looking grey and black heron. Adult has black crown, mantle and back, with 1–3 long white feathers on nape. White forehead extends to form a white line above eye. Grey on side of neck, wings and tail. Underwings grey in flight, rest of underparts plain buffish white. Iris red, bill black with base of lower mandible greenish, legs and feet yellowish green. When breeding, bill is entirely black and legs turn to pink (shown). **DISTRIBUTION** Almost throughout the world's temperate and tropical regions, except for

Breeding

E Indonesia, Australasia and the Pacific islands. Widespread and locally common resident throughout Borneo. Race: *N. n. nycticorax*. **HABITS AND HABITAT** A nocturnal feeder, sleeping by day in tree roosts and colonies, and becoming active from dusk, when birds will fly to their feeding grounds. Birds actively carrying nesting materials have been recorded in daytime. Feeds at sides of drains, streams, paddy fields, marshes, ponds and canals. Roosting and nesting colonies often include other egrets and, occasionally, Rufous Night Heron (below).

Rufous Night Heron ■ *Nycticorax caledonicus* 55–60cm
(Malay: Pucung-kuak Merah. Indonesian: Kowak-malam Merah)

DESCRIPTION Large rufous-brown heron, similar to Black-crowned Night Heron (above). Adult has black crown to nape with white nape-plumes; rest of upperparts and wings plain, deep chestnut-brown. Throat to breast chestnut-brown; belly to vent whitish. Iris yellow, facial skin greenish, bill black, legs and feet dull yellowish green. When breeding, has bluish facial skin, pink legs and feet, and plain buff underparts (shown).

Breeding

DISTRIBUTION Philippines, Java, New Guinea, Australia, New Zealand, W Pacific. Used to be scarce in Borneo but recently became locally common. Breeding has been recorded in Sabah. Race: *N. c. manillensis*. **HABITS AND HABITAT** A nocturnal feeder, sleeping by day in tree roosts and colonies. Active from dusk, when birds will circle the roosting area before leaving for their feeding grounds. Feeds at sides of drains, streams, paddy fields, marshes, ponds and canals. Roosting and nesting colonies often include Black-crowned Night Heron and other egrets.

Javan Pond Heron ■ *Ardeola speciosa* 45–52cm
(Malay: Pucung-padi Emas. Indonesian: Blekok Sawah)

DESCRIPTION Breeding bird has orange-buff head, neck and upper breast; mantle and back black with long black plumes extending towards tail. Wings and tail white. Chin and throat white, graduating to deep cinnamon breast, which is cleanly demarcated from white belly and vent. Non-breeding bird has blackish-brown head heavily streaked buff, and light brown upperparts with white wings. Neck and breast buff, boldly streaked dark brown. Non-breeding bird has yellow iris, dark-tipped yellowish bill with dark culmen, and greenish-yellow legs and feet; breeding bird has black-tipped yellow bill and yellow legs. In non-breeding plumage, indistinguishable in the field from **Chinese Pond Heron** *A. bacchus*, which is a rare winter visitor to NW Borneo. **DISTRIBUTION** Southeast Asia, Sundas, Sulawesi, Mindanao. Common resident in SE Borneo, regular non-breeding visitor in Sabah. Race: *A. s. speciosa*. **HABITS AND HABITAT** Estuarine mangroves, freshwater swamps, lakes, rivers and paddy fields. Perches singly on floating vegetation, clambering about, catching insects and small fish. Also forages for worms on freshly ploughed paddy fields.

Non-breeding

Purple Heron ■ *Ardea purpurea* 70–90cm
(Malay: Pucung Serandau. Indonesian: Cangak Merah)

DESCRIPTION Adult is a mixture of chestnut, black and grey, with prominent black and chestnut lines running down side of neck from face to chest. Cap and nape black, upperparts grey with long, pale greyish and chestnut back plumes. Prominent chestnut shoulder-patch turns purple when breeding. Chin whitish, foreneck rufous with dark streaking, long greyish plumes on lower hindneck, thigh chestnut and rest of underparts dark grey. Iris yellow, bill yellow with dark culmen, legs and feet yellow-brown. **DISTRIBUTION** Africa, Madagascar, Palaearctic to Indian sub-continent, Southeast Asia, Taiwan, Philippines, Wallacea. Widespread, locally common Bornean resident and also a scarce non-breeding winter visitor. Race: *A. p. manilensis*. **HABITS AND HABITAT** Coasts, estuaries, rivers, freshwater swamps, marshes, ponds, paddy fields. Single or in loose flocks; waits motionless for fish in shallow water for long periods. Less restricted to coastal areas than **Grey Heron** *A. cinerea*.

Great Egret ▪ *Ardea alba* 85–104cm
(Malay: Bangau Besar. Indonesian: Kuntul Besar)

DESCRIPTION A large white egret, largest of all the white egrets occurring in the region. Heavy bill, characteristic kink in neck and gape line that goes behind eye are diagnostic. Non-breeding bird has yellow bill and iris, orange yellow facial skin and dark legs. Bird in breeding plumage has extensive lacy back plumes (none on breast), black bill, deep greenish-blue facial skin and pinkish-red legs. Similar to the smaller **Intermediate Egret** *A. intermedia* which has a shorter bill, and gape line does not extend beyond eye. **DISTRIBUTION** South Asia, East Asia, Southeast Asia, Australia. Common winter visitor throughout Borneo, with a small resident breeding population in Sabah and E Kalimantan. Race: *A. a. modesta*. **HABITS AND HABITAT** Wetlands, mangroves, paddy fields, streams, rivers, ponds, mudflats, shallow coastal waters. Feeds singly or in scattered loose flocks, standing in shallow water or on a floating log to catch fish. Often mixes with other egrets.

Non-breeding

Chinese Egret ▪ *Egretta eulophotes* 65–68cm
(Malay: Bangau Cina. Indonesian: Kuntul Cina)

DESCRIPTION A mid-sized all-white egret, usually larger than Little Egret (p. 49) and with proportionally shorter neck and legs. Non-breeding bird has blackish bill with dull yellow base. Iris yellow, facial skin greenish yellow, legs and feet dull greenish. Breeding

bird has long nape-plumes, together with a lacy breast and lower back plumes, bright blue facial skin, reddish-orange bill, black legs and yellow-green toes. **DISTRIBUTION** East and Southeast Asia, Sundas. Breeds on islets off E China; winters in Philippines, Indonesia, Borneo. Regular non-breeding winter visitor in small numbers to NE coast of Borneo. Monotypic. **HABITS AND HABITAT** Wetlands, estuaries, mudflats, bays, lagoons, rocky coasts. Usually seen singly, feeding with other white egrets at water's edge on tidal mudflats. Actively hunts and chases for prey disturbed by incoming wavelets.

Little Egret ▪ *Egretta garzetta* 55–65cm
(Malay: Bangau Kecil. Indonesian: Kuntul Kecil)

DESCRIPTION An elegant mid-sized white egret, smaller than **Intermediate Egret**
Ardea intermedia. Non-breeding bird has black legs and bill, with pale greenish-yellow
base to lower mandible. Iris yellow with greenish facial skin. Winter visitor *E. g. garzetta*
has greenish-yellow feet (shown); resident race *E. g. nigripes* has black feet. A number
of records have emerged in E and SE Asia indicating a rare dark form having bluish grey
plumage with varying amount of white in the
head and chin, could be mistaken as a **White-
faced Heron** *E. novaehollandiae*. **DISTRIBUTION**
Europe, Africa, Asia, Australasia. Races: *E. g.
garzetta* is a widespread and common winter visitor
throughout Borneo; residential *E. g. nigripes* is less
common. **HABITS AND HABITAT** Wetlands,
mangroves, wet paddy fields, streams, ponds,
mudflats, shallow coastal waters, drains. Feeds
singly or in scattered loose flocks, often mixing
with other egrets. Habitually stirs up prey in mud
or water with feet. Can be seen feeding along
ditches and drains in urban habitats.

Pacific Reef Egret ▪ *Egretta sacra* 58–66cm
(Malay: Bangau Batu Pasifik. Indonesian: Kuntul Karang)

DESCRIPTION White morph adult is overall white, about the size of Little Egret (above),
but has shorter neck and legs, and bill thicker at base and less pointed. Bill colour varies
from dark bluish grey to pale yellow, usually with dark culmen. Iris yellow; facial skin
varies from blue-grey to yellowish. Legs yellowish green, sometimes with yellower toes.
Dark morph adult is unmistakable as it is the only egret that occurs in this habitat with
such a dark greyish-blue colour scheme. **DISTRIBUTION**
Indian Ocean to W Pacific, East and Southeast Asia, Sundas,
Philippines, Wallacea. Locally common resident throughout
Borneo's coast and islands. Dark morph
population is more numerous than white
morph birds. Race: *E. s. sacra*. **HABITS
AND HABITAT** Rocky coasts, atolls,
mudflats, islands, sandy beaches. Usually
seen singly, occasionally in pairs or loose
flocks, foraging at water's edge, stalking
for prey in a crouched posture. Also seen
flying over, and feeding off, shoals of
small fish that jump off into the air when
escaping from larger predating fish.

LEFT: *Dark morph.* RIGHT: *White morph*

Black-winged Kite ■ *Elanus caeruleus* 31–37cm
(Malay: Helang-tikus Biasa. Indonesian: Elang Tikus)

DESCRIPTION An elegant white, grey and black kite with largish owl-like head. Adult has white forehead and pale grey crown; mantle, back and rest of upperparts dark grey with black wing coverts forming a distinctive shoulder-patch; long primaries exceed tail tip. Large eyes with blackish eye-patch. Underparts white. Iris reddish orange, cere yellow, bill black, legs and feet yellow. **DISTRIBUTION** Mediterranean, Africa, Saudi Arabia, Iran, Indian sub-continent to Southeast Asia, Philippines, Greater Sundas, New Guinea. Once quite scarce in Borneo except in S Kalimantan, now a locally common lowland resident throughout and spreading. Race: *E. c. hypoleucus.* **HABITS AND HABITAT** Dry open country, grasslands, paddy fields, lightly wooded areas; also suburban gardens and oil-palm plantations. The only resident kite that hovers like a kestrel. Often perches on exposed bare branches and overhead power cables and poles.

Crested Serpent-eagle
■ *Spilornis cheela* 48cm
(Malay: Helang-kuik Biasa. Indonesian: Elang-ular Bido)

DESCRIPTION The commonest forest raptor in Borneo. Adult has black crown and short puffy crest at nape. Upperparts dark greyish brown, wing coverts sparsely dotted white. Face and throat grey, breast plain brown, belly, flanks and vent brown with white spots. Tail black with a single broad whitish-grey bar. Iris yellow, cere and bare facial skin yellow, bill blue-grey, legs and feet pale yellow. **DISTRIBUTION** Indian sub-continent to Southeast Asia, S China, Taiwan, Greater Sundas, Palawan. A common resident throughout Borneo, 0–c. 1,200m; its altitude range overlaps with the darker but much rarer Mountain Serpent-eagle (p. 51) from about 800m. Race: *S. c. pallidus* (shown) in N Borneo, *S. c. richmondi* in the S. **HABITS AND HABITAT** Forests, swamps, plantation forests, forest clearings, residential areas adjacent to forests. Often seen circling singly or in pairs, calling loudly in 2 or 3 notes, *kwee-wee*. Habitually perches singly on branches overlooking open patches of ground where it can ambush its prey.

Mountain Serpent-eagle

■ *Spilornis kinabaluensis* 55–58cm
(Malay: Helang-kuik Kinabalu.
Indonesian: Elang-ular Kinabalu)

DESCRIPTION A serpent-eagle similar
to Crested Serpent-eagle (p. 50) but very
much darker. Upper parts and wing coverts
very dark brown. Crown, nape, face and
throat black. Upper breast plain dark brown.
Lower breast, belly, vent and flanks dark
brown with dense white rectangular spots.
Tail black with single bold whitish bar. Iris,
cere and bare facial skin yellow, bill blue-
grey, legs and feet yellow. **DISTRIBUTION**
Rare montane endemic along central
Bornean mountain ranges, typically from
1,100–2,900m, rarely down to 800m,
which overlaps with Crested Serpent-eagle.
Monotypic. **HABITS AND HABITAT**
Montane forests, best chance to see is when
birds are circling singly or in pairs.

Bat Hawk ■ *Macheiramphus alcinus* 41–51cm
(Malay: Lang Malam. Indonesian: Elang Kelelawar)

DESCRIPTION A mid-sized pied kite resembling
a falcon. Adult has dark crest, white throat with
thick black median throat stripe, white chest and,
sometimes, white belly. Rest of body plumage brown-
black, with long wings that almost touch tail tips
when perched. Iris golden yellow with crescent-
shaped white eyebrow. White lower eyelid sometimes
partially closed to resemble white crescent below
eyes. Bill and cere grey-black. Legs and feet dark grey.
Flight feathers and unbarred tail all brown-black in
flight. **DISTRIBUTION** Africa, Madagascar, Sumatra,
Thai–Malay Peninsula, Sulawesi, New Guinea.
Uncommon lowland resident throughout Borneo.
Race: *M. a. alcinus*. **HABITS AND HABITAT** Feeds
on bats, including fruit bats and insectivorous bats, as
well as cave swiftlets, thus often associates with woods
near limestone caves. Mainly crepuscular to coincide
with its prey.

Rufous-bellied Eagle ■ *Lophotriorchis kienerii* 42–61cm
(Malay: Helang Perut Merah. Indonesian: Elang Perut-karat)

DESCRIPTION A medium-sized, handsome raptor. Adult has short crest on black hood; nape and entire upperparts black. Chin and throat white. Wings long, almost reach tail-tip when perched. Upper breast feathers white tinged rufous with bold dark shaft streaks. Lower breast and belly feathers rufous with dark shaft streaks, vent rufous. In flight shows black-mottled rufous underwing-coverts, remiges and tail barred, with broader subterminal band. Iris dull yellow, cere yellow, bill dark grey, legs and feet greenish yellow with feathered tarsi. **DISTRIBUTION** India and Sri Lanka to SE Asia, Greater Sundas, Philippines and Sulawesi. Uncommon resident and possible winter visitor, from sea level to 1,530m. Race: *L. k. formosus*. **HABITS AND HABITAT** Riverine, lowland and hill dipterocarp, regenerating forests, forest plantations, mangroves. Usually single, sometimes circling above canopy to feed on small birds and mammals, and also observed hunting bats amongst Bat Hawks (opposite).

Black Eagle ■ *Ictinaetus malaiensis* 65–80cm
(Malay: Helang Hitam Asia. Indonesian: Elang Hitam)

DESCRIPTION A large, magnificent black eagle, unmistakable in flight. Adult is blackish overall with indistinct grey barring on long tail. Iris brown, cere yellow, bill black, legs

feathered black with yellow feet. In flight, yellow feet, gape and cere, together with pale carpel patch and faint pale barring on remiges, are distinctive against the otherwise entirely black bird. **DISTRIBUTION** India, Sri Lanka, Southeast Asia, Fujian, Taiwan, Greater Sundas, Sulawesi, Malukus. Scarce but widely distributed Bornean resident, occurring from the coast up to 1,525m in Kinabalu National Park. Race: *I. m. malaiensis*. **HABITS AND HABITAT** Primary, secondary and hill forests, including plantation forests. Usually seen in pairs, gliding effortlessly in circles over the forest canopy, checking it for nests. Feeds on eggs/nestlings and, possibly, canopy-dwelling mammals and reptiles.

Changeable Hawk Eagle ■ *Nisaetus limnaeetus* 63–77cm
(Malay: Helang-hintik Biasa. Indonesian: Elang Brontok)

DESCRIPTION A polymorphic eagle. Pale morph adult has buff head streaked brown with short nuchal crest. Upperparts brown with buff-fringed feathers; throat whitish with median stripe and moustache. Breast whitish buff, boldly streaked brown. Tail has 3 dark bands plus a broader sub-terminal band. Iris brownish yellow, cere and bill dark grey. Tarsi feathered rufous, feet yellow. Flight feathers barred brown in flight. Dark morph adult is overall blackish brown to black. Iris brown, cere and bill black. Feet yellow. In flight, underwing coverts are darker than the barred

flight feathers. **DISTRIBUTION** Himalayas, Andamans, Southeast Asia, Greater Sundas, Philippines.Widespread and common resident throughout Borneo, 0–1,400m. Both pale and dark morph birds are regularly seen; in certain locations 1 form predominates. Intermediate-phase birds are possibly juveniles. Race: *N. l. limnaeetus.* **HABITS AND HABITAT** Lowland primary and secondary forests, open woodlands, occasionally coastal and mangrove forests. Chiefly a forest bird, usually seen circling, but may raid fowls in villages. Hunts for birds, lizards and small mammals.

ABOVE: *Dark morph.* BELOW: *Pale morph*

Wallace's Hawk Eagle ■ *Nisaetus nanus* 45–49cm
(Malay: Helang-hintik Kecil. Indonesian: Elang Wallace)

DESCRIPTION A smallish hawk eagle. Adult has black crown with white-tipped long crest; dark-streaked brown head; brown upperparts, wings darker brown with pale-fringed feathers; brown median stripe on paler brown throat. Breast buff, boldly streaked dark brown; belly, thigh and vent barred brown. Has 3 black bands on tail. Iris yellow, cere and bill black, tarsi feathered and feet yellow. In flight, flight feathers are narrowly barred and underwing coverts rufous, mottled black. Juvenile is almost indistinguishable from juvenile **Blyth's Hawk Eagle** *N. alboniger*, a very uncommon resident. **DISTRIBUTION** Thai–Malay Peninsula, Sumatra. Local and scarce Bornean resident, 0–1,000m. Race: *N. n. nanus.* **HABITS AND HABITAT** Lowland forests around floodplains, riverine and swamp forests, plantation forests. Habits similar to other hawk eagles. Preys on birds, reptiles and small mammals.

White-bellied Fish-eagle ■ *Icthyophaga leucogaster* 65–75cm
(Malay: Helang-laut Putih. Indonesian: Elang-laut Perut-putih)

DESCRIPTION A large white, grey and black raptor. Adult has white head and nape, rest of upperparts dark greyish brown with black primaries. Wedge-shaped tail white with dark base. Throat and rest of underparts white. In flight, white underwing coverts contrast with dark flight feathers. Iris brown, cere grey, bill grey with dark tip. Legs and feet pale yellow. **DISTRIBUTION** India, East and Southeast Asia, Philippines, Greater Sundas, Wallacea,

Australia. Widespread and common resident along the entire coast and island groups of Borneo; less common on large rivers and lakes inland. Monotypic. **HABITS AND HABITAT** Estuaries, fishing jetties, mangroves, lakes, swamps, rocky coasts, offshore islands. Often seen soaring over the coast or perching on tall trees. Hunts by snatching sea snakes and fish from surface; scavenges for floating dead fish and refuse. Also robs food from other raptors.

Lesser Fish-eagle ■ *Ichthyophaga humilis* 48cm
(Malay: Helang-kanguk Kecil. Indonesian: Elang-ikan Kecil)

DESCRIPTION A compact grey, brown and white fish-eagle. Adult has grey head, neck and upper breast. Mantle, back and wings greyish brown, with buff-fringed scapulars and wing coverts. Lower breast brownish; belly to vent white; brownish-grey tail lacks terminal band. Iris yellow, bill and cere grey, legs and feet pale grey. The very similar but larger **Grey-headed Fish-eagle** *I. ichthyaetus*, an uncommon resident, has a white tail with a broad black terminal band. **DISTRIBUTION** Himalayas, Southeast Asia, Sumatra, Sulawesi. Scarce resident along less disturbed and forested rivers in the interior lowlands and hills of Borneo, up to 1,000m. Occasionally near the coast. Race: *I. h. humilis*. **HABITS AND HABITAT** Riverine forests. Perches on trees along forested rivers; often flushed out by moving boats, flying ahead and perching again on another overhanging branch. Solitary. Feeds on freshwater fish, swooping on prey from near surface and midstream rocks.

Brahminy Kite ▪ *Haliastur indus* 45cm
(Malay: Helang-tembikar Merah. Indonesian: Elang Bondol)

DESCRIPTION Distinctive mid-sized white
and chestnut-brown kite. Adult has plain white
head and neck, and white mantle and breast
with fine black shaft streaks. Rest of upperparts
chestnut with long black primaries. Belly, vent
and unbarred tail chestnut. In flight, underwing
coverts darker chestnut and flight feathers
paler. Iris brown, cere yellow, bill blue-grey, legs
and feet yellow. **DISTRIBUTION** Indian sub-
continent to East and Southeast Asia, Greater
Sundas, Philippines, Wallacea, New Guinea to
Solomons, Australia. The commonest raptor in
Borneo; more often found along the coast, also
inland up to 1,100m. Race: *H. i. intermedius*.
HABITS AND HABITAT Open country, logged
forests, oil-palm plantations, mangroves, coasts,
inland along large rivers and lakes, paddy fields;
also villages and suburban areas. Predator and
scavenger, feeding on fish, snakes, lizards, large
insects, rats and refuse.

Crested Goshawk ▪ *Lophospiza trivirgata* 35–46cm
(Malay: Helang-sewah Besar Berjambul.
Indonesian: Elang-alap Jambul)

DESCRIPTION A powerful accipiter, but when perched
on a tree is about the size of a green pigeon. Adult has grey
head and short grey nuchal crest, and greyish-brown mantle
and wings. Throat and chin white with black median and
lateral stripes. Chest white, streaked or sometimes heavily
blotched rufous; belly barred rufous. Longish tail evenly
barred black. Flight feathers and tail banded in flight. Iris and
cere yellow, bill grey, legs and feet yellow. **DISTRIBUTION** S
India, Himalayas, Southeast Asia, S China, Taiwan, Greater
Sundas, S Philippines. Locally common lowland Bornean
resident, once recorded up to 2,015m. Race: *L. t. microsticta*.
HABITS AND HABITAT Primary and secondary dipterocarp
forests, peat-swamp forests, plantation forests, forest edges.
Hunts for small birds, nestlings, rodents, reptiles, etc., from
a still perch, often a low branch over a river or path. If not
spooked, can be quite approachable.

Oriental Bay Owl ■ *Phodilus badius* 27cm
(Malay: Pungguk-api Biasa. Indonesian: Serak Bukit)

DESCRIPTION A beautiful small owl. Heart-shaped pinkish-buff facial disc of adult is distinctive; thick, broad 'ridge' above bill to forehead, with brown feathers from lores onto the inside edge of eyes extending eyebrow-like to top edge of facial disc. Edge of facial disc narrowly fringed chestnut-brown. Crown, nape and back chestnut-brown, speckled with black spots. Wings chestnut-brown, dotted with black spots and bordered buff on wing coverts. Underparts pinkish buff, spotted with black-bordered buff. Legs feathered buff to toes, feet yellowish buff, bill ivory. **DISTRIBUTION** Southeast Asia, S China, Greater Sundas. Scarce Bornean resident, sparingly distributed throughout lowland and hill forests, up to 750m. Race: *P. b. badius*. **HABITS AND HABITAT** Lowland and hill dipterocarp forests, secondary forests, bamboo and plantation forests. Recorded in oil-palm estates next to forests in Sepilok, Sabah. A shy, nocturnal forest owl, inhabiting middle and lower storeys of the forest. It likes to perch on vertical trunks of medium-sized trees and saplings.

Collared Scops Owl ■ *Otus lempiji* 20–25cm
(Malay: Jampuk Biasa. Indonesian: Celepuk Reban)

DESCRIPTION Most common of lowland scops owls. Rufous morph adult has blackish forehead and crown, and prominent buffish ear-tufts. Facial disc brown fringed with black. Upperparts and wings have cryptic plumage, with paler feathers at nape forming indistinct collar, visible only when neck is extended forwards. Underparts buff-brown with fine brown vermiculations and discontinuous dark streaks. Iris yellow, bill and claws greenish-grey, legs feathered to toes, feet pale grey. A polymorphic owl, with brown, rufous and grey (rare) morphs. **DISTRIBUTION** India, SE Asia to E Asia, Greater Sundas. Common resident in lowland forests, recorded up to 1,500m. Race: *O. l. lemurum* (shown) in N Borneo, *O. l. lempiji* elsewhere. **HABITS AND HABITAT** Nocturnal, single-syllable *wook* call can be heard repeated every 10–15 seconds. Not afraid of humans, and may stay on the same perch for several minutes even after being spotted. Occurs in primary and secondary forests, including parks and city gardens, and plantations. Feeds on mice, nestlings, insects and geckos.

Reddish Scops Owl ■ *Otus rufescens* 15–18cm
(Malay: Jampuk Merah. Indonesian: Celepuk Merah)

DESCRIPTION A small reddish-brown owl. Adult has indistinct buffish-brown facial disc with dark brown fringe, and long, dark brown hairs on face and around eyes. Crown, nape and back chestnut-brown with streaks formed by black and buff spots. Wing coverts darker, with black and buff streaks; brown flight feathers barred buff. Underparts rufous with black spots. Legs feathered buff to toes, feet pale yellow, bill ivory. **DISTRIBUTION** Thai–Malay Peninsula, Greater Sundas. Scarce lowland Bornean resident, up to 1,985m. Race: *O. r. rufescens*. **HABITS AND HABITAT** Lowland and hill dipterocarp forests, lower montane, logged and secondary forests. A small, shy, nocturnal owl, which inhabits the lower and middle storeys. Diet is poorly known, but it probably feeds mostly on insects.

Barred Eagle Owl
■ *Bubo sumatranus* 40–46cm
(Malay: Burung-hantu Bertanduk Belang Melayu. Indonesian: Beluk Jampuk)

DESCRIPTION One of the 3 large owls of Borneo; the least common. Adult has prominent long, horizontal ear tufts, which together with forehead and nape are finely barred dark brown and buff. Back to rump dark brown, barred rufous. Wings richly patterned dark brown and rufous with whitish lower scapular feathers. Throat and breast densely barred rufous and brown, belly pale white with less dense dark brown barrings. Legs feathered to toes, feet and bill yellow. Juvenile bird can be completely white. **DISTRIBUTION** Thai–Malay Peninsula, Greater Sundas. Sparsely distributed scarce lowland Bornean resident, up to 1,000m. Race: *B. s. strepitans*. **HABITS AND HABITAT** Lowland and hill dipterocarp forests, gardens, kerangas, plantation and secondary forests. Nocturnal but can occasionally be found roosting in thick foliage during the day. Feeds on birds, snakes and rats.

Buffy Fish Owl ■ *Bubo ketupu* 38–45cm
(Malay: Tumbuk-ketampi Biasa. Indonesian: Beluk Ketupa)

DESCRIPTION The commonest of the 3 large Bornean owls. Adult has long, horizontal ear tufts and pale forehead 'V' above bill. Head dark brown with rufous streaks. Upperpart feathers rich orange-brown, heavily mottled with dark streaks and buff edges. Flight feathers broadly barred brown and buff. Underparts rufous, breast broadly streaked dark brown, belly with finer streaks. Iris yellow, bill dark grey. Unfeathered legs and feet greenish grey. **DISTRIBUTION** India, Southeast Asia, Greater Sundas. Locally common lowland resident throughout Borneo, including nearby islands, up to 945m. Race: *B. k. pageli* in NW Borneo, *B. k. ketupu* elsewhere. **HABITS AND HABITAT** Swamps, paddy fields, plantation forests, riverine forests, mangroves, seashores. The most common owl to be seen in Danum Valley, lower Kinabatangan and Tabin. It is not uncommon to see a few together, especially in open wooded localities near water. Usually preys on fish and frogs; also seen feeding on rats and recorded to come to lights on buildings to hunt insects.

Sunda Wood Owl ■ *Strix leptogrammica* 40–55cm
(Malay: Carik-kafan Coklat. Indonesian: Kukuk-beluk Coklat)

DESCRIPTION The 2nd commonest large owl of Borneo. Adult *S. l. vaga* underparts quite similar to those of Barred Eagle Owl (p. 57), but facial disc rufous with dark brown edging, appearing like a spectacle with dark shadows around eyes. Upperparts densely barred dark brown and rufous, flight feathers and tail with similar broader barring. Throat to upper breast rufous brown, densely barred dark brown; belly buffish white and similarly barred. Legs feathered to toes, feet grey, bill black. *S. l. leptogrammica* is generally smaller and brighter. **DISTRIBUTION** Borneo and Java. Uncommon lowland resident throughout Borneo, to above 1,500m in Kinabalu National Park. Races: *S. l. vaga* (shown) in Sabah, *S. l. leptogrammica* elsewhere. **HABITS AND HABITAT** Lowland and hill dipterocarp forests, secondary forests, forest edges, plantation forests, coastal vegetation. Nocturnal, feeding on small mammals, birds, reptiles and large insects. If disturbed, might compress its plumage to look like a piece of dead wood.

Brown Boobook ■ *Ninox scutulata* 27–33cm
(Malay: Pungguk Betemak Biasa.
Indonesian: Pungguk Coklat)

DESCRIPTION A hawk-like owl, with a rounded head that
lacks a flat facial disc. Adult has greyish-brown upperparts
with blackish-brown head; tail tipped white and broadly barred
black and brown. Underparts whitish, densely and broadly
streaked brown, streaks sparser at belly. Iris yellow, bill dark
grey with greenish culmen. Legs feathered to toes, feet yellow.
The similar **Northern Boobook** *N. japonica* is slightly paler
and has a different call; it is a scarce winter visitor to offshore
islands of N Borneo. **DISTRIBUTION** Indian sub-continent to
Southeast Asia, S China, Taiwan, Greater Sundas. Widespread
and locally common lowland Bornean resident, up to 1,530m.
Race: *N. s. borneensis*. **HABITS AND HABITAT** Lowland
forests, forest edges, secondary forests, mangroves, plantation
forests, scrub. Feeds mostly on moths, beetles, dragonflies
and other insects. Nocturnal and occasionally crepuscular. Its
2-note call, *boo-book, boo-book*, with the 2nd note higher, is
one of the most frequently heard owl calls in the night forest.

Red-naped Trogon ■ *Harpactes kasumba* 31–34cm
(Malay: Kesumba Tengkuk Merah. Indonesian: Luntur Kasumba)

DESCRIPTION A large trogon with a conspicuous red nape. Adult male has black
forehead to hind-crown. Blue facial and orbital skin broken by black patch behind eye.
Broad red nape stripe running from just behind blue orbital skin. Mantle to uppertail
golden brown with tail tipped black. Black and white vermiculations on
wing coverts, with black primaries. Throat to upper breast black, bordered
below by white breast-band. Rest of underparts bright red. Under-tail
feathers patterned black and white. Iris dark brown,
bill blue, legs and feet bluish grey. Adult female has
grey-brown head, breast and upperparts; broader buff
vermiculations on wing coverts; yellow-brown breast
and belly. **DISTRIBUTION** Thai–Malay Peninsula,
Sumatra. Locally common lowland resident
throughout Borneo, up to 1,220m. Race: *H. k.
impavidus*. **HABITS AND HABITAT** Lowland and
hill dipterocarp forests, bamboo, plantation forests,
kerangas, peat swamps, lower montane forests.
Usually seen singly or in pairs. Prefers upper and
mid-storeys of undisturbed forests, where it hunts for
large insects and caterpillars.

LEFT: *Female*. RIGHT: *Male*

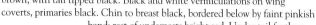

Diard's Trogon ■ *Harpactes diardii* 30–35cm
(Malay: Kesumba Tengkuk Jambu. Indonesian: Luntur Diard)

DESCRIPTION A large trogon with a pink nape. Adult male has reddish-black forehead to hind-crown, purple orbital skin, and broad pink nape stripe. Mantle to uppertail golden brown, with tail tipped black. Black and white vermiculations on wing coverts, primaries black. Chin to breast black, bordered below by faint pinkish band; rest of underparts bright red. Under-tail feathers white, densely flecked black. Iris orange-brown, bill blue with dark culmen and tip, legs and feet bluish grey. Adult female is similar but with grey-brown head and breast, buff vermiculations on wing coverts, and rest of underparts pinkish, and without pink nape stripe. **DISTRIBUTION** Thai–Malay Peninsula, Sumatra. Locally common lowland resident throughout Borneo, up to 1,220m. Race: *H. d. diardii*. **HABITS AND HABITAT** Lowland and hill dipterocarp forests, plantation forests, logged and riparian forests, peat swamps, kerangas, lower montane forests. Habits are like those of Red-naped Trogon (above) but prefers the forest understorey.

LEFT: *Male*. RIGHT: *Female*

Scarlet-rumped Trogon ■ *Harpactes duvaucelii* 23–26cm
(Malay: Kesumba kecil Pinggul Merah. Indonesian: Luntur Putri)

DESCRIPTION The smallest of the Bornean trogons. Adult male has a black head, throat and nape; mantle and back cinnamon with distinctive scarlet rump and uppertail coverts. Uppertail feathers cinnamon with black tip. Black and white vermiculations on wing coverts; primaries black. Iris brown, eyelid cobalt-blue; bill blue with dark culmen and tip, legs and feet light grey. Adult female is similar but black on entire head is replaced by brown, yellow-brown breast grades to pinkish orange on rest of underparts, and has black and yellow vermiculations on wing coverts. Scarce resident **Cinnamon-rumped Trogon** *H. orrophaeus* is similar but slightly larger, with an almost uniform cinnamon rump as on back. **DISTRIBUTION** Thai–Malay Peninsula, Sumatra. Common lowland resident throughout Borneo, up to 1,005m or occasionally 1,500m. Monotypic. **HABITS AND HABITAT** Lowland and hill dipterocarp forests, secondary forests, kerangas, peat swamps, mangroves, forest plantations. Habits are essentially similar to those of other trogons, but this species is not as shy and is quite comfortable to perch in the open.

LEFT: *Male*. RIGHT: *Female*

Orange-breasted Trogon ■ *Harpactes oreskios* 26–31cm
(Malay: Kesumba Harimau. Indonesian: Luntur Harimau)

DESCRIPTION The only trogon whose male lacks red in its plumage. Adult male has olive-green head, nape, throat and upper breast; mantle to uppertail rich chestnut, tail tipped black. Black and white vermiculations on wing coverts, primaries

black. Lower breast yellow-orange, belly to under-tail coverts yellow. Under-tail feathers patterned black and white. Iris brown with blue eye-ring, bill blue with dark culmen and tip, legs and feet pale grey. Adult female is similar but has olive-brown head and mantle, black and buff vermiculations on wing coverts, and underparts less orange overall. **DISTRIBUTION** SW China, Southeast Asia, Greater Sundas. Scarce, mainly sub-montane Bornean resident, 200–1,500m. Race: *H. o. dulitensis.* **HABITS AND HABITAT** Hill and sub-montane forests, and secondary forests, particularly on slopes. Habits are essentially like those of other trogons, but this species is not shy of humans; if one is spotted, it can be approached and observed quite closely.

LEFT: *Female.* RIGHT: *Mle*

Whitehead's Trogon ■ *Harpactes whiteheadi* 30–33cm ⓔ
(Malay: Kesumba Gunung Kinabalu. Indonesian: Luntur Kalimantan)

DESCRIPTION The only montane trogon of Borneo with a distinctive grey breast. Adult male has scarlet forehead, crown and nape; cinnamon mantle to uppertail, black and white vermiculations on wing coverts, black primaries. Chin and throat black, breast grey, rest of underparts scarlet, under-tail feathers white. Iris brown with blue orbital skin,

bill blue with dark culmen and tip, legs and feet pale grey. Adult female is similar but all scarlet is replaced by cinnamon-brown, and has black and yellow vermiculations on wing coverts. **DISTRIBUTION** Uncommon endemic montane resident, 900–2,500m. Monotypic. **HABITS AND HABITAT** Primary montane forests from G. Kinabalu and G. Trus Madi along the spinal range to G. Mulu, the Usun Apau Plateau and G. Dulit. A very shy bird, often sitting quietly on higher branches and making short flights from perch to perch.

LEFT: *Female.* RIGHT: *Male*

Wreathed Hornbill ▪ *Rhyticeros undulatus* 100cm
(Malay: Enggang Gunung Biasa. Indonesian: Julang Emas)

DESCRIPTION A large hornbill with a gular pouch. Adult male (centre and right bird in photo) has dark brown crown-stripe and mane, yellowish-white head and neck, and yellow gular pouch. Rest of plumage black with plain white tail. Bill white with ridged brownish base, and corrugated low casque. Iris orange-yellow with orbital skin red, legs and feet dark grey. Adult female is similar but has blue gular pouch (left bird in photo), and black

replaces all the brown and white in the male's head and neck. Both male and female have a black stripe on gular pouch. **DISTRIBUTION** NE India to SW China, Southeast Asia, Greater Sundas. Widespread and locally common resident throughout Borneo, chiefly sub-montane, up to 3,050m. Monotypic. **HABITS AND HABITAT** Lowland and hill dipterocarp forests, kerangas, montane forests, peat-swamp forests. The only Bornean hornbill that occurs in higher montane forests. Usually in groups or pairs, flying long distances in search of fruiting trees. Feeds mainly on fruits, also on small animals.

Rhinoceros Hornbill ▪ *Buceros rhinoceros* 110cm
(Malay: Enggang Badak. Indonesian: Rangkong Badak)

DESCRIPTION A large hornbill with an orange casque. Other than white belly, thighs and rump, body plumage of adult is black overall. The only Bornean hornbill to have a broad black band at centre of white tail. Bill pale yellow, base of lower mandible black; middle of upper mandible yellow, graduating to orange-red at base. Upturned and protruding casque reddish orange on upper surface, yellow on front. Legs and feet greenish. Adult female (left in photo) has white iris; adult male (right in photo) has red iris and black stripe at side of casque. **DISTRIBUTION** Thai–Malay Peninsula, Greater Sundas. Locally common lowland Bornean resident, up to 2,000m. Race: *B. r. borneoensis*. **HABITS AND HABITAT** Lowland and hill dipterocarp forests, secondary forests, lower montane forests, plantation forests, riverine and peat-swamp forests. Usually seen in pairs. Flies long distances to search for fruiting trees, returning to feed on the same trees until the fruits are exhausted. Makes a loud series of calls before taking flight.

Helmeted Hornbill ■ *Rhinoplax vigil* 120cm + 50cm elongated central tail
streamers (Malay: Enggang Gading. Indonesian: Rangkong Gading)

DESCRIPTION A large hornbill with elongated tail streamers. Adult male has black crown and nape, and brown ear-coverts. Bare and wrinkled skin on side of neck to throat red. Upperparts dark brown. Breast blackish brown; belly, thigh and vent dirty white. Tail white with broad, dark sub-terminal band; elongated central tail feathers grey-brown with dark sub-terminal band and white tip. Conspicuous white tips to flight feathers. Bill yellow with red basal half; short, blunt-fronted casque red. Iris brown, legs and feet olive-brown. Adult female is similar but bare skin at neck and throat is bluish white. **DISTRIBUTION** Thai–Malay Peninsula, Sumatra. Uncommon lowland resident throughout Borneo, up to 915m. Monotypic. **HABITS AND HABITAT** Lowland and hill dipterocarp forests, lowland alluvial forests, including forests over limestone. Usually solitary or in pairs. Feeds mainly on fruits, also on birds, lizards and other small vertebrates. Has a peculiar call that starts in slow *wook* notes a few seconds apart but gaining in speed to end in maniacal *kekekeke* laughter.

LEFT: *Female*. RIGHT: *Male*

Wrinkled Hornbill
■ *Rhabdotorrhinus corrugatus* 65–70cm (Malay: Enggang Berkedut Melayu. Indonesian: Julang Jambul-hutan)

DESCRIPTION A handsome hornbill with a gular pouch, male bird (shown) is attractive with multi-coloured head. Male has black mane, ochre neck with paler gular pouch. Wrinkled casque and base of upper mandible red, basal half of lower mandible deep brown and ridged, rest of bill ochre. Orbital skin blue. Legs and feet dark brownish-grey. Female has blue pouch and black neck, uniform yellow bill with smaller casque. **DISTRIBUTION** Thai–Malay Peninsula, Sumatra, Borneo. Scarce lowland resident, up to 300m. Monotypic. **HABITS AND HABITAT** Usually seen in pairs, sometimes in small groups, flying over forest; feeds at fruiting trees with other hornbills.

Male

White-crowned Hornbill

■ *Berenicornis comatus* 85cm
(Malay: Enggang Bulu. Indonesian: Enggang Jambul)

DESCRIPTION One of the rarer hornbills in Borneo. Adult male has a distinctive tall, bushy white crest made up of erect, shaggy feathers. Head to nape white. Back to rump and wings glossy black. Throat to upper belly white, lower belly to vent black. Entire tail white. Bill and insignificant casque dark grey with paler base. Iris yellow; bare skin around eye, gape and malar areas bluish. Legs and feet black. Adult female is similar but has black on throat to belly. **DISTRIBUTION** Tenasserim Range in peninsular Myanmar and peninsular Thailand, Annam, Cochinchina, Thai–Malay Peninsula, Sumatra. Uncommon, sparingly distributed lowland resident throughout Borneo, up to 1,800m; scarce in Kalimantan. Monotypic. **HABITS AND HABITAT** Lowland and hill dipterocarp forests, lower montane forests, kerangas, peat-swamp forests, occasionally secondary forests. Usually found in small family groups or pairs. Feeds mainly on large insects, lizards and other small animals, and on fruits.

Female

Bushy-crested Hornbill ■ *Anorrhinus galeritus* 65–70cm
(Malay: Enggang Buluh. Indonesian: Enggang Klihingan)

DESCRIPTION The only hornbill that has no white in its plumage. Adult has feathers from crown to rump including wings, which are black. Throat and breast black, belly dark grey. Basal two-thirds of tail brownish-grey with terminal third black. Gular

and orbital skin behind eye pale blue. Male has entirely black bill and casque; female has variable amount of yellow on both upper and lower mandibles. Iris red, legs and feet black. **DISTRIBUTION** Thai-Malay peninsula, Greater Sundas. Common resident throughout lowland and submontane forests, up to 1,100m. Monotypic. **HABITS AND HABITAT** Usually seen in noisy flocks of up to 15 birds foraging near canopy in primary as well as logged forests. Arboreal frugivore and omnivore, feeding on figs, fruits, large insects, frogs and lizards.

LEFT: *Male*. RIGHT: *Female*

Oriental Pied Hornbill ■ *Anthracoceros albirostris* 75cm
(Malay: Kelingking Biasa. Indonesian: Kangkareng Perut-putih)

DESCRIPTION A smallish pied hornbill. Other than white on belly, vent and under-tail, the adult plumage is glossy black. Bare skin on cheek and around eye bluish white. Bill yellowish ivory. Adult male has black at base of bill and casque, and black at lower front of protruding casque. Adult female has black on base of lower mandible, front of upper mandible, cutting edges of both mandibles and on front portion of small, non-protruding casque. White tips to flight feathers conspicuous in flight. Iris brown, legs and feet dark grey. **DISTRIBUTION** India to S China, Southeast Asia, Greater Sundas. Widespread and locally common lowland Bornean resident, commoner on islands and coasts, up to 500m. Race: *A. a. convexus*. **HABITS AND HABITAT** Mangroves, coastal vegetation, peat-swamp forests, plantation forests, forest edges, riverine forests. Often seen in small parties. Prefers more open habitats, and feeds on fruits and insects. Flight consists of a few wing flaps followed by gliding with extended wings, this repeated.

LEFT: *Female*. RIGHT: *Male*

Black Hornbill ■ *Anthracoceros malayanus* 75cm
(Malay: Kelingking Hitam. Indonesian: Kangkareng Hitam)

DESCRIPTION Other than the broad white tips to the under-tail feathers, the plumage is entirely black. Adult male has pale yellowish-cream bill and protruding casque. Adult female is similar in plumage, but has small pinkish malar patch and bare skin around eye, and less protruding casque, which together with bill is dark grey instead of creamy white. Iris reddish brown, legs and feet dark grey. There is a variant form for both male and female, where bird has a prominent white or grey supercilium extending to nape. **DISTRIBUTION** Thai–Malay Peninsula, Sumatra. Common and widespread lowland Bornean resident, up to 1,000m. Monotypic. **HABITS AND HABITAT** Lowland and hill dipterocarp forests, secondary forests, kerangas, peat-swamp and coastal forests, riverine forests, mangroves, oil-palm plantations. Usually seen in pairs. Forages in upper storey of forests, feeding on fruits, large insects and lizards.

LEFT: *Female*. RIGHT: *Male*

Bornean Barbet ■ *Psilopogon eximius* 15–16cm (e)
(Malay: Takur Tukang Gunung. Indonesian: Tekur Leher-hitam)

DESCRIPTION The smallest of the Bornean barbets. Adult has black forehead and bright red crown. Turquoise-blue loral spot, supercilium and ear-coverts; yellow spot below eye. Black chin and throat bordered turquoise below. Red spot on side of neck with small, dull red breast-patch. Upperparts brilliant green, underparts paler green. Iris brown, bill black, legs and feet olive-green. Immature has bluish throat and forehead, with duller red on crown; was previously thought to be a separate race found only on G. Kinabalu. **DISTRIBUTION** Uncommon endemic resident along the central Bornean mountain ranges, typically 1,050–2,140m, with extreme records from 425m. Monotypic. **HABITS AND HABITAT** Hill dipterocarp forests, lower and higher montane forests. Usually found with Mountain Barbet (p. 67) but at lower altitudes than Golden-naped Barbet (above). Feeds on fruits. Call is series of 3 *tooks*, with a pause after the 2nd *took*.

Gold-whiskered Barbet ■ *Psilopogon chrysopogon* 30cm
(Malay: Takur Besar Biasa. Indonesian: Takur Gedang)

DESCRIPTION The largest barbet in Borneo. Adult has red lores and forehead, yellow forecrown, and blue crown speckled red and black. Rest of upperparts brilliant green. Black face extends to ear-coverts, bordered below and with extensive bright yellow malar patch. Chin and upper throat grey, edged blue below. Rest of underparts pale green, under-tail blue.

Iris reddish brown, bill greyish black with black bristles at base, legs and feet olive-green. **DISTRIBUTION** Thai–Malay Peninsula, Sumatra. Common resident throughout Borneo's lowlands and sub-montane habitats, up to 1,525m. Race: *P. c. chrysopsis*. **HABITS AND HABITAT** Lowland and hill dipterocarp forests, kerangas, plantation forests, secondary forests, peat-swamp forests. Often seen singly. Forages in upper and middle storeys, or may perch openly on a bare branch at forest edge. Feeds mainly on fruits, occasionally on small vertebrates.

Red-throated Barbet
■ *Psilopogon mystacophanos* 23cm
(Malay: Takur Rengkung Merah Biasa.
Indonesian: Takur Warna-warni)

DESCRIPTION The only Bornean barbet whose sexes
differ in plumage. Adult male has red loral spots, narrow
black forehead-band, orange-yellow forecrown and red
hind-crown. Black supercilium is broader behind eye.
Blue cheek below eye, bordered below by small yellowish
malar patch. Rest of upperparts brilliant green. Chin and
throat red, bordered blue below and with red spot on side
of breast. Rest of underparts pale green, under-tail light
blue. Iris brown, bill black with bristles at base, legs and
feet olive. Adult female is duller green overall, and has
dull red crown-patch and loral spots, bluish cheek, and
paler base to lower mandible. Red spots on side of breast
small or absent. See similar Mountain Barbet (below).
DISTRIBUTION Thai–Malay Peninsula, Sumatra.
Common lowland resident throughout Borneo, up to
1,380m. Race: *P. m. mystacophanos*. **HABITS AND
HABITAT** Lowland and hill dipterocarp forests, plantation
forests, kerangas, secondary forests, peat-swamp forests.
Forages in upper and middle storeys, feeding mainly on
fruits and on insects.

ABOVE: *Male*. BELOW: *Female*

Mountain Barbet ■ *Psilopogon monticola* 20–22cm ⓔ
(Malay: Takur Bukit Borneo. Indonesian: Takur Gunung)

DESCRIPTION Unlike other Bornean barbets, lacks gaudy colours on its head. Adult
has yellowish-green forehead, and streaked greyish-blue crown with a red patch at centre
of crown to nape. Ear-coverts greenish blue with malar area grey-yellowish blue. Rest of
upperparts brilliant green. Throat pale yellowish and grey, tinged blue at lower throat, with
small red spot at breast side. Rest of underparts pale green.
Iris brown, bill black with bristles at base, legs and feet olive-
green. Where their ranges overlap, could be confused with
female Red-throated Barbet (above), but that bird has red
loral spots, greener throat and longer bill. **DISTRIBUTION**
Endemic, locally common resident of montane forests,
750–2,200m. Monotypic. **HABITS AND HABITAT** Hill
dipterocarp forests, montane forests, kerangas, forest edges,
orchards and cultivated lands at appropriate altitude. Feeds
mainly on fruits and insects. Call is easy to identify, being a
series of rapid *tooks*, interspersed with slower *tukuks*.

Golden-naped Barbet ■ *Psilopogon pulcherrimus* 20–21.5cm
(Malay: Takur Topeng Hitam Gunung. Indonesian: Takur Tengkuk-emas)

DESCRIPTION The only Bornean barbet that has no red in its plumage. Adult has turquoise-blue forehead and central crown to hind-neck; face and side of crown yellowish green. Black lores connect to eyes, which are bordered by turquoise-blue. Nape golden yellow, with rest of upperparts brilliant green; feathers on wings coverts fringed paler, creating a scaly effect. Chin and upper throat turquoise-blue, rest of underparts pale green with breast tinged yellow. Iris greyish brown, bill black with bristles at base, legs and feet olive-green. **DISTRIBUTION** Locally common endemic resident of montane forests, usually at 1,100–2,500m but with extreme records at 600–3,200m. Monotypic. **HABITS AND HABITAT** Primary and secondary montane forests, usually higher up than Mountain Barbet (p. 67). Feeds mainly on fruits and insects. Not afraid of humans, and can be approached quite closely. Occasionally perches and feeds on low branches.

Bornean Brown Barbet ■ *Calorhamphus fuliginosus* 17–18cm
(Malay: Takur-dahan Borneo. Indonesian: Ampis Kalimantan)

DESCRIPTION A brownish barbet. Adult *C. f. tertius* male (shown) has brown or reddish-brown forehead to nape, rest of upperparts t o tail darker brown. Chin and throat reddish rufous, breast to vent greyish buff, sometimes with variable faint rufous tinge on breast. Iris olive-yellow; bill rufous, with culmen and basal half of upper mandible blackish; legs and feet orange-red. Adult *C. f. fuliginosus* male is similar to *C. f. tertius* counterpart but has black bill and rufous wash on breast to belly. Adult females of both races are respectively similar to males

but entire bill is rufous. **DISTRIBUTION** Common lowland endemic throughout Borneo, up to 1,450m. Races: *C. f. tertius* in Sabah, Brunei and N Sarawak; *C. f. fuliginosus* elsewhere in Borneo. **HABITS AND HABITAT** Lowland and hill dipterocarp forests, secondary forests, forest edges, peat swamps, mangroves, coastal vegetation, plantation forests. Does not behave like other green barbets, and often seen in family groups. Feeds on fruits and insects, foraging from tree to tree.

LEFT: *Male*. RIGHT: *Female*

Rufous Piculet ■ *Sasia abnormis* 9–10cm
(Malay: Belatuk-kerdil Api Melayu. Indonesian: Tukik Tikus)

DESCRIPTION Tiny, short-tailed woodpecker. Adult male has yellow forehead. Crown and rest of upperparts olive-green, uppertail black. Face, ear-coverts, neck and underparts orange-rufous. Iris orange with bare skin around eye pink, upper mandible black, lower mandible yellow, legs and feet orange. Adult female is similar but forehead is concolourous with underparts. **DISTRIBUTION** Southern Myanmar to Thai–Malay Peninsula, Sumatra, Java. Common resident throughout lowland and sub-montane Borneo, up to 1,590m. Race: *S. a. abnormis*. **HABITS AND HABITAT** Lowland and hill dipterocarp forests, lower montane forests, kerangas, peat-swamp forests, secondary forests, forest edges, plantation forests, bamboo. Prefers disturbed forests, usually in middle or lower storeys, where it taps quietly on lower stems of undergrowth.

Male

Grey-and-buff Woodpecker ■ *Hemicircus concretus* 13–14cm
(Malay: Belatuk-daun Dahi Merah. Indonesian: Caladi Cikotok)

DESCRIPTION A small grey woodpecker with a triangular crest. Adult male has forehead to top of crest crimson, rest of head dark grey, nape feathers tipped buff. Faint buff line runs down side of neck. Upperparts' feathers black, fringed buff, creating a striking scalloped pattern. Primary feathers black. Underparts dark grey, lower flanks and vent mottled black and buff. Short tail black. Iris reddish brown; bill, legs and feet dark grey. Adult female is similar but has dark grey forehead to crest. **DISTRIBUTION** Thai–Malay Peninsula, Greater Sundas. Widespread and locally common resident of Borneo's lowlands, up to 1,530m. Race: *H. c. sordidus*. **HABITS AND HABITAT** Lowland dipterocarp forests, secondary forests, peat swamps, forest edges, plantation forests, gardens. Usually in pairs or small groups, especially in secondary forests, foraging on trunks, small branches and foliage in top storey. A bark-gleaning insectivore; also feeds on fruits.

Male

Buff-rumped Woodpecker ■ *Meiglyptes tristis* 15–18cm
(Malay: Belatuk-batu Biasa. Indonesian: Caladi Batu)

DESCRIPTION A smallish, densely barred woodpecker. Adult male has black and buff vermiculations on head, crown and neck. Eye-ring and lores buff with bright red malar patch.

Mantle and back broadly barred buff and black, rump plain buff. Wings black with buff bars. Tail barred buff and black. Underparts barred buff and black,

breast with finer barring. Iris brown, bill black, legs and feet dark grey. Adult female similar but lacks red malar patch. **DISTRIBUTION** Thai–Malay Peninsula, Greater Sundas. Common resident throughout Borneo's lowlands and islands, up to 1,100m. Race: M. *t. grammithorax.* **HABITS AND HABITAT** Primary and secondary forests, forest edges, coastal vegetation, kerangas, plantation forests, peat-swamp forests. Bark- and foliage-gleaning insectivore, sometimes joining mixed-species feeding flocks. Forages quietly on smaller branches of the upper storey, feeding mainly on ants, termites and grubs.

LEFT: *Female.* RIGHT: *Male*

Buff-necked Woodpecker ■ *Meiglyptes tukki* 21cm
(Malay: Belatuk-batu Leher Kuning. Indonesian: Caladi Badok)

DESCRIPTION A smallish buff and brown woodpecker. Adult male has brown head and red malar patch. Prominent plain buff patch is sandwiched by 2 blackish patches at side

of neck. Upperparts dark brown, narrowly barred buff. Throat finely barred dark brown and buff; lower throat blackish. Rest of underparts barred brown and buff. Iris reddish brown; upper mandible dark

grey, lower pale grey; legs and feet brownish grey. Adult female is similar but lacks red malar patch. **DISTRIBUTION** Thai–Malay Peninsula, Greater Sundas. Common resident throughout Borneo's lowlands and islands, up to 1,225m. Race: M. *t. tukki* (shown), M. *t. percnerpes* in S Borneo. **HABITS AND HABITAT** Lowland dipterocarp and secondary forests, forest edges, kerangas, coastal vegetation, plantation forests, peat and freshwater swamps. Usually seen in pairs and in mixed-species flocks, foraging in middle and lower storeys for ants and termites. Population seems unaffected by logging.

LEFT: *Male.* RIGHT: *Female*

Orange-backed Woodpecker ■ *Chrysocolaptes validus* 30cm
(Malay: Belatuk Dada Merah. Indonesian: Pelatuk Kundang)

DESCRIPTION Adult male has short reddish crest with dark brown speckles. Side of head and neck orange-brown. Lower nape to back white, graduating into orange rump; tail black. Wings blackish brown with broad orange bars on primaries and secondaries. Throat and underparts red, mottled orange-brown. Iris yellow, upper mandible dark grey, lower mandible yellow, legs and feet pale orange. Adult female is similar but has dark grey instead of red, and grey instead of orange, on body plumage; cream instead of yellow lower mandible; dark grey instead of pale orange legs and feet.
DISTRIBUTION Thai–Malay Peninsula, Greater Sundas. Locally common resident throughout Borneo's lowlands and montane areas, up to 1,985m. Race: *C. v. xanthopygius*. **HABITS AND HABITAT** Lowland and hill dipterocarp forests, montane forests, kerangas, peat swamps, mangroves, riparian and secondary forests, forest edges, plantation forests. Often seen in pairs and small family parties. Forages at middle to upper storeys, feeding on insects, including their larvae.

LEFT: *Female.* RIGHT: *Male*

Olive-backed Woodpecker ■ *Chloropicoides rafflesii* 25cm
(Malay: Belatuk-pinang Rimba. Indonesian: Pelatuk Raffles)

DESCRIPTION An olive, medium-sized woodpecker. Adult male (shown) has red crown and nuchal crest, edged below by thin black lateral crown stripe. Grey-white supercilium from above eye to nape. Broad black eye-stripe connects to nape, broad white stripe from cheek to side of neck bordered below by black malar stripe that broadens down to side of neck. Spine of nape, primaries and uppertail feathers black; mantle, back and rest of upperparts olive-green. Lores and cheeks orange buff, with paler orange chin and throat; breast, belly and rest of underparts olive-green with white spots on flanks. Iris brown, bill black, legs and feet grey-olive. Adult female is similar but has black crown and crest. **DISTRIBUTION** Thai-Malay Peninsula, Sumatra and Bangka. Widespread uncommon resident throughout lowlands, up to 1,590m. Race: *C. r. dulitensis*. **HABITS AND HABITAT** Lowland and hill dipterocarp forests, peat-swamp, kerangas, secondary forests, forest plantation and nipah. Bark-gleaning and woodpecking insectivore, usually seen singly or in pairs, feeds mainly on ants, termites and ant larvae. Occasionally joins mixed foraging flocks.

Male

Common Flameback ■ *Dinopium javanense* 28–30cm
(Malay: Belatuk-pinang Biasa. Indonesian: Pelatuk Besi)

DESCRIPTION A large woodpecker. Adult male has crimson extending from forehead to upper nape, black lower nape to upper mantle. Broad white supercilium to nape bordered below by a broad black eye-band, which connects to hind-neck. Broad white loral stripe extends from lores to cheek down neck side, black malar stripe broadens at neck side. Lower mantle and wings greenish yellow, back and rump crimson, tail black. Throat buff; breast to vent feathers buff with curvy black barrings, giving them unevenly scaled

appearance. Iris brown, bill dark grey with paler base, legs and feet dark grey. Adult female is similar but has shorter black crest with white specks. **DISTRIBUTION** India to Southeast Asia, SW China, Greater Sundas. Locally common resident in coastal lowlands, up to 500m. Race: *D. j. raveni* (shown) in Sabah and, possibly, E Kalimantan; *D. j. borneonense* elsewhere. **HABITS AND HABITAT** Peat swamps, coastal forests, riparian and secondary forests, plantation forests, gardens. Usually seen in pairs. Feeds mainly on ants and other insects, plus small reptiles.

LEFT: *Male*. RIGHT: *Female*

Rufous Woodpecker ■ *Micropternus brachyurus* 21–25cm
(Malay: Belatok Biji Nangka. Indonesian: Pelatuk Kijang)

DESCRIPTION A mid-sized all-rufous woodpecker. Adult is overall rusty rufous with dark sub-terminal lines on scapulars and mantle feathers; primaries, secondaries and wing

coverts barred black. Chin and throat finely speckled buff. Flanks and belly to vent narrowly barred black. Tail barred black and rufous, with terminal half black. Iris dark brown, bill black, legs and feet dark grey. Adult male has red wash around eye and cheek, while adult female has buffish wash. **DISTRIBUTION** Himalayas and India to Southeast Asia, S China, Greater Sundas. Locally common resident in Borneo's lowlands and uplands, up to 1,740m. Race: *M. b. badiosus.* **HABITS AND HABITAT** Lowland and hill dipterocarp forests, secondary forests, peat swamps, plantation forests, orchards, coastal vegetation. Usually seen singly or in pairs. Feeds mainly on tree ants and termites, foraging from low levels up to canopy.

LEFT: *Male*. RIGHT: *Female*

Banded Yellownape ■ *Chrysophlegma miniaceum* 23–26cm
(Malay: Belatuk-hijau Merah. Indonesian: Pelatu Merah)

DESCRIPTION A medium-sized red woodpecker. Adult male has a red head; darker red on crown and nape, with yellow-tipped nuchal crest. Reddish patch around eye and on cheek. Mantle to rump olive-green, faintly mottled buff; tail black. Wings red, with primaries broadly barred brown and buff. Chin to breast red-chestnut, rest of underparts narrowly barred brown and buff. Iris reddish brown, bill dark grey with whitish-grey lower mandible, legs and feet dark grey. Adult female is similar but lacks reddish forehead and cheek, these instead finely spotted with buff. **DISTRIBUTION** Thai–Malay Peninsula, Greater Sundas. Common resident in lowland and upland Borneo, up to 1,675m. Race: *C. m. malaccense*. **HABITS AND HABITAT** Lowland and hill dipterocarp forests, secondary forests, peat swamps, mangroves, forest edges, gardens, plantation forests. Usually seen singly or in small parties. A bark-gleaning insectivore, feeding mainly on ants, termites and their eggs.

LEFT: *Male*. RIGHT: *Female*

Crimson-winged Woodpecker
■ *Picus puniceus* 25cm
(Malay: Belatuk-hijau Paruh Kuning.
Indonesian: Pelatuk Sayap-merah)

DESCRIPTION Adult male (shown) has forehead, crown and nuchal crest crimson; upright feathers behind crown extending down to hindneck bright yellow. Lores black with broad crimson malar patch, bold bluish eye ring. Wings crimson, tail feathers blackish brown. Mantle, back, rump and underparts olive green, with sparse whitish bars on flanks. Adult female is similar but lacks crimson malar patch. **DISTRIBUTION** Thai-Malay Peninsula and Greater Sundas. Widespread but scarce resident of lowlands and uplands, sea level to 1,700m. Race: *P. p. observandus*. **HABITS AND HABITAT** Lowland and hill dipterocarp forests, peat-swamp, kerangas, secondary forests, occasionally gardens. Bark-gleaning insectivore, forages for ants, termites, their eggs and larvae on trunks, main branches, and in dense clumps of epiphytes and foliage on smaller branches.

Male

Great Slaty Woodpecker ■ *Dryocopus pulverulentus* 51cm
(Malay: Belatuk-kelabu Besar. Indonesian: Pelatuk-kelabu Besar)

DESCRIPTION The largest woodpecker in Borneo. Adult male is overall slate-grey, with no crest of any form. Wings and tail darker grey, head and neck speckled white, buffish-orange chin and throat with red malar patch, vent tinged brown. Iris dark brown, bill pale grey with darker tip, legs and feet dark grey. Adult female is similar but lacks red malar patch. **DISTRIBUTION** Himalayas to Southeast Asia, Greater Sundas, Palawan. Generally scarce resident throughout Borneo, up to 1,300m. Race: *D. p. pulverulentus*. **HABITS AND HABITAT** Lowland and hill dipterocarp forests, secondary forests, kerangas, peat swamps, mangroves, riparian forests, gardens. Usually in pairs or small family groups, foraging in upper canopy. Loud drumming can be heard from a distance. Bark-gleaning and wood-pecking insectivore, feeding mainly on ants and grubs.

LEFT: *Male*. RIGHT: *Female*

White-bellied Woodpecker ■ *Dryocopus javensis* 40–48cm
(Malay: Belatuk-hitam Perut Putih. Indonesian: Pelatuk Ayam)

DESCRIPTION An unmistakable large black and white woodpecker. Adult male has elaborate crimson crest extending from forehead to nape. Head, neck and throat black with fine white streaks. Broad crimson malar patch, with rest of upperparts plain black.

Breast black, belly dirty white, thigh and vent mottled black and white, tail black. Iris white, bill black, legs and feet dark grey. Adult female is similar but lacks crimson malar patch and crimson crest. **DISTRIBUTION** W China, India to Southeast Asia, Korea, Greater Sundas, Philippines. Widespread and common lowland resident throughout Borneo, including islands, up to 600m. Race: *D. j. javensis*. **HABITS AND HABITAT** Primary and secondary forests, mangroves, kerangas, plantation forests, gardens, orchards. Usually seen in pairs or small family groups. Drumming is loud and audible from afar. Forages for a variety of insects by bark-gleaning and wood-pecking.

LFFT: *Female*. RIGHT: *Male*

Sunda Pygmy-woodpecker ▪ *Picoides moluccensis* 13cm
(Malay: Belatuk-belacan Kecil Biasa. Indonesian: Caladi Tilik)

DESCRIPTION A small brown and white woodpecker. Adult has dark brown to blackish forehead, crown and nape. Broad, dark brown eye-stripe extends from forehead across eye to side of neck, bordered above by broad white supercilium that extends to nape. Lores and cheek white with prominent dark brown sub-moustachial stripe. Mantle, back and scapulars barred dark brown and white; rest of wings dark brown, spotted white. Chin white; rest of underparts greyish white, streaked brown. Iris brown, bill black, legs and feet dark grey. Adult male has red spot on side of crown. **Grey-capped Pygmy-woodpecker** *P. canicapillus*, locally common throughout Borneo, is similar but has darker upperparts and a rufous wash on underparts. **DISTRIBUTION** India, Thai–Malay Peninsula, Greater Sundas. Locally common resident of coastal areas and islands of Borneo. Race: *P. m. moluccensis*. **HABITS AND HABITAT** Secondary forests, gardens, parks, mangroves, riparian and peat-swamp forests, coastal vegetation. Usually seen singly or in pairs drumming on dead branches; not easy to locate owing to its small size.

Rufous-collared Kingfisher
▪ *Actenoides concretus* 23–24cm
(Malay: Pekaka-rimba Melayu. Indonesian: Cekakak-hutan Melayu)

DESCRIPTION An attractive forest kingfisher. Adult male has green cap, broad black eye-stripe from lores to nape, and thin chestnut supercilium. Rufous cheek stripe from gape connects to orange-rufous collar, bordered below by broad, dark blue malar patch. Back and wings azure-blue, tail darker blue, rump light turquoise. Chin to breast bright orange-rufous, graduating to yellowish belly and vent. Brown iris with contrasting thin yellow eye-ring, bill yellow with dark culmen, legs and feet yellow. Adult female is similar but back and wings are dark olive-green, spotted buff. **DISTRIBUTION** Thai–Malay Peninsula, Sumatra. Locally common resident throughout Borneo, 0–1,680m. Race: *A. c. borneanus*. **HABITS AND HABITAT** Lowland and hill dipterocarp forests, secondary and riverine forests. A forest kingfisher, not necessarily associated with water. Usually seen perched in the lower storey of dense forests, silent and motionless. Feeds on lizards, frogs, baby snakes and insects.

LEFT: *Female*. RIGHT: *Male*

Stork-billed Kingfisher

■ *Pelargopsis capensis* 35cm
(Malay: Pekaka-emas Biasa. Indonesian: Pekaka Emas)

DESCRIPTION This unmistakable bird is the largest of the Bornean kingfishers. Adult has buff-yellow head and neck, some with a slightly grey-brown cap and nape. Mantle greenish blue, back to rump turquoise; tail and wings azure-blue, primaries black. Chin pale buff, rest of underparts orange-yellow. Iris brown with thin orangish eye-ring; thick, stocky bill bright red with dark tip; legs and feet red. **DISTRIBUTION** India to Southeast Asia, Greater and Lesser Sundas, Philippines. Common lowland resident throughout Borneo, 0–400m. Race: *P. c. innominata*. **HABITS AND HABITAT** Swamp forests, Nipah palms, mangroves, paddy fields, coastal wetlands, large drains, forests next to rivers and ponds. Often solitary. Perches quite conspicuously in the open near water, where it hunts for crabs, fish and other small vertebrates. Aggressive and territorial when breeding.

Ruddy Kingfisher ■ *Halcyon coromanda* 23cm
(Malay: Pekaka Belacan. Indonesian: Cekakak Merah)

DESCRIPTION A distinctive ruddy-orange kingfisher. Adult *H. c. major*, when viewed in good light, has dark purplish-rusty forehead, face and side of neck. Rest of upperparts

violet, tinged orange, with pale whitish-turquoise rump-patch. Breast purplish, graduating to orange-yellow belly. Iris dark grey with contrasting thin orange eye-ring; bill bright red; legs and feet duller red. Resident *H. c. minor* appears rufous-brown with much less violaceous upperparts. **DISTRIBUTION** NE India, East and Southeast Asia, Greater Sundas, Philippines. Widespread but uncommon, mainly coastal Bornean resident, up to 765m; also a rare non-breeding winter visitor to N Borneo. Commoner in Sabah and Brunei than elsewhere on the island. Races: *H. c. minor* (resident), *H. c. major* (shown, migrant). **HABITS AND HABITAT** Coastal swamps, Nipah palms, mangroves, riparian and secondary forests, plantation forests. Hunts for small crabs, lizards, frogs and fish from low perches.

Collared Kingfisher ■ *Todiramphus chloris* 23–25cm
(Malay: Pekaka Bakau Biasa. Indonesian: Cekakak Sungai)

DESCRIPTION A white and turquoise kingfisher. Adult has white loral spot, greenish-turquoise cap, blackish eye-stripe from lores to nape. White throat connects to broad white collar, back greenish blue; wings, rump and tail deep turquoise. Underparts plain white. Iris dark brown; bill dark grey, with lower base of lower mandible pale; legs and feet dark grey. **DISTRIBUTION** Red Sea and Arabian coasts, India to Southeast Asia, Greater Sundas, Wallacea, Philippines, N Australia, Melanesia. Common to abundant resident throughout Borneo; used to be coastal but now commonly encountered quite far inland, occasionally up to 1,500m. Race: *T. c. laubmannianus*. **HABITS AND HABITAT** Mangroves, swamps, beaches, coastal vegetation, gardens, plantation forests, paddy fields, ponds, villages, towns. Noisy bird that is often seen perching on overhead power cables uttering its loud, harsh *kek…kek…kek* call. The easiest kingfisher to see in Borneo, as it frequents housing areas. Feeds on lizards, frogs, insects and young hatchlings.

Rufous-backed Dwarf-kingfisher ■ *Ceyx rufidorsa* 14cm
(Malay: Rajaudang-api Biasa. Indonesian: Raja-udang Api)

DESCRIPTION A small brightly coloured forest kingfisher. Adult has head and upperparts rich rufous with varying amount of lilac sheen. No blue/black mantle. Prominant white neck-side patch, with smaller patch above made up of varying amounts of black/blue/lilac. Throat whitish, rest of underparts orange-yellow. Iris brown, bill, legs and feet red. *C. r. motleyi* (shown) has black/blue scapular and wing coverts with black flight feathers. *C. r. rofidorsa* has rufous/mauve wing coverts with dark flight feathers. **DISTRIBUTION** Sundaic, Palawan. A common and widespread lowland resident throughout, up to 1,200m. Race: *C. r. motleyi* in N Borneo, and *C. r. rofidorsa* elsewhere. Similar **Black-backed Dwarf-kingfisher** *C. erithaca*, which has diagnostic blue/black mantle, is a possible migrant to Borneo. **HABITS AND HABITAT** Lowland primary and secondary forests, mangroves, peat swamps, plantation forests, scrub, seashores. Often seen singly. Frequents areas near water; also regularly observed darting with tremendous speed through the understorey of forests uttering its *tse…tseeee…tseeee* cry.

Blue-banded Kingfisher ■ *Alcedo euryzona* 18cm
(Malay: Rajaudang Bukit Melayu. Indonesian: Raja-udang Kalung-biru)

DESCRIPTION Adult male has black forehead, faintly barred turquoise blue; black crown and nape. Mantle to rump bright turquoise blue. Rufous loral spot, white neck-side stripe. Wing converts black spotted turquoise, flight feathers black-edged turquoise. Throat white; broad breast band mottled turquoise-blue; white belly, flanks and vent. Bill black, iris brown, legs and feet pink/red. Adult female is similar but has less blackish upperparts, has rufous cheeks and neck-side stripe, with plain bright orange breast and rest of underparts slightly paler; has orange lower mandible instead of black. Adult female is similar to **Common Kingfisher** A. *atthis*, which has greenish-blue upperparts and white neck-side

stripe. **DISTRIBUTION** Tenasserim, Thai-Malay Peninsula, Sumatra and Borneo. Uncommon resident, sea level to 1,400m. Race: A. *e. peninsulae*. **HABITS AND HABITAT** On rocks and overhanging branches along flowing rocky streams and at edges of body of water in primary and secondary lowland and lower montane dipterocarp forests. Usually seen singly, perched on rock or low branch close to water. Feeds on fish, crustaceans and insects.

LEFT: *Male*. RIGHT: *Female*

Blue-eared Kingfisher ■ *Alcedo meninting* 15–17cm
(Malay: Rajaudang Meninting. Indonesian: Raja-udang Meninting)

DESCRIPTION A small, bright metallic blue kingfisher. Adult has bright, deep blue head with densely barred forecrown, and white throat and neck-side patch. Mantle to uppertail turquoise blue, wing coverts dark blue with paler spots, primaries black. Underparts orange-rufous. Iris brown, legs and feet scarlet. Bill colour varies: young birds have entirely scarlet

bill; older birds may have black-tipped scarlet-based bill or entirely black bill. Similar to **Common Kingfisher** A. *atthis* but is deeper blue overall and has blue ear-coverts. **DISTRIBUTION** India to SW China, Southeast Asia, Greater Sundas, Philippines, Wallacea. Common lowland resident throughout Borneo, up to 1,375m. Race: A. *m. verreauxii*. **HABITS AND HABITAT** Primary and secondary forests along streams and rivers, mangroves, coastal swamps, occasionally plantation forests. Prefers overhung or tunnel-like brooks. Feeds only on small fish, perching still on low branches overhanging water, watching intently for prey that might come in range, then plunge-diving to catch it.

Red-bearded Bee-eater = *Nyctyornis amictus* 27–31cm
(Malay: Beberek-tunggal Janggut Merah. Indonesian: Cirik-cirik Kumbang)

DESCRIPTION A large, unmistakable forest bee-eater with a square tail. Adult male has lilac forehead and crown, uniformly bright green nape to uppertail. Light blue feathers ring the base of bill, throat to upper breast bright red. Belly to vent yellowish green. Under-tail feathers golden yellow with broad terminal band, outer-tail feathers black. Iris orange, decurved bill black with pale base, legs and feet grey. Adult female is similar but forehead is concolourous with chin. **DISTRIBUTION** Tenasserim Range in peninsular Myanmar and peninsular Thailand, Malay Peninsula, Greater Sundas, Philippines. Locally common lowland resident throughout Borneo, up to 1,200m. Monotypic. **HABITS AND HABITAT** Lowland dipterocarp, peat-swamp and secondary forests, kerangas, plantation forests. Usually seen singly, unlike other bee-eaters. Rarely perches openly on exposed bare twigs, more often on leafy lower and middle storeys. Sallies out to catch passing insects, but rarely returns to same perch. Brightly coloured front might trick bees to believe it is a flower in bloom.

LEFT: *Male.* RIGHT: *Female*

Blue-throated Bee-eater
= *Merops viridis* 30–31cm
(Malay: Berek-berek Rengkung Biru. Indonesian: Kirik-kirik Biru)

DESCRIPTION The commonest bee-eater in Borneo. Adult has deep chestnut crown to mantle, green wings. Broad black stripe from lores to ear-coverts. Lower back and rump pale turquoise-blue, uppertail and long central streamers darker blue. Throat and cheek turquoise-blue, breast to vent light greenish blue. Under-tail dark grey. Iris dark brown, decurved bill black, legs and feet grey. The similar **Blue-tailed Bee-eater** M. *philippinus* is a very rare visitor, with a green crown and mantle, yellow chin and rufous throat. **DISTRIBUTION** S China, Southeast Asia, Greater Sundas, Philippines. Common lowland resident throughout Borneo, up to 800m. Monotypic. **HABITS AND HABITAT** Open country, sandy areas, mangroves, kerangas, oil-palm plantations, forest edges, paddy fields, gardens, secondary forests, scrub. Migrates locally, breeding in sandy coastal areas and dispersing to forests afterwards. Usually seen in small flocks, hawking for flying bees, wasps and dragonflies from open perches in low and middle storeys, and from overhead power cables along roads adjacent to forests.

White-fronted Falconet
■ *Microhierax latifrons* 15–17cm
(Malay: Rajawali-belalang Dahi Putih. Indonesian: Alap-alap Dahi-putih)

DESCRIPTION Smallest raptor in the world. A tiny black and white falcon, similar to **Black-thighed Falconet** M. *fringillarius*, which occurs elsewhere in Borneo in the S. Adult male has white forehead and cheek. Crown, nape and rest of upperparts black. Broad black eye-band from lores across eye to crown. Throat and upper breast white, belly pale buffish. Vent to tail black. Iris, bill and legs black. Adult female has chestnut-rufous forehead. **DISTRIBUTION** Endemic resident in lowlands of N Borneo, up to c. 1,200m. Widespread but scarce. Occurs south to northern Kalimantan Timur on the E coast and south to Lawas in Sarawak on the W coast, not recorded in other Kalimantan provinces. Monotypic. **HABITS AND HABITAT** Lowland and hill dipterocarp forests, secondary forests, plantation forests, forest edges and clearings. Perches on dead branches on tall trees singly or in small parties, often allopreening. Makes dashing sallies for insects and small birds in flight.

Blue-rumped Parrot
■ *Psittinus cyanurus* 18cm
(Malay: Nuri Puling. Indonesian: Nuri Tanau)

ABOVE: *Female*. BELOW: *Male*

DESCRIPTION A short-tailed, plump-looking parrot. Adult male has dull blue head and nape, and purplish-grey mantle with blue lower back and rump. Wing feathers dark green, edged yellow, with red shoulder-patch. Throat grey, rest of underparts green. Iris greyish white; upper mandible red, lower mandible brown; legs and feet pale greenish. Adult female is similar but has brownish-grey head, green mantle and rump, and dark brown bill. **DISTRIBUTION** Thai–Malay Peninsula, Sumatra. Generally scarce and local resident throughout Borneo's lowlands, up to 500m. Race: *P. c. cyanurus*. **HABITS AND HABITAT** Lowland dipterocarp and secondary lowland forests, kerangas, plantation forests. Flies high over upper canopy, often in small flocks. Feeds on fruits, seeds, berries and small palm nuts. Its sharp, shrill call, *chi-chi-chi*, is often made in flight.

Blue-naped Parrot ■ *Tanygnathus lucionensis* 31cm
(Malay: Nuri-kelapa Tengkuk Biru. Indonesian: Betet-kelapa Filipina)

DESCRIPTION A largish parrot. Adult has diagnostic blue crown and nape, green upperparts, and yellowish-green underparts with dull yellow under-tail. Wing feathers darker green, shoulder blackish blue, greater wing coverts fringed yellow, median coverts broadly edged yellow. Adult male has brighter blue on head. Iris 2-toned, with creamy-white outer ring and honey-gold inner ring. Bill red, legs and feet grey. **DISTRIBUTION** Philippines, Talaud Islands of Indonesia. On the main island of Borneo, found only in Tanjung Aru, Kota Kinabalu, where there is an established feral population of less than 100 birds; also found in Lawas, Sarawak, and on Maratua, Tiga, Mantanani and Si Amil islands. Races: *T. l. horrisonus* in Maratua, *T. l. salvadorii* (shown) elsewhere. **HABITS AND HABITAT** Coastal vegetation, Casuarina trees, forests and gardens at sea-level. Often perches exposed on protruding branches of Casuarina and other trees. Feeds on various fruits, tree bark, seeds, young shoots and buds. Flies fast and straight, calling loudly.

Long-tailed Parakeet ■ *Psittacula longicauda* 40–48cm
(Malay: Bayan Melayu. Indonesian: Betet Ekor-panjang)

DESCRIPTION A long-tailed, largish green parakeet. Adult male has green forehead and crown, and rosy-pink side of head and nape. Mantle and back paler green, rump darker green, long tail feathers blue. Wings green with bluish primaries. Black chin-patch extends to side of neck. Underparts yellowish green. Iris 2-toned, with creamy-white outer ring and yellow inner ring. Upper mandible red, lower mandible grey. Legs and feet grey. Adult female resembles male but has green nape and overall dark grey bill. **DISTRIBUTION** Andamans, Nicobars, Southeast Asia, Sumatra. Locally common resident throughout Borneo's lowlands, particularly in coastal areas, up to 200m. Race: *P. l. longicauda*. **HABITS AND HABITAT** Secondary forests, kerangas, peat-swamp forests, open woodlands, plantation forests, oil-palm estates, mangroves, coastal forests, forest edges, gardens. Often seen in noisy flocks in flight. Generally a bird of the canopy, where it feeds on fruits and young shoots; may sometimes descend to garden fruit trees and oil palms to feed.

ABOVE: *Male.* BELOW: *Female*

Blue-crowned Hanging Parrot

■ *Loriculus galgulus* 12cm
(Malay: Serindit Melayu. Indonesian: Serindit Melayu)

DESCRIPTION A small, mainly green and scarlet parrot. Adult male has green head, blue spot on crown, golden-yellow patch on mantle, and green back with yellow patch bordering bright scarlet rump and uppertail. Underparts green throughout except for scarlet throat-patch. Adult female is similar but has duller blue and yellow, and lacks scarlet throat-patch. Iris brown, bill black, legs and feet brown to grey. **DISTRIBUTION** Thai–Malay Peninsula, Sumatra. Locally common resident throughout Borneo's lowlands, including some islands; recorded up to 1,620m on G. Kinabalu. Being a popular cagebird, wild population is scarce in forests accessible to trappers. Monotypic. **HABITS AND HABITAT** Primary and secondary forests, mangroves, plantation forests, woodland, gardens. Well hidden when perched owing to its small size and green colour. Usually utters a high-pitched note on the wing while flying over treetops. Hangs upside-down like a bat to sleep.

ABOVE: *Male*. BELOW: *Female*

Green Broadbill ■ *Calyptomena viridis* 14–18cm
(Malay: Seluwit Biasa. Indonesian: Madi-hijau Kecil)

DESCRIPTION A chunky green broadbill. Adult male is overall iridescent green, with forehead feathers covering most of bill; black bean-shaped ear-patch, 3 black wing bars; dark-tipped primaries edged black. Iris dark brown, bill dark grey with yellow tip, legs and feet grey-olive. Adult female is similar but green is less brilliant, has a pale yellowish eye-ring, has a more exposed bill, and lacks black ear-patch and wing bars. **DISTRIBUTION** Thai–Malay Peninsula, Sumatra. Widespread and common resident throughout Borneo, generally below 700m but occasionally up to 1,300m. Race: *C. v. gloriosa*. **HABITS AND HABITAT** Lowland and hill dipterocarp forests, lower montane forests, riverine and tidal swamp forests, kerangas, plantation forests. Not an easy bird to observe owing to its overall green colour, which blends in well with the canopy foliage. Usually seen singly or in pairs, foraging in lower storey for fruits (mainly figs) and, occasionally, insects.

LEFT: *Male*. RIGHT: *Female*

Whitehead's Broadbill ■ *Calyptomena whiteheadi* 24–27cm
(Malay: Seluwit Rengkung Hitam. Indonesian: Madi-hijau Whitehead)

DESCRIPTION The largest green broadbill of Borneo. Adult male is overall bright iridescent green, tuft at forehead covers most of bill. Black ear-patch and spot at side of forehead. Dark-based feathers of forecrown make it appear black-spotted. Broad black streaks on mantle, scapular and wing coverts. Black edges to flight feathers; tail green with broad black tip. Chin green, black patch at throat; broad black streaks at breast, flanks and belly. Under-tail black. Iris dark brown, bill dark grey, legs and feet grey-olive. Adult female is similar but is duller green overall, has a yellowish-grey bill, lacks black at side of forehead, and has obscure blackish ear-covert patch and plain green underparts.

DISTRIBUTION Uncommon endemic montane resident along the N-central mountain ranges, 600–1,850m. Monotypic. **HABITS AND HABITAT** Montane forests. Frequents lower storey, generally feeding on fruits. Small parties often feed in fruiting trees, and are sometimes quite vocal.

LEFT: *Female*. RIGHT: *Male*

Black-and-red Broadbill
■ *Cymbirhynchus macrorhynchos* 20–24cm
(Malay: Hujan-hujan Merah.
Indonesian: Sempur-hujan Sungai)

DESCRIPTION A comparatively slender-looking broadbill. Adult has black forehead, nape, mantle and back; wings black with long white bar on scapulars, bright orange edge of alula visible when perched. Rump maroon, black tail. Black chin bordered below by deep maroon throat-patch that extends to side of neck. Black band across upper breast. Rest of underparts deep maroon. Iris dark brown to blue, upper mandible turquoise-blue, lower mandible yellow with blue edges, legs and feet greyish blue. **DISTRIBUTION** Southeast Asia, Sumatra. Widespread and common lowland resident throughout Borneo, up to 900m. Race: *C. m. macrorhynchos*.
HABITS AND HABITAT Lowland dipterocarp forests, secondary forests, riverine and peat-swamp forests, kerangas, mangroves, Nipah swamps, forest edges, gardens, plantation forests. Often seen in pairs, usually close to water and streams – the only broadbill not restricted to forest. Feeds on insects, riverine organisms and berries. Population seems unaffected by logging.

Male

Banded Broadbill ■ *Eurylaimus javanicus* 21–23cm
(Malay: Hujan-hujan Ungu. Indonesian: Sempur-hujan Rimba)

DESCRIPTION Adult male has black forecrown and lores, deep greyish-burgundy crown to nape. Mantle to rump black, heavily marked with bright yellow plumes throughout; tail black. Wings black with broad yellow streaks on coverts, transverse wing bars made up of yellow spots across primaries and secondaries. Throat greyish burgundy, separated from less greyish belly by narrow blackish breast-band. Under-tail black with white-tipped feathers. Iris greyish white; bill turquoise-blue with cutting edges of both mandibles black; legs and feet bluish grey. Adult female is similar but has less black on forehead and lacks blackish breast-band. **DISTRIBUTION** Southeast Asia, Greater Sundas. Widespread lowland resident throughout Borneo, commoner in some areas, up to 1,220m. Race: *E. j. brookei*. **HABITS AND HABITAT** Lowland and hill dipterocarp forests, secondary forests, kerangas, peat-swamp forests, lower montane forests, plantation forests. Usually seen in pairs, and frequents upper and middle storeys. Often sits quietly on an open perch in middle storey, and feeds mainly on insects.

Black-and-yellow Broadbill ■ *Eurylaimus ochromalus* 13–15cm
(Malay: Hujan-hujan Kecil. Indonesian: Sempur-hujan Darat)

DESCRIPTION A cute, chunky little broadbill. Adult male has black head and neck, encircled by white collar-ring. Mantle to rump black, heavily marked with bright yellow plumes throughout; tail black. Wings black with broad yellow streaks on coverts; transverse wing bars made up of yellow streaks across primaries and secondaries. Narrow black breast-band below white collar-ring. Pink breast graduating into yellowish vent. Under-tail black with white-tipped feathers. Iris yellow; bill turquoise-blue with cutting edges of both mandibles black; legs and feet pink. Adult female is similar but has incomplete black breast-band. **DISTRIBUTION** Thai–Malay Peninsula, Sumatra. Common lowland resident throughout Borneo, up to 1,800m. Monotypic. **HABITS AND HABITAT** Lowland and hill dipterocarp forests, secondary forests, kerangas, riverine and peat-swamp forests, plantation forests. The most often heard broadbill in Borneo forests, usually seen in pairs and small parties, making its cicada-like trill. Forages for insects from upper and middle storeys.

LEFT: *Male*. RIGHT: *Female*

Bornean Banded Pitta ▪ *Hydronis schwaneri* 22cm ⓔ
(Malay: Burung-pacat Belang Borneo. Indonesian: Paok Pancawarna)

DESCRIPTION Jewel of the Bornean rainforest. Adult male (shown) has black crown, bright broad yellow supercilium from forehead to connect at nape, bordered below by broad, black eye band extending to nape. Mantle and back plain chestnut-brown, with slight purplish tinge on flight feathers, thick white line on black wing-coverts, tail purplish-blue. Throat yellow, paler at chin; breast and flanks blackish-blue heavily barred bright yellow, deep blue belly with yellow barrings restricted to flanks. Bill black, iris brown, legs and feet flesh colour. Adult female is similar, but has duller yellow with black at crown and face not as black; underparts uniformly blackish-blue heavily barred yellow. **DISTRIBUTION** Uncommon endemic occurring from near sea level to 1,680m, but more often encountered above 650m. Monotypic. **HABITS AND HABITAT** Lowland and hill dipterocarp forests, occasionally in selectively logged forests. Very shy and elusive bird, generally on the ground, hopping along trails and on fallen logs, and occasionally perching on low branches. Flight is low and short. A terrestrial insectivore.

Male

Blue-headed Pitta ▪ *Hydromis baudii* 17cm ⓔ
(Malay: Burung-pacat Biru Borneo. Indonesian: Paok Kepala-biru)

DESCRIPTION Jewel of the Bornean rainforest floor. Adult male has forehead to nape dark neon blue, broad black mask from lores to nape, throat and sides of neck white, back and rest of upperparts red-brown; thick white line on black wing-coverts, navy blue on rump and short tail. Breast dark purplish-blue, lighter at belly and vent. Bill black, iris grey, legs and feet flesh colour. Adult female lacks blue crown and black mask, instead has reddish-brown head; with throat and entire underparts light-brown instead of white and purplish-blue. **DISTRIBUTION** Locally common to uncommon endemic in lowland primary and secondary forests, including forest plantation, sea level to 610m. Monotypic. **HABITS AND HABITAT** Generally on the ground, hopping along forest trails, and occasionally perching on low branches. Flight is low and short, usually taken to cross streams. A terrestrial feeder, jabbing and scattering leaf litter searching for worms, insects, grubs, molluscs, etc. Occasionally encountered hopping ahead of hikers on forest trails and can effectively be followed for quite a while if safe distance is kept in between.

ABOVE: *Male*. BELOW: *Female*

Blue-banded Pitta ■ *Erythropitta arquata* 15–17cm ⓔ
(Malay: Burung-pacat Rantai Biru. Indonesian: Paok Kalung-biru)

DESCRIPTION Jewel of the Bornean rainforest slopes, an unmistakable bird. Sexes alike, adult has crown to nape red-crimson; forehead, throat and side of neck red-orange, narrow distinct turquoise-blue line behind eye down side of neck. Upperparts dark green with narrow turquoise-blue patch at wing coverts, blue on short tail. Breast and rest of underparts red crimson, with turquoise-blue, chain-like band across upper breast. Bill black, iris grey, legs and feet blackish grey. **DISTRIBUTION** Rare endemic preferring hilly terrains mainly in sub-montane forests throughout, from 150m to 1,520m, not recorded in Brunei. Monotypic. **HABITS AND HABITAT** A slope specialist, always encountered on steep hill ridges. Very shy and elusive bird, generally on the ground, hopping along forest trails and on fallen logs, and occasionally perching on low branches. Flight is low and short. A terrestrial insectivore. Its low, monotone whistle is similar to **Garnet Pitta** *E. granatina*, Black-crowned Pitta (below) and **Rail-babbler** *Eupetes macrocerus*.

Black-crowned Pitta
■ *Erythropitta ussheri* 14–16cm ⓔ
(Malay: Burung-pacat Delima Sabah.
Indonesian: Paok Sabah)

DESCRIPTION A striking purple-blue and red pitta. Adult has black head and neck; 2 long, thin turquoise lines run from eyebrow to nape. Nape deep purplish blue, graduating to blackish-blue rump and tail. Wing coverts turquoise-blue. Throat and breast black, latter with reddish wash; rest of underparts deep crimson. Iris dark brown, bill black, legs and feet bluish grey. Similar and parapatric to **Garnet Pitta** *E. granatina*, which has crimson cap and nape, and occurs over the rest of lowland Borneo. Both species have a similar call, which is a long whistle, with Black-crowned Pitta's slightly longer. **DISTRIBUTION** Locally common endemic lowland resident in N Borneo, up to 200m. Monotypic. **HABITS AND HABITAT** Lowland dipterocarp forests, selectively logged and secondary forests, plantation forests. Ground-dwelling forest bird. Shy and elusive, favouring thickly covered forest floors, but considered the most approachable of Borneo's pittas.

Asian Hooded Pitta ■ *Pitta sordida* 16–19cm
(Malay: Burung-pacat Hijau. Indonesian: Paok Hijau)

DESCRIPTION A smallish green pitta. Adult has entirely black head and neck, appearing like a black hood. Mantle to back green, rump turquoise-blue, tail black. Wings green with turquoise-blue patch on coverts. In flight, white wing-patches visible against black primaries. Underparts green with faint bluish wash on breast, belly to vent bright red. Iris dark brown, bill black, legs and feet dark grey. **DISTRIBUTION** NE Indian sub-continent, Southeast Asia, Greater Sundas, Philippines, Sulawesi, New Guinea. Locally common lowland Bornean resident, with local movements that are poorly understood, up to 400m. Races: *P. s. muelleri* (shown) and a possible northern winter visitor *P. s. cucullata*, which has deep brown crown. **HABITS AND HABITAT** Lowland dipterocarp forests, selectively logged and secondary forests, kerangas, plantation forests, peat-swamp and mangrove forests, Nipah thickets, gardens, bamboo. Usually found near water. Forages on the ground, feeding on worms and insects. Will occasionally come out in the open.

Golden-bellied Gerygone ■ *Gerygone sulphurea* 9–10.5cm
(Malay: Kelicap-perepat Asia. Indonesian: Remetuk Laut)

DESCRIPTION A small, active bird. Adult has brownish-grey forehead, crown, nape and upperparts; white lores extend to above eye. Chin, throat and breast pale yellow, fading into whitish belly and vent. Iris dark brown, bill black; legs and feet dark grey, and has a visibly long tarsus. Can be mistaken for a female sunbird in the field, but should be easy to differentiate by its grey upperparts and short, straight bill. **DISTRIBUTION** Southeast Asia, Greater Sundas, Philippines, Sulawesi. Locally common lowland Bornean resident, commoner on offshore islands, up to 1,700m. Race: *G. s. sulphurea.* **HABITS AND HABITAT** Lowland and hill dipterocarp forests, peat-swamp and riparian forests, coastal vegetation, mangroves, plantation forests, kerangas, open country. Active feeder that forages in middle and upper storeys for worms and insects.

Erpornis ▪ *Erpornis zantholeuca* 11–13cm
(Malay: Kelicap-berjambul. Indonesian: Yuhina Perut-putih)

DESCRIPTION A small, nondescript olive-green bird. Adult has olive-green forehead, short crest and upperparts. Lores, face and ear-coverts greyish olive. Throat to belly plain, pale buffish white; under-tail coverts yellow; under-tail feathers olive, fringed yellow. Iris black, bill pinkish with dark grey culmen, legs and feet pink. **DISTRIBUTION** Himalayas to Southeast Asia, SE China, Taiwan, Sumatra. Scarce, chiefly sub-montane Bornean resident, commoner in Sabah, 0–1,750m. Race: *E.z.brunnescens*. **HABITS AND HABITAT** Lowland and hill dipterocarp forests, kerangas, peat-swamp and secondary forests, plantation forests. Usually seen singly or in small flocks, occasionally joining mixed feeding flocks. Foliage-gleaning insectivore and partial frugivore.

Black-hooded Oriole ▪ *Oriolus xanthornus* 20–23cm
(Malay: Kunyit Tudung Asia. Indonesian: Kepudang Kerudung-hitam)

DESCRIPTION Adult has black head, upper nape and throat, resembling a black hood with a longer front. Lower nape and rest of body bright yellow. Wing coverts yellow with

black at base of primary coverts, rest of wings black with narrow yellow fringing on primaries, and extensive yellow edging on secondaries and tertials. Tail yellow with an extensive black rectangular patch at middle. Iris reddish brown, bill deep pink, legs and feet grey. **DISTRIBUTION** India, Sri Lanka to SW China, Indochina, Thailand, NE Sumatra. Uncommon to rare lowland resident of E coast of Borneo, patchily from Sandakan to Tawau, P. Maratua, Sangkulirang Peninsula and Sungai Wain, up to 305m. Race: *O. x. tanakae*. **HABITS AND HABITAT** Secondary forests, plantation forests, forest edges, riverine and coastal forests, cultivated areas. Foliage-gleaning insectivore and frugivore, usually seen singly or in pairs foraging in upper canopy.

Black-and-crimson Oriole ■ *Oriolus consanguineus* 21–22cm
(Malay: Kunyit Hitam Biasa. Indonesian: Kepudang Melayu)

DESCRIPTION Other than the deep crimson rectangular patch on breast and upper belly, and the crimson wing-patch at primary wing coverts, adult has overall black plumage. Upperpart and throat feathers have bluish sheen. Iris dark brown, bill silvery grey, legs and feet dark grey. In juvenile crimson at breast is replaced by dark chestnut streaks. Female has sooty grey underparts without crimson patch on breast, upper belly and wing. **DISTRIBUTION** Malay Peninsula, Greater Sundas. Common montane resident on mountain spine from NE to central Borneo, 600–2,300m. Race: *O. c. vulneratus*. **HABITS AND HABITAT** Lower and upper montane forests. Usually seen singly or in pairs; also joins mixed feeding flocks. Feeds on fruits and insects, including their lavae, often in upper storey.

Dark-throated Oriole ■ *Oriolus xanthonotus* 18–20cm
(Malay: Kunyit-bongsu Biasa. Indonesian: Kepudang Hutan)

DESCRIPTION Adult male *O. x. consobrinus* has black head, nape and throat, resembling a black hood. Rest of upperparts bright yellow; wings black, with primaries fringed white and secondaries fringed yellow. Tail black, tipped yellow. Breast to belly white, boldly streaked black; vent yellow. Under-tail feathers yellow with black base. Iris reddish brown, bill deep pink, legs and feet dark grey. Adult female has greyish to green-olive upperparts with dark grey wings, yellow eye-ring. Chin and throat greyish white, finely streaked black; rest of underparts similar to male. Adult male *O. x. xanthonotus* has less yellow on tail; adult female has less greyish throat and breast, and less streaked underparts. **DISTRIBUTION** Thai–Malay Peninsula, Southeast Asia, Greater Sundas, Palawan. Common and widespread lowland resident throughout Borneo, up to 1,315m. Races: *O. x. xanthonotus* in S Borneo, *O. x. consobrinus* (shown) in N Borneo. **HABITS AND HABITAT** Lowland and hill dipterocarp forests, kerangas, peat-swamp and secondary forests, plantation forests. Usually seen singly or in pairs, but joins mixed feeding flocks to forage in upper canopy for insects and fruits.

LEFT: *Male*. RIGHT: *Female*

Bornean Whistler ■ *Pachycephala hypoxantha* 16cm 🄴
(Malay: Murai-siul Emas Borneo. Indonesian: Kancilan Kalimantan)

DESCRIPTION Adult has olive-green upperparts, dark lores; wing coverts and tail darker green, dark primaries and secondaries with paler edges. Underparts yellow with faint

greenish wash, darker at breast. Under-tail dark olive-green. Iris dark brown, bill black, legs and feet grey. *P. h. sarawacensis* has more uniform yellow underparts. **DISTRIBUTION** Locally common endemic montane resident, from G. Kinabalu along central mountain ranges to upper Telen, G. Pueh and G. Nyiut, 650–2,920m. Races: *P. h. sarawacensis* on Pueh Range and G. Nyiut, Sarawak; *P. h. hypoxantha* (shown) elsewhere. **HABITS AND HABITAT** Hill dipterocarp forests, montane forests, forest edges and clearings. Often seen on lower branches, actively foraging from perch to perch; also makes sallies to catch insects in mid-air and joins mixed feeding flocks.

Black-winged Flycatcher-shrike ■ *Hemipus hirundinaceus* 13.5–15cm
(Malay: Rembah Sayap Hitam. Indonesian: Jingjing Batu)

DESCRIPTION Adult male has glossy dark bluish-black upperparts except for white rump. Chin, throat and rest of underparts white with greyish wash on breast. Iris dark brown, bill black, legs and feet dark grey. Adult female is similar but has dark bluish-brown upperparts. The mainly sub-montane and montane **Bar-winged Flycatcher-shrike** *H. picatus* is similar

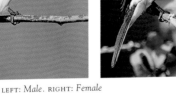

but has a prominent white wing bar. **DISTRIBUTION** Thai–Malay Peninsula, Greater Sundas. Widespread and common lowland Bornean resident, up to 1,200m. Monotypic. **HABITS AND HABITAT** Lowland and hill dipterocarp forests, kerangas, peat-swamp forests, forest edges, secondary forests, gardens, mangroves. Usually seen singly or in pairs; also in small parties and joins mixed feeding flocks. A foliage gleaner, also sallying for insects in flight.

LEFT: *Male*. RIGHT: *Female*

Large Woodshrike
■ *Tephrodornis virgatus* 17–18cm
(Malay: Rembah-rimba Besar. Indonesian: Jingjing Petulak)

DESCRIPTION Adult male has grey forehead to nape, bordered below from lores to
ear-coverts by broad black eye-band. Mantle to back grey, rump white, tail dark grey.
Underparts greyish white, with more grey at
breast. Iris pale brown, bill black, legs and feet
dark grey. Adult female is similar but has browner
upperparts and yellowish brown at base of bill.
DISTRIBUTION India, S China, Southeast Asia,
Greater Sundas. Locally common lowland resident
throughout Borneo, up to 1,150m. Race: *T. v.
frenatus*. **HABITS AND HABITAT** Lowland and
hill dipterocarp forests, logged and secondary forests,
kerangas, plantation forests, forest edges, clearings,
gardens. Usually in pairs and noisy small parties.
Forages by gleaning foliage or hawking for insects in
the canopy, and makes short flights from tree to tree.

Male

Rufous-winged Philentoma
■ *Philentoma pyrhoptera* 15–17cm
(Malay: Rembah-batu Kecil. Indonesian: Philentoma Sayap-merah)

DESCRIPTION Medium-sized philentoma. Adult male in typical morph has dull blue head
to mantle and throat to breast, rufous wings with dark grey on scapulars and some coverts,
blackish-grey primaries, rufous tail. Lower breast to vent buff, under-tail rufous. Iris red,
bill black, legs and feet dark grey. Adult female is similar but has dark grey head, mantle
and back, buff chin and throat; rest of underparts buff with dark grey patch on breast side,
bill brownish grey. Male in rare blue morph is entirely dull
blue with paler belly and vent; may be confused with female
Maroon-breasted Philentoma (p. 92). **DISTRIBUTION**
S Indochina, Thai–Malay
Peninsula, Sumatra. Locally
common resident throughout
Borneo, up to 1,530m. Race:
P. p. pyrhoptera. **HABITS
AND HABITAT** Lowland
and hill dipterocarp forests,
peat-swamp and secondary
forests, kerangas, plantation
forests. Usually seen singly
or in pairs. Foliage-gleaning
insectivore in dense lower
storey, also sallying for insects
and foraging on the ground.

LEFT: *Female.* RIGHT: *Male*

Maroon-breasted Philentoma ■ *Philentoma velata* 18–20cm
(Malay: Rembah-batu Dada Ungu. Indonesian: Philentoma Kerudung)

DESCRIPTION Adult male has black forehead, extending over eye to ear-coverts and down to upper throat. Crown, nape and rest of upperparts dull blue. Lower throat to breast deep maroon, rest of underparts dull blue. Iris red, bill black, legs and feet dark grey. Adult female is entirely dull blue with darker lores, throat and breast, by which it is distinguished from blue morph Rufous-winged Philentoma (p. 91). **DISTRIBUTION** Thai–Malay Peninsula, Greater Sundas. Uncommon lowland Bornean resident, up to 1,530m. Race: *P. v. caesia*. **HABITS AND HABITAT** Lowland and hill dipterocarp forests, kerangas, peat-swamp and secondary forests, plantation forests. Usually seen singly or in pairs, hawking for insects. Noisy and conspicuous, and almost always near water.

LEFT: *Male*. RIGHT: *Female*

Bristlehead ■ *Pityriasis gymnocephala* 25–26cm Ⓔ
(Malay: Tiong-batu Kepala Merah. Indonesian: Tiong-batu Kalimantan)

DESCRIPTION Unmistakable black and red bird with a very large bill. Adult male (shown) has bristle-like orange-yellow feathers on crown, from which it gets its name. Face, throat and neck bright scarlet. Black ear-patch protrudes like the ear piece of a headphone. Thigh feathers red, rest of upperparts and underparts black; feathers on mantle, back and breast are fringed darker, making them appear scaly. Iris red-brown, massive bill black, legs and feet pink-flesh. Adult female is similar but has red patches on flanks. **DISTRIBUTION** Uncommon endemic lowland Bornean resident, up to 1,220m. Monotypic. **HABITS AND HABITAT** Lowland and hill dipterocarp forests, kerangas, peat-swamp and mangrove forests, secondary forests, plantation forests. Nomadic. Usually seen in small family parties, but also in mixed feeding flocks. Moves rather slowly over upper and middle storeys while feeding, quite undisturbed by any human presence.

Male

Common Iora ■ *Aegithina tiphia* 12–14cm
(Malay: Kunyit-kecil Biasa. Indonesian: Cipoh Kacat)

DESCRIPTION There is much variation in colour according to age and season. Adult male *A. t. aequanimis* has yellow forehead and crown, greenish-yellow nape to rump. Wings black with 2 broad white wing bars; yellowish-white edges to primaries, secondaries and tertials. Tail black. Underparts yellow. Iris white, bill pale bluish grey, legs and feet bluish grey. Adult female is similar but duller, and has deep olive-green wings and tail. *A. t. viridis* has greener head and face, and shows a more contrasting yellow eye-ring.
DISTRIBUTION Indian sub-continent, Sri Lanka, SW China, Southeast Asia, Greater Sundas, Palawan. Common and widespread lowland resident throughout Borneo, including offshore islands, up to 610m. Races: *A. t. aequanimis* (shown) in Sabah, *A. t. viridis* elsewhere. **HABITS AND HABITAT** Forest edges, peat swamps, logged and secondary forests, mangroves, coastal scrub forests, open country, kerangas, gardens. Usually seen singly or in pairs. Forages for worms and insects by gleaning amongst foliage in the forest canopy and shrubs, hopping from branch to branch.

Male

White-breasted Woodswallow ■ *Artamus leucorynchus* 16.5–18.5cm
(Malay: Layang-hujan Biasa. Indonesian: Kekep Babi)

DESCRIPTION Adult has slaty-grey forehead to back, white rump, slaty-grey tail and wings. Chin and throat slaty grey, sharply demarcated from plain white breast and rest of underparts; under-tail slaty grey. Iris dark brown, bill light blue, legs and feet dark grey.
DISTRIBUTION Andamans, Thai–Malay Peninsula, Greater Sundas, Philippines, Wallacea, New Guinea, Australia, W Pacific. Common resident throughout Borneo, including offshore islands, up to 2,000m. Race: *A. l. leucorynchus*. **HABITS AND HABITAT** Open country, woodland edges, open areas in towns and villages. Often seen in small family parties, perching on open branches, high wires, lamp-posts, radio mast or other high structures. Makes brief sorties after flying insects, and will harass birds, and other animals, including humans, that come near.

Sunda Cuckooshrike ■ *Coracina larvata* 22–23cm

(Malay: Selancang-punai Sunda. Indonesian: Kepudang-sungu Gunung)

DESCRIPTION Adult male has black forehead, face, ear-coverts and throat. Rest of body plumage slate-grey with blackish primaries and tail. Iris and bill black, legs and feet grey.

Adult female is similar but has grey throat and paler face mask. **DISTRIBUTION** Sumatra, Java. Common resident in montane forests of central Bornean mountain ranges from G. Kinabalu to G. Dulit, Usun Apau plateau and Barito Ulu. Race: *C. l. normani*. **HABITS AND HABITAT**

Disturbed and undisturbed lower and upper montane forests. Usually seen singly or in pairs, feeding in upper storey, often in mixed hunting parties. Conspicuous in its habitat, as it is one of the largest birds. Foliage-gleaning insectivore, also feeding on geckos and fruits.

LEFT: *Male*. RIGHT: *Female*

Lesser Cicadabird

■ *Lalage fimbriata* 17.5–20cm
(Malay: Selancang-kelabu Melayu.
Indonesian: Kepudang-sungu Kecil)

ABOVE: *Male*. BELOW: *Female*

DESCRIPTION Adult male is dark grey overall, with a blackish head resembling a hood. Nape to rump grey, tail black. Scapulars grey, wings black. Throat black; rest of underparts grey, paler at under-tail coverts and with under-tail feathers tipped white. Iris dark brown, bill black, legs and feet dark grey. Adult female has grey upperparts; lacks blackish hood of male but has blackish eye-stripe; wings and tail darker grey; underparts white, extensively barred dark grey; under-tail darker grey with white-tipped feathers. **DISTRIBUTION** Thai–Malay Peninsula, Greater Sundas. Common lowland resident throughout Borneo, up to 1,036m. Race: *L. f. schierbrandi*. **HABITS AND HABITAT** Lowland and hill dipterocarp forests, kerangas, alluvial and peat-swamp forests, coastal vegetation, secondary forests, gardens, plantation forests. Canopy bird that hunts for insects and caterpillars; joins mixed feeding flocks.

Pied Triller ■ *Lalage nigra* 16cm
(Malay: Selancang Melayu. Indonesian: Kapasan Kemiri)

DESCRIPTION A smallish black and white triller. Adult male has white forehead that connects to supercilium, bordered below by black lores and eye-stripe. Forecrown to mantle black. Back to rump pale grey, tail black. Black wings with large white patch on coverts, broad white fringes on primaries and secondaries. Underparts white. Iris dark brown; bill, legs and feet black. Adult female is similar but black in upperparts is replaced by brownish grey; underparts greyer, with throat, breast and flanks finely barred. **DISTRIBUTION** Nicobars, Thai–Malay Peninsula, Greater Sundas, Philippines. Widespread and very common lowland resident throughout Borneo, including islands, up to 500m. Race: *L. n. nigra*. **HABITS AND HABITAT** Coastal vegetation, kerangas, mangroves, gardens, plantation forests, open country. Usually seen singly or in pairs. Forages for insects and worms in lower or middle storeys of beach vegetation, or even down to the ground.

LEFT: *Female.* RIGHT: *Male*

Scarlet Minivet ■ *Pericrocotus flammeus* 17–19cm
(Malay: Burung-matahari Besar Biasa. Indonesian: Sepah Hutan)

DESCRIPTION Adult male has black head and mantle. Back and rump scarlet. Uppertail black with scarlet outer feathers. Wing black with scarlet wing-patch and an additional smaller scarlet wing marking between tertials and secondaries. Throat black, rest of underparts scarlet with pale patch in between thighs. Iris dark brown; bill, legs and feet black. Distinguished from Grey-chinned Minivet (p. 96) by darker chin and additional wing marking. Adult female has yellow forehead and face with dark loral stripe. Crown to mantle grey, back and rump yellow. Uppertail grey with yellow outer feathers. Underparts yellow with pale patch at belly. Distinguished from respective Grey-chinned by yellow forehead and face and additional wing marking. To distinguish from Fiery Minivet, p. 96. **DISTRIBUTION** India to Southeast Asia, S China, Greater Sundas, Lombok, Philippines. Locally common lowland resident throughout Borneo, up to 1,300m. Race: *P. f. insulanus.* **HABITS AND HABITAT** Lowland and hill dipterocarp forests, secondary forests, plantation forests, occasionally montane forests. Usually seen in small family parties, foraging for insects from tree to tree, often at canopy level.

LEFT: *Male.* RIGHT: *Female*

Grey-chinned Minivet ■ *Pericrocotus solaris* 16–17cm

(Malay: Burung-matahari Gunung Biasa. Indonesian: Sepah Dagu-kelabu)

DESCRIPTION Adult male has black head and mantle, scarlet back and rump, black

ABOVE: *Male*. BELOW: *female*

uppertail with scarlet outer feathers. Black wings with scarlet wing-patch. Throat dark grey, rest of underparts scarlet with buffish patch at belly in between thighs, under-tail feathers scarlet. Iris dark grey; bill, legs and feet black. Adult female has dark grey forehead to nape, paler grey face. Mantle and back grey, back and rump yellow. Uppertail dark grey at centre, yellow at side. Wing coverts grey with darker primaries and secondaries, wing-patch yellow. Throat grey, rest of underparts yellow with pale patch at centre of belly. Similar to Scarlet Minivet (p. 95). **DISTRIBUTION** E Himalayas to Southeast Asia, S China, Taiwan, Sumatra. Common montane resident from G. Kinabalu along Borneo's central mountain ranges to G. Mulu and G. Dulit, 650–2,450m. Race: *P. s. cinereigula*. **HABITS AND HABITAT** Primary and secondary hill and montane forests. Often seen in small parties, joining mixed feeding flocks. Gleans foliage for insects, occasionally making sallies for flying insects.

Fiery Minivet ■ *Pericrocotus igneus* 15–15.5cm

(Malay: Burung-matahari Kecil Biasa. Indonesian: Sepah Tulin)

DESCRIPTION Adult male has black head and mantle, bright reddish-orange back and rump, black uppertail with orange outer feathers. Wings black with bright reddish-orange wing-patch. Throat black, rest of underparts reddish orange. Pale yellow patch at belly in between thighs, under-tail feathers orange. Iris dark brown; bill, legs and feet black. Adult female has yellow forehead, face and chin; dark loral stripe; grey crown to mantle; yellow-orange back and rump. Uppertail grey at centre, orange-red at side. Wing coverts grey with darker primaries and secondaries, wing-patch yellow. Throat to belly yellow; pale patch at centre of belly and strong orange-red wash at under-tail. Distinguished from similar

LEFT: *Male*. RIGHT: *Female*

Scarlet Minivet (p. 95) by smaller size and different colour scheme on female. **DISTRIBUTION** Thai–Malay Peninsula, Sumatra, Palawan. Locally common lowland resident throughout Borneo, up to 600m. Race: *P. i. igneus*. **HABITS AND HABITAT** Lowland dipterocarp forests, kerangas, riparian and peat-swamp forests, plantation forests. Usually seen in small family parties, noisily foraging from canopy to canopy.

Spotted Fantail ▪ *Rhipidura perlata* 18cm
(Malay: Murai-gila Berbintik Melayu. Indonesian: Kipasan Mutiara)

DESCRIPTION A lowland fantail that prefers remoter forests. Adult
has blackish-grey head and nape, thin white supercilium running from
lores to above eye, nape to rump blackish grey, wings and uppertail
feathers blackish-brown. Neck and breast blackish-grey spotted white,
belly and lower flanks plain white. Graduated undertail feathers
blackish-grey with broad white tips resembling a hand fan when spread
out. Iris brown, bill, legs and feet black. Sexes alike. **DISTRIBUTION**
Thai-Malay Peninsula and Greater Sundas. Locally common lowland
and sub-montane resident, sea level to 1,680m. Monotypic. **HABITS
AND HABITAT** Lowland and hill dipterocarp forests, old logged
and secondary forests, kerangas. Generally in primary lowland forest,
less common in secondary forest, usually seen singly or in pairs,
occasionally in small groups. A sallying insectivore, sometimes joins
mixed feeding flocks.

White-throated Fantail ▪ *Rhipidura albicollis* 17.5–20.5cm
(Malay: Murai-gila Gunung Biasa. Indonesian: Kipasan Gunung)

DESCRIPTION A black and white montane fantail. Adult *R. a. kinabalu* has dark
forehead, lores and face, prominent white supercilium, dark grey crown and nape. Mantle
and rest of upperparts brownish grey. Chin grey, white throat tapers to side of neck, rest
of underparts dark grey; under-tail feathers dark grey, broadly tipped white, and forming
a semicircular-shaped tail when fanned out. Iris brown, bill black, legs and feet dark grey.
R. a. sarawacensis is paler below and has a narrower white throat stripe. **DISTRIBUTION**
Himalayas, India to SW China, Southeast Asia, Sumatra. Common Bornean montane
resident from G. Kinabalu to
G. Murud and G. Mulu, plus
isolated population on G. Pueh
Range, 700–2,750m. Races:
R. a. sarawacensis on G. Pueh
Range, *R. a. kinabalu* (shown)
elsewhere. **HABITS AND
HABITAT** Hill dipterocarp
forests, gardens, montane
and secondary forests, scrub.
Active bird that catches
insects on the wing, generally
foraging in lower and middle
storeys. Often in mixed feeding
flocks; not a shy bird, and can
be very approachable.

Sunda Pied Fantail
■ *Rhipidura javanica* 17–19.5cm
(Malay: Murai-gila Biasa. Indonesian: Kipasan Belang)

DESCRIPTION An active lowland black and white fantail. Adult has blackish-grey head and nape, and short white supercilium. Mantle and upperparts brownish grey. Chin dark grey; throat white, bordered below by broad, dark grey breast-band and breast side. Lower breast to vent white. Under-tail feathers dark grey, broadly tipped white; they are

of progressive length and when fanned out form a semicircular-shaped tail. Iris brown, bill black, legs and feet black. **DISTRIBUTION** Southeast Asia, Greater Sundas. Common and widespread lowland resident throughout Borneo, including coastal islands, up to 1,550m. Race: *R. j. longicauda*. **HABITS AND HABITAT** Peat-swamp and secondary forests, forest edges, gardens, plantation forests, mangroves, coastal vegetation. Feeds on insects, foraging in lower and middle storeys. Active and noisy, constantly fanning out tail.

Greater Racket-tailed Drongo
■ *Dicrurus paradiseus* 30cm + 30cm tail rackets
(Malay: Cecawi Anting-anting Besar. Indonesian: Srigunting Batu)

DESCRIPTION Unmistakable, as it is the only drongo in Borneo that has rackets. Adult has all-black plumage. Short black crest on forehead made up of bristles, upperparts glossy blue-black, underparts lack blue gloss. Tail slightly forked, with 2 elongated outer feathers, bare-shafted for most of its length until the terminal racket. When birds are observed in the field, the rackets are usually in various stages of development. When rackets are absent, may be confused with the passage migrant and winter visitor **Crow-billed Drongo** *D. annectans*,

which has a deeper forked tail and turned-up tail tips, and is commoner in the N. **DISTRIBUTION** Indian sub-continent, SW China, Southeast Asia, Greater Sundas. Common and widespread lowland resident throughout Borneo, including islands, up to 650m. Race: *D. p. brachyphorus* on main island of Borneo. **HABITS AND HABITAT** Lowland and hill dipterocarp forests, kerangas, peat-swamp and secondary forests, riparian forests, coastal scrub, forest plantations, gardens. Often noisy and conspicuous. Sallies for larger insects from upper storey, also joining mixed feeding flocks.

Ashy Drongo ■ *Dicrurus leucophaeus* 25–29cm
(Malay: Cecawi Kelabu. Indonesian: Srigunting Kelabu)

DESCRIPTION Unmistakable grey drongo of montane habitats. Adult has black forehead and white lores, rest of body plumage grey. Wing coverts bluish grey, with primaries and secondaries darker grey; long, dark grey tail deeply forked. Iris reddish orange, bill black, legs and feet black. **DISTRIBUTION** Afghanistan to China, Southeast Asia, Greater Sundas, Lombok, Palawan. Very common sub-montane and montane resident throughout Borneo's highlands, 150–2,200m. Race: *D. l. stigmatops*. **HABITS AND HABITAT** Forest edges, clearings, paddy fields, villages at suitable altitude. Perches conspicuously on treetops, power cables or bare branches, and sallies out to catch insects on the wing, often returning to the same spot to feed.

Black-naped Monarch ■ *Hypothymis azurea* 13–16cm
(Malay: Murai-ranting Biasa. Indonesian: Kehicap Ranting)

DESCRIPTION Active and noisy flycatcher. Adult male has cobalt-blue head and upperparts, black band at bill base, roundish black patch on nape. Throat and breast cobalt-blue, graduating into whitish belly and vent, and with black stripe across upper breast. Under-tail greyish blue. Iris black with thin, bright blue eye-ring; bill blue; legs and

feet bluish grey. Adult female has duller blue head and nape, rest of upperparts and wings brown. Bill varies from black to blue. Breast greyish, washed blue, and graduating to white belly and vent; tail brown. **DISTRIBUTION** Indian sub-continent to S China, Taiwan, Southeast Asia, Sundas, Philippines. Widespread and common Bornean lowland resident, including offshore islands. Races: *H. a. prophata* (shown) on mainland Borneo, various others on offshore islands. **HABITS AND HABITAT** Lowland and hill dipterocarp forests, kerangas, peat-swamp and secondary forests, coastal scrub,

plantation forests. Usually seen singly or in pairs, foraging for grasshoppers, stick insects, beetles and other insects in middle or lower storeys.

LEFT: *Male*. RIGHT: *Female*

Blyth's Paradise-flycatcher

■ *Terpsiphone affinis* Body only 22cm, elongated tail up to 45cm
(Malay: Murai-gading Biasa. Indonesian: Seriwang Asia)

Male

DESCRIPTION Adult male (shown) has black head and throat resembling a black hood, has short crest made up of slightly elongated nuchal feathers. Rest of plumage white, with fine dark shaft streaks on mantle and wing-coverts, bold dark shaft streaks on tertials. Primaries and secondaries broadly edged black. Tail feathers finely edged black with fine dark shaft streaks, central tail feathers very much elongated, occasionally double the body length. Iris dark, bold bare blue skin around eye, bill blue with dark tip, legs and feet blue-grey. Adult female is like male, but hood is duller black graduating into grey breast, upperparts and non-elongated tail rufous-brown instead of white, belly and flanks pale rufous. The very rare rufous morph male has colour scheme like female but has elongated central tail feathers. **DISTRIBUTION** From S China to Sumatra, S E Asia, Greater and Lesser Sundas. A widespread common resident throughout lowlands, up to 1,432m. Race: *T. a. borneensis.* **HABITS AND HABITAT** Lowland and hill dipterocarp forests, secondary forests, peat-swamp, kerangas, forest plantations. Joins mixed feeding flocks, gleaning for insects, also sallying for insects from inconspicuous perch. The male with its long, flowing, white tail is very conspicuous and often seen flying through forests and across streams.

Long-tailed Shrike ■ *Lanius schach* 23–25cm
(Malay: Tirjup Ekor Panjang Asia. Indonesian: Bentet Kelabu)

DESCRIPTION Adult *L. s. bentet* has black face mask from forehead to ear-coverts that tapers down at side of neck. Crown to mantle grey, back and rump rufous, long tail black. Wings black with white fringes to tertials and white on base of primaries. Chin and rest of underparts whitish, with rufous wash on belly, deeper rufous on flanks. Iris dark brown, bill black, legs and feet dark grey. Adult *L. s. nasutus* has black crown and nape, appearing like a black helmet. **DISTRIBUTION** Iran to Southeast Asia, Greater Sundas, Wallacea, Philippines, New Guinea. Two races occur in Borneo: *L. s. bentet* (shown), common resident in SE Borneo, has migrated N and is now locally common in E Sabah; rare migrant *L. s. nasutus* in N Borneo only; sea-level to 1,600m in Kundasang. **HABITS AND HABITAT** Paddy fields, swamps, forest edges, oil-palm plantations, open scrub, cultivated areas. Usually solitary. Perches on fences, tall grass stalks and low branches in open country, pouncing on insects on the ground.

Jay Shrike ■ *Platylophus galericulatus* 25–28cm
(Malay: Burung-menjerit. Indonesian: Tangkar Ongklet)

DESCRIPTION Another unmistakable bird. Adult has overall rich, dark brown plumage. Distinctive white patch at side of neck is edged by blackish feathers on 3 sides away from eye. Blackish-brown vertical/forward-pointing crest. Has 2 tiny white patches behind each eye, 1 at tail of eyebrow and other facing it below. Iris dark grey, bill dark grey with paler/yellow base, legs and feet deep bluish grey.

DISTRIBUTION Thai–Malay Peninsula, Greater Sundas. Locally common lowland resident throughout Borneo, up to 1,680m. Races: *P. g. lemprieri* (shown) in N Borneo, *P. g. coronatus* elsewhere.

HABITS AND HABITAT Lowland and hill dipterocarp forests, kerangas, secondary forests, plantation forests, forest edges. Its presence is often revealed by its call. Usually seen in pairs or small parties, sometimes joining mixed feeding flocks. A foliage-gleaning insectivore at lower and middle storeys.

Bornean Treepie ■ *Dendrocitta cinerascens* 40cm ⓔ
(Malay: Gagak-pohon Borneo. Indonesian: Tangkar-uli Kalimantan)

DESCRIPTION Adult has blackish-brown forehead, lores and cheek, crown to nape and rest of upperparts silvery grey, wings black with white wing-patch at base of primaries. Long uppertail feathers grey with broad black terminal band. Neck and rest of underparts fawn-brown. Black under-tail feathers are of progressive length and much shorter than uppertail feathers. Iris reddish brown; bill, legs and feet black. **DISTRIBUTION** Locally common sub-montane and montane endemic resident of N and central mountains, 305–2,900m.

Monotypic. **HABITS AND HABITAT** Hill dipterocarp forests, lower and upper montane forests, kerangas, clearings, scrub. Usually seen in pairs or small parties. Feeds on fruits and insects, occasionally on the ground. In Kinabalu National Park, boldly feeds on moths and large insects at low branches near the power station and around Park Headquarters.

Bornean Green Magpie ▪ *Cissa jefferyi* 32cm ⓔ
(Malay: Gagak-gunung Borneo. Indonesian: Ekek-geling Kalimantan)

DESCRIPTION An unmistakable bird in montane forests. Adult is a striking, bright green bird with black mask from lores to nape, with longish crown feathers which usually cover

the black nape. Contrasting maroon-red wings, with inner side to terminal end of tertial feathers prominently white resembling two broad white bands running down its back. Entire underparts bright green as on back, graduated undertail feathers grey tipped white with black subterminal band, resembling a broadly barred, black and white undertail. Iris white with pink/red eye-ring; bill, legs and feet bright red. **DISTRIBUTION** Common endemic along the central Bornean mountain ranges, mainly from 900 to 2,735m, occasionally down to 305m. Monotypic. **HABITS AND HABITAT** Lower and upper montane forests and forest edges. Noisy birds with varied voices including melodious series of notes. Usually seen in small groups or in mixed foraging parties; feeds on insects, snails, frogs, as well as young nestlings of smaller birds.

Grey-headed Canary-flycatcher
▪ *Culicicapa ceylonensis* 12–13 cm
(Malay: Sambar-kenari Kepala Kelabu. Indonesian: Sikatan kepala-abu)

DESCRIPTION Small bird that perches conspicuously in upper and middle storeys. Adult has plain grey head, and pale eye-ring. Mantle and rest of upperparts olive-green, flight feathers edged yellow. Throat to breast grey, rest of underparts brighter olive-green than upperparts. Iris dark, bill black with basal half orange, legs and feet orange. Sexes alike. **DISTRIBUTION** Pakistan, India to E Asia, Greater and Lesser Sundas. Common lowland and submontane resident from sea level to 1,700m. Race: *C. c. antioxantha*. **HABITS AND HABITAT** Usually single or in pairs, sitting on open branches and sallying for insects; not shy. Occasionally joins mixed feeding flocks. Insectivore, feeding on insects, including beetles and wasps.

Hairy-backed Bulbul ■ *Tricholestes criniger* 15–17cm
(Malay: Merbah Tengkuk Berbulu. Indonesian: Brinji Rambut-tunggir)

DESCRIPTION A small yellow-brown bulbul
with a distinctive yellow patch around eye.
Adult has olive-brown forehead to nape, more
olive mantle, and olive-brown back and rest of
upperparts. Pale yellow doughnut-shaped area
around eye. Chin and throat yellow, breast and
flanks yellow with olive wash, rest of underparts
dull yellow. Under-tail feathers dark olive-brown,
tipped pale yellow. Iris black, bill pink, legs and
feet pinkish buff. **DISTRIBUTION** Thai–Malay
Peninsula, Sumatra. Widespread and common
lowland resident throughout Borneo, up to 900m.
Race: *T. c. viridis*. **HABITS AND HABITAT**
Lowland and hill dipterocarp forests, secondary
forests, plantation forests. Usually seen singly or
in small parties, also joining mixed feeding flocks.
Feeds on fruits and insects.

Cinereous Bulbul ■ *Hemixos cinereus* 18–20cm
(Malay: Merbah-kelabu Biasa. Indonesian: Brinji Kelabu)

DESCRIPTION A mid-sized grey and olive
bulbul. Adult has greyish-brown head with
short, bristle-like feathers. Nape, face, mantle
and back grey-brown; wings, rump and tail
bright olive-yellow. White feathers of chin
often puffed out; lower throat and breast grey,
fading into paler belly. Vent and under-tail
bright olive-yellow. Iris deep grey; bill black,
legs and feet dark grey. **DISTRIBUTION**
Thai-Malay Peninsula, Sumatra, Greater
Sundas. Chiefly montane, locally common
Bornean resident, up to 2,800m, occasionally
found in lowlands. Race: *H. c. connectens*.
HABITS AND HABITAT Lowland and hill
dipterocarp forests, lower and upper montane
forests, secondary forests, kerangas. Usually
seen in noisy groups, and congregates at
fruiting trees with other bulbuls and barbets.
Feeds on fruits and insects, snatching fruits in
hovering flight.

Streaked Bulbul ■ *Ixos malaccensis* 20–22cm
(Malay: Bebarau-bukit Melayu. Indonesian: Brinji Bergaris)

DESCRIPTION The only bulbul that has a boldly streaked breast. Adult has olive-green crown to nape and mantle to rump. Feathers on head short and bristly. Wings and tail feathers darker olive. Chin, throat and breast dark grey, boldly streaked white, fading into buffish-washed white belly, flanks and vent. Iris yellow-orange, bill dark grey with yellow on basal half of lower mandible, legs and feet olive-grey. **DISTRIBUTION** Thai–Malay Peninsula, Sumatra. Widespread but uncommon lowland resident throughout Borneo, up to 1,200m. Monotypic. **HABITS AND HABITAT** Lowland and hill dipterocarp forests, peat-swamp and secondary forests, kerangas, bamboo. Usually seen in pairs or small flocks, congregating at fruiting trees with other bulbuls and barbets. Snatches fruits in hovering flight; also feeds on insects.

Bold-striped Tit Babbler ■ *Mixornis bornensis* 12–13cm
(Malay: Kekicau-berjalur Timur. Indonesian: Ciung-air Coreng)

DESCRIPTION A small, noisy chestnut babbler. Adult *M. b. montanus* has finely streaked buff and dark brown forehead; streaked, dark grey and brown crown. Nape and rest of upperparts chestnut with blackish at tips of primaries and terminal half of tail feathers. Lores bluish with dark streaks; face and ear-coverts streaked blackish and buff. Chin to upper breast buffish white with bold black streaks, belly and flanks buff-yellow with faint streaking. Iris yellow, bill dark grey with paler lower mandible, legs and feet pale grey. Adult *M. b. bornensis* has richer chestnut crown and upperparts. **DISTRIBUTION** Borneo, Java, Bangka, Belitung, Lingga. Widespread and common Bornean lowland resident, up to 1,300m. Races: *M. b. montanus* (shown) in Sabah and E Kalimantan, *M. b. bornensis* elsewhere. **HABITS AND HABITAT** Scrub, gardens, cultivated areas, oil palm, kerangas, mangroves, peat-swamps, coastal vegetation. More often heard than seen, as it skulks and forages in dense foliage and undergrowth. Usually in small parties. Feeds on insects and, occasionally, fruits.

Fluffy-backed Tit Babbler ■ *Macronus ptilosus* 15–17cm
(Malay: Kekicau-berbulu Pong-pong. Indonesian: Ciung-air Pongpong)

DESCRIPTION A largish brown babbler. Adult has bright chestnut forehead to nape; rest of upperparts duller brown, wings olive-black with olive-brown wing coverts, tail feathers blackish brown. Long blackish plumes on rump occasionally visible in the field. Lores and orbital area before eyes turquoise, ear-coverts brown. Chin and throat black with turquoise bare skin at neck side. Breast brown, graduating to darker belly and vent. Iris reddish brown; bill, legs and feet black. **DISTRIBUTION** Thai–Malay Peninsula, Belitung, Sumatra. Common lowland resident throughout Borneo, up to 1,070m. Race: M. *p. trichorrhos*. **HABITS AND HABITAT** Lowland and hill dipterocarp forests, peat-swamp and secondary forests, kerangas, mangroves, forest edges, plantation forests. Noisily skulks and forages in dense foliage and undergrowth, usually in pairs or small parties, feeding on insects.

Bicoloured Babbler ■ *Cyanoderma bicolor* 12–13.5cm ⓔ
(Malay: Kekicau-kecil Kelip. Indonesian: Tepus Merbah-sampah)

DESCRIPTION A smallish chestnut, grey and blue babbler. Adult C. *b. bicolor* has slate-grey head and nape; rest of upperparts deep chestnut with dark grey at inner web of primaries and secondaries. Turquoise wash on lores and orbital area; turquoise bare skin visible at side of neck while singing. Chin, face, throat, neck side and breast dark grey; lower breast paler grey, graduating into buffish-brown belly and vent. Iris reddish brown, bill dark grey, legs and feet pale grey. **DISTRIBUTION** Widespread and common lowland endemic throughout Borneo, up to 1,220m. Races: C. *b. bicolor* (shown) in N and W Borneo, C. *b. rufum* in S and E Borneo. **HABITS AND HABITAT** Lowland and hill dipterocarp forests, peat-swamp and secondary forests, kerangas, mangrove edges, plantation forests. Usually seen in small, noisy foraging parties; also joins mixed feeding flocks. Foliage gleaner in dense undergrowth, feeding on insects.

Bare-headed Scimitar Babbler ■ *Melanocichla calva* 25–26cm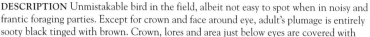
(Malay: Kekicau-raya Hitam Botak. Indonesian: Cica-kopi Botak)

DESCRIPTION Unmistakable bird in the field, albeit not easy to spot when in noisy and frantic foraging parties. Except for crown and face around eye, adult's plumage is entirely sooty black tinged with brown. Crown, lores and area just below eyes are covered with

bare yellow skin, hence its name. Blue gular skin inflates and is visible when singing. Bill red, legs and feet olive-grey. Sexes alike. **DISTRIBUTION** Scarce and uncommon endemic along north central mountain ranges, from G. Kinabalu to G. Dulit, at 750–1,900m. Monotypic. **HABITS AND HABITAT** Primary submontane and montane forests. Creeps in middle and lower storeys, foraging for crickets, cicadas and other insects among dense creepers. Usually in small groups, sometimes joining mixed foraging parties. Aboreal foliage-gleaning and substrate-gleaning insectivore.

Chestnut-rumped Babbler ■ *Stachyris maculata* 17–18.5cm
(Malay: Kekicau-kantan Besar Biasa. Indonesian: Tepus Tunggir-merah)

DESCRIPTION A largish babbler with a distinctive breast pattern. Adult has finely streaked black and white forehead; crown and rest of upperparts olive-brown; bright brown on rump and basal half of tail feathers. Bluish lores and orbital skin; grey cheek and ear-

coverts. Chin black with bluish malar patch. Feathers on throat and upper breast black, broadly fringed white, creating attractive diamond-shaped pattern. Feathers on lower breast and belly white, broadly streaked black. Vent brown, under-tail feathers olive-brown. Iris yellow, bill dark grey with paler lower mandible, legs and feet bluish grey. **DISTRIBUTION** Thai–Malay Peninsula, Sumatra. Common lowland resident throughout Borneo, up to 950m. Race: *S. m. maculata*. **HABITS AND HABITAT** Lowland and hill dipterocarp forests, peat-swamp and secondary forests, kerangas, plantation forests, forest edges. A noisy, skulking bird that is more often heard than seen. Usually in small parties, often in mixed feeding flocks. Feeds on insects, foraging on tree bark.

Black-throated Babbler

■ *Stachyris nigricollis* 15–16cm
(Malay: Kekicau-kantan Rantai Putih.
Indonesian: Tepus Kaban)

DESCRIPTION A mid-sized babbler with a striking dark throat. Adult has finely streaked black and white forehead; crown and nape dark grey, washed brown. Rest of upperparts rich chestnut-brown; dark grey at tail tip, wing-tips and inner web of primaries. Lores and face black, with contrasting white supercilium and white malar patch; ear-coverts to side of neck dark grey. Massive black patch demarcated by broken white line covering chin, throat and upper breast; rest of underparts dark grey. Iris reddish brown, bill black with greyish blue at base of lower mandible, legs and feet dark grey.
DISTRIBUTION Thai–Malay Peninsula, Sumatra. Locally common Bornean lowland resident, up to 490m. Monotypic.
HABITS AND HABITAT Lowland and hill dipterocarp forests, peat-swamp and secondary forests, kerangas, mangroves, plantation forests. Usually seen in small parties, occasionally joining mixed feeding flocks. A foliage gleaner in dense lower storey and undergrowth, feeding on insects.

Moustached Babbler ■ *Malacopteron magnirostre* 16–18cm
(Malay: Kekicau-cangkuk Bermisai. Indonesian: Asi Kumis)

DESCRIPTION A plain, nondescript babbler with a distinct moustache. Adult has dark greyish-brown forehead to nape, rest of upperparts dull brown with brighter chestnut-brown at tail. Pale eye-ring; lores, face and ear-coverts grey, bordered below by distinct dark grey moustachial stripe. Underparts greyish white, paler at chin and throat, darker at breast and flanks. Iris brown, bill grey, legs and feet greyish blue. Similar to the widespread lowland resident **Sooty-capped Babbler** M. *affine*, but that has no dark moustachial stripe.
DISTRIBUTION Thai–Malay Peninsula, Sumatra. Locally common lowland resident throughout Borneo, up to 1,220m. Race: M. *m. cinereocapilla*. **HABITS AND HABITAT** Lowland and hill dipterocarp forests, peat-swamp and secondary forests, kerangas, plantation forests, forest edges. Usually seen singly or in small groups, sometimes in mixed feeding flocks. Forages for insects in middle storey of undergrowth within the forest.

Rufous-crowned Babbler ■ *Malacopteron magnum* 17–19cm
(Malay: Kekicau-cangkuk Berapi Besar. Indonesian: Asi Besar)

DESCRIPTION A medium-sized brown babbler. Adult has rufous forehead to crown, black nape. Mantle and rest of upperparts olive-brown, tail rufous with darker terminal half. Lores, face and orbital skin greyish. Underparts greyish white with faint dark grey streaks on breast, under-tail feathers dark grey. Iris reddish brown; bill grey, paler on lower mandible; legs and feet bluish grey. **Scaly-crowned Babbler** M. *cinereum*, also a common lowland resident, is similar but has pink legs and black-tipped crown feathers.

DISTRIBUTION Thai–Malay Peninsula, Sumatra, Palawan. Common lowland resident throughout Borneo, up to 1,000m. Races: M. *m. saba* (shown) in Sabah, M. *m. magnum* elsewhere. **HABITS AND HABITAT** Lowland and hill dipterocarp forests, peat-swamp and secondary forests, kerangas, plantation forests, forest edges. Skulking bird with a melodious song; more often heard than seen. Often forages for insects in small groups in mid-storey with other birds in mixed hunting party.

Bornean Swamp Babbler ■ *Pellorneum macropterum* 14–15cm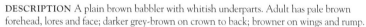
(Malay: Kekicau-telunjuk Dada Putih Borneo. Indonesian: Pelanduk Rawa)

DESCRIPTION A plain brown babbler with whitish underparts. Adult has pale brown forehead, lores and face; darker grey-brown on crown to back; browner on wings and rump.

Tail feathers pale brown at base and blackish at terminal half. Underparts white with breast sides and flanks washed greyish. Iris brown, bill dark grey, legs and feet pinkish grey. Upperpart colours are variable, with some individual exhibiting more brown and less grey. **DISTRIBUTION** Locally common lowland endemic throughout Borneo, up to 1,100m. Monotypic. **HABITS AND HABITAT** Lowland dipterocarp forests, peat-swamp and secondary forests, kerangas, mangroves, coastal vegetation, banks of rivers and streams, plantation forests. Usually seen in pairs. Often forages for insects terrestrially on banks of rivers and streams, sometimes very close to stationary observers.

Ferruginous Babbler

■ *Pellorneum bicolor* 16–18cm
(Malay: Kekicau-telunjuk Api.
Indonesian: Pelanduk Merah)

DESCRIPTION A smallish rufous and cream babbler.
Adult has rufous-brown forehead to nape and rest of
upperparts, with greyish wash on mantle and brighter
rufous on tail. Lores and area around eye pale buffish,
forming a small, pale eye-patch. Underparts creamy
white with buffish wash on breast and flanks; under-tail
feathers rufous. Iris brown, bill dark grey with yellow at
side of mandibles, legs and feet pink. **DISTRIBUTION**
Thai–Malay Peninsula, Sumatra. Locally common
lowland resident throughout Borneo, up to 1,300m.
Monotypic. **HABITS AND HABITAT** Lowland and hill
dipterocarp forests, peat-swamp and secondary forests,
kerangas, plantation forests. Inconspicuous skulker, more
often heard than seen. Seldom perches in the open,
and more often seen singly. Forages for insects in the
understorey, and climbs about in dense thickets.

Leaflitter Babbler ■ *Pellorneum poliogene* 12.5–14.5cm ⓔ
(Malay: Kekicau Sampah Dedaun. Indonesian: Pelanduk Pipi-kelabu)

DESCRIPTION A small, short-tailed babbler. Adult
has brown forehead to crown; rest of upperparts
olive-brown, washed dark grey; wings and tail feathers
rufous brown. Pale grey lores and area around eye,
bordered below by prominent dark moustachial stripe;
ear-coverts darker grey. Chin and throat buffish
white, breast sides and flanks buff with pale brown
wash, belly buff, vent light brown. Iris red-brown, bill
dark grey with paler lower mandible, legs and feet
pinkish. Identical to **Glissando Babbler** *P. saturatum*
which occurs elsewhere in Borneo. **DISTRIBUTION**
Widespread and common lowland endemic
throughout Sabah, E and S Kalimantan. Monotypic.
HABITS AND HABITAT Lowland and hill
dipterocarp forests, peat-swamp and secondary forests,
kerangas, plantation forests. Usually seen singly or in
pairs. Terrestrial litter-gleaning insectivore, difficult
to spot owing to its small size and habit of foraging in
dense undergrowth.

Bornean Black-capped Babbler

■ *Pellorneum capistratoides* 15–17cm ⓔ
(Malay: Kekicau-tanah Ubun Hitam Borneo. Indonesian: Pelanduk Kepala-hitam)

DESCRIPTION A plump-looking terrestrial babbler. Adult has black forehead to nape, bordered below by white supercilium that runs from bill base to nape. Dark grey lores, face and ear-coverts. Rest of upperparts rich chestnut-brown. Chin and throat white; breast and rest of underparts chestnut-brown, paler at breast. Iris red-brown; black upper mandible

with black tip, pale grey lower mandible; legs and feet dark grey. **DISTRIBUTION** Widespread and common lowland endemic throughout Borneo, up to 1,410m. Races: *P. c. morrelli* (shown) in Sabah, *P. c. capistratoides* elsewhere. **HABITS AND HABITAT** Lowland and hill dipterocarp forests, peat-swamp and secondary forests, kerangas, plantation forests, mangroves. Forages for insects and small invertebrates terrestrially and at lower storey in undergrowth. Usually seen singly or in pairs, walking about on the ground and making short flights to nearby thickets.

Horsfield's Babbler ■ *Malacocincla sepiaria* 14cm
(Malay: Kekicau-belukar Paruh Tebal. Indonesian: Pelanduk Semak)

DESCRIPTION A small, short-tailed babbler. Adult has dark, brownish-grey forehead and crown; nape and ears paler with faintly streaked ear coverts. Lores and supercilium grey, mantle and back olive-brown, wings and short tail feathers walnut-brown. Chin and throat greyish-white with faint streaks; tawny-rufous on side of breast to flanks, and on undertail coverts; belly white. Iris brown, bill dark grey, legs and feet greyish-pink. Sexes alike. Similar to **Abbott's Babbler** M. *abbotti* which appears brighter brown overall as it has much less dark grey on crown, no grey-olive on upperparts, and has more enhanced tawny-

rufous on flanks and tail; legs coral red instead of pinkish grey. **DISTRIBUTION** Thai-Malay Peninsula and Greater Sundas. Locally common lowland resident throughout, from sea level to 1,700m. Race: M. *s. harterti* in Sabah and adjacent part of E Kalimantan, M. *s. rufiventris* elsewhere. **HABITS AND HABITAT** Lowland and hill dipterocarp forests, old logged and secondary forests, forest plantations, peat-swamp. Foliage-gleaning insectivore, often heard along forest trails where it occurs in small groups, foraging for insects in thick undergrowth.

Striped Wren Babbler ■ *Kenopia striata* 14cm
(Malay: Kekicau Muka Putih. Indonesian: Berencet Loreng)

DESCRIPTION A striking babbler. Adult has broad black crown that tapers at forehead, forming a front-pointing black arrow; bold white streak from centre of crown to nape. Lores and feathers above bill buff; face greyish-white with dark smears. Rest of upperparts dark-brown with contrasting bold white streaks on mantle and wing coverts, no streaks on wings and tail. Underparts white with breast sides mottled black, flanks rufous. Bill black, paler at base of lower mandible, iris brown, legs and feet pale pink. Sexes alike. DISTRIBUTION Thai-Malay Peninsula and Sumatra. Sparingly distributed, uncommon to rare lowland resident throughout, sea level to 1,220 m. Monotypic. HABITS AND HABITAT Lowland and hill dipterocarp forests, kerangas, occasionally secondary forests. Terrestrial insectivore also gleaning for insects close to ground in lower storey foliage and undergrowth. The easiest lowland wren babbler to observe in Sabah.

Sunda Fulvetta ■ *Alcippe brunneicauda* 14–15cm
(Malay: Kekicau Sampah Malayu. Indonesian: Wergan Coklat)

DESCRIPTION A nondescript small greyish-brown babbler. Adult has grey forehead to nape; rest of upperparts greyish brown, with wings and tail olive-brown. Face and ear-coverts grey. Underparts buffish white; throat and breast with indistinct whitish streaks, dark grey wash at breast sides and flanks. Iris grey, bill grey, legs and feet dark grey. DISTRIBUTION Thai–Malay Peninsula, Sumatra. Locally common lowland and sub-montane resident throughout Borneo, up to 1,432m. Race: *A. b. eriphaea*. HABITS AND HABITAT Lowland and hill dipterocarp forests, kerangas, secondary forests, plantation forests. Usually seen in small parties, foraging in lower to middle storeys of dense foliage. An active bird, hopping about in search of insects and fruits.

Sunda Laughingthrush ■ *Garrulax palliatus* 24–25cm
(Malay: Kekicau-raya Cenuk Kerak. Indonesian: Poksai Mantel)

DESCRIPTION A large grey and chestnut thrush. Adult has slate-grey head to mantle. Back, wings and tail dark chestnut. Lores black, and contrasting bluish-white orbital skin appearing as broad eye-ring. Chin to breast slate-grey; belly, flanks and vent dark chestnut.

Iris reddish brown; bill, legs and feet black. **DISTRIBUTION** Sumatra. Locally common montane resident along Borneo's N-central mountain ranges, 300–3,500m. Race: G. *p. schistoclamys*. **HABITS AND HABITAT** Primary and secondary sub-montane and montane forests and scrub. Usually seen in small parties, often allopreening. Chiefly feeds on fruits, occasionally taking insects. Sometimes occurs in mixed feeding flocks; may also feed terrestrially.

Chestnut-hooded Laughingthrush
■ *Garrulax treacheri* 23–25cm ⓔ
(Malay: Kekicau-raya Borneo. Indonesian: Poksai Kalimantan)

DESCRIPTION A large grey and chestnut laughingthrush. Adult has rich chestnut forehead to nape, with visible white flecks on forehead; rest of upperparts slate-grey. Whitish wing-patch formed by white outer web of primaries. Lores, chin, face and ear-coverts rich chestnut. Crescent-shaped yellow orbital skin behind and below eye. Throat and breast buffish grey with fine whitish streaks, belly and flanks slate-grey, vent rich

chestnut, under-tail slate-grey. Iris black, bill yellow-orange, legs and feet dull orange. **DISTRIBUTION** Common endemic montane resident along Borneo's central mountain ranges. Races: G. *t. treacheri* (shown) in Sabah S to G. Dulit, G. *t. griswoldi* in central Borneo, G. *t. damnatus* elsewhere. **HABITS AND HABITAT** Primary and secondary sub-montane and montane forests and scrub. Feeds on insects and fruits. Usually seen in small groups, foraging conspicuously from lower to upper storeys. Often joins mixed feeding flocks; may also feed terrestrially.

Chestnut-crested Yuhina ▪ *Staphida everetti* 14–15cm ⓔ
(Malay: Kekicau-berjambul Borneo. Indonesian: Yuhina Kalimantan)

DESCRIPTION A small, active, short-crested bird of montane forests. Adult has chestnut forehead to nape, with a short nuchal crest; rest of upperparts slate-grey, darker at wings and tail. Lores and short supercilium white, ear-coverts chestnut. Chin and throat white with indistinct dark malar stripe, rest of underparts and under-tail feathers plain white. Iris reddish brown, bill dark grey, legs and feet brown. **DISTRIBUTION** Common sub-montane and montane endemic resident along Borneo's N-central mountain ranges, from close to sea-level in valleys in mountainous areas up to 2,800m. Monotypic. **HABITS AND HABITAT** Lowland and hill dipterocarp forests, primary and secondary sub-montane and montane forests, kerangas, forest edges. Always in flocks, at times comprising up to 30 birds, noisily foraging across canopy, feeding on seeds and insects. Also joins mixed feeding flocks.

Pygmy Heleia ▪ *Apalopteron squamifrons* 9cm ⓔ
(Malay: Kelicap-kacamata Burik Kerdil. Indonesian: Opior Kalimantan)

DESCRIPTION Adult has dark olive-grey forehead with broken white bars, appearing like neatly aligned whitish speckles; crown and rest of upperparts olive-grey, darker at wings and tail. Lores, face and ear-coverts pale greyish, with thin buff eye-ring. Chin pale yellow; throat, breast and flanks yellow with grey wash. Belly and vent brighter yellow. Iris grey-white, bill black, legs dark grey, feet olive. **DISTRIBUTION** Scarce endemic resident, chiefly sub-montane and montane areas, 50–2,150m. Monotypic. **HABITS AND HABITAT** Primary and secondary sub-montane and montane forests and scrub, kerangas, forest edges, village clearings. Usually seen in small flocks, often of mixed species, arriving at vegetation in waves to feed. Fast and active. Feeds on fruits and insects.

Mountain Black-eye ■ *Zosterops emiliae* 12–14cm ⓔ
(Malay: Kelicap-kacamata Gunung Borneo. Indonesian: Opior Mata-hitam)

DESCRIPTION Adult *Z. e. emiliae* has olive-green upperparts; darker olive on forehead, crown, wings and tail. Black lores and orbital area bordered above by short yellow supercilium. Underparts uniform olive-green as upperparts, under-tail feathers dark

grey. Iris brown, bill yellow-orange with dark culmen, legs and feet yellow-orange. The other races have varying amount of yellow in the underparts: *Z. e. trinitae* has paler greenish yellow; *Z. e. fusciceps* has yellow; *Z. e. moultoni* has more intense yellow. **DISTRIBUTION** Common endemic montane resident in Borneo's N-central mountain ranges, 1,265–4,000m. Races: *Z. e. emiliae* (shown) on G. Kinabalu and *Z. e. trinitae* on G. Trus Madi, Sabah; *Z. e. fusciceps* on G. Maga, Sarawak; *Z. e. moultoni* elsewhere. **HABITS AND HABITAT** Primary and secondary montane forests and scrub. Usually seen in small parties, conspicuously foraging for insects, fruits and nectar at the branches of small trees and bushes.

Hume's White-eye ■ *Zosterops auriventer* 9.5–11.5cm
(Malay: Kelicap-kacamata Rimba Melayu. Indonesian: Kacamata belukar)

DESCRIPTION Adult has olive-green forehead, crown and rest of upperparts; wing tipped black, with visible black primaries; terminal half of tail blackish. Chin, throat and face olive-green with black lores and prominent broad, bright white eye-ring. Broad grey breast-band connects to grey side of belly and flanks; broad olive-yellow ventral stripe at centre of belly connects to olive-yellow under-tail coverts; under-tail feathers dark grey.

Iris brown, bill black, legs and feet dark grey. The very scarce lowland resident **Swinhoe's White-eye** *Z. simplex* is similar but has a yellow forehead, paler grey flanks and narrower ventral stripe. **DISTRIBUTION** Thai–Malay Peninsula. Locally common, chiefly sub-montane Bornean resident, 0–1,700m. Race: *Z. a. medius*. **HABITS AND HABITAT** Lowland and hill dipterocarp forests, lower montane and secondary forests, plantation forests. Usually seen in flocks, arriving at vegetation to feed in waves. Actively forages at middle and upper storeys of secondary growth for insects, fruits and nectar.

Black-capped White-eye ■ *Zosterops atricapilla* 10–11cm
(Malay: Kelicap-kacamata Gunung Sunda. Indonesian: Kacamata Topi-hitam)

DESCRIPTION Unmistakable in the field. Adult has diagnostic black lores and forehead; crown and rest of upperparts olive-green, tail dark grey. Chin, throat and ear-coverts olive-green; prominent broad white eye-ring. Broad grey breast-band connects to grey side of belly and flanks; broad olive-yellow ventral stripe at centre of belly connects to olive-

yellow under-tail coverts; under-tail feathers dark grey. Iris greyish white, bill dark grey with pale base to lower mandible, legs and feet dark grey. **DISTRIBUTION** Borneo, Sumatra. Locally common sub-montane and montane resident in Borneo's N-central mountain ranges, 885–2,150m. Race: *Z. a. clarus*. **HABITS AND HABITAT** Primary and secondary sub-montane and montane forests and scrub. Usually seen in small flocks, occasionally singly, foraging in middle and lower storeys. Feeds on insects, fruits and nectar.

Mountain Leaf Warbler ■ *Seicercus trivirgatus* 10–11cm
(Malay: Cekup-daun Kunyit Gunung. Indonesian: Cikrak Daun)

DESCRIPTION A small greenish leaf warbler with a distinctive head pattern. Adult *S. t. kinabaluensis* has blackish crown split by broad, pale yellow median crown-stripe. Broad yellowish supercilium bordered below by broad black lores and eye-stripe. Rest of upperparts greyish green with darker tail and wing feathers, and no wing bar. Underparts

pale yellow with faint grey wash at breast and flanks. Iris dark grey, bill dark grey with pale orange tip, legs and feet dark grey. Adult *S. t. sarawacensis* has much more green on upperparts and brighter yellow on underparts. **DISTRIBUTION** Thai–Malay Peninsula, Greater Sundas. Common montane resident in Borneo's N-central mountain ranges, 1,100–3,350m. Races: *S. t. kinabaluensis* (shown) on G. Kinabalu, *S. t. sarawacensis*. **HABITS AND HABITAT** Primary and secondary lower and upper montane forests and scrub. Usually seen in small parties, also joining mixed feeding flocks. Actively forages for insects.

Sunda Warbler ■ *Phylloscopus grammiceps* 9–10cm
(Malay: Cekup-kacamata Sunda. Indonesian: Cikrak Muda)

DESCRIPTION An attractive montane chestnut and yellow warbler. Adult has rufous-chestnut crown, face and nape, and blackish lateral crown-stripe from mid-crown to nape. Rest of upperparts deep olive-green, darker at wing coverts and tail; 2 yellow wing bars; primaries and secondaries fringed yellow. Underparts bright yellow with olive-green under-tail. Prominent white eye-ring, brown iris; bill yellow-orange with dark grey culmen; legs and feet

grey-brown. **DISTRIBUTION** Thai–Malay Peninsula, Lesser Sundas, Sumatra, Palawan. Common montane resident in Borneo's N-central mountain ranges, 1,036–2,450m. Race: *P. g. montis.* **HABITS AND HABITAT** Primary and secondary lower and upper montane forests and scrub, highland swamps. Usually seen in small parties, also joining mixed feeding flocks. Actively forages for insects.

Yellow-bellied Warbler ■ *Abroscopus superciliaris* 9cm
(Malay: Cekup-buluh Perut Kuning. Indonesian: Cikrak bambu)

DESCRIPTION Adult has dark-grey forehead, face and crown. Hind-neck and rest of upperparts olive. Prominent white supercilium extends well behind eye. Throat white, breast, belly and rest of underparts bright yellow. Iris dark brown, bill black with pale tip. Legs and feet yellowish-grey. Sexes alike. **DISTRIBUTION** NE India, SE Asia, Thai-Malay Peninsula, Borneo, Java. Widespread and fairly common mainly as submontane resident, at 500–1,500m. Race: *A. s. schwaneri.* **HABITS AND HABITAT** Usually in groups or in mixed foraging flocks. Quite vocal. Occurs in middle and lower storeys and secondary growth, in forests associated with bamboo, actively foraging among dense leaves. Aboreal foliage-gleaning insectivore; also feeds on spiders.

Sunda Bush Warbler ▪ *Horornis vulcanius* 12–13cm
(Malay: Cekup-semak Biasa. Indonesian: Ceret Gunung)

DESCRIPTION A small, deep brown warbler. Adult has dark brown crown and rest of upperparts; wings and tail feathers blackish brown, fringed paler brown. Contrasting grey supercilium bordered below by broad, dark lores and eye-stripe. Throat to ear-coverts greyish, breast and belly brown with greyish wash. Vent and under-tail dark brown. Iris brown, bill dark grey with yellow at side of mandibles, legs and feet blackish brown.

DISTRIBUTION Sumatra, Java, Bali, Lesser Sundas, Palawan. Common montane resident of Borneo's N-central mountain ranges, from G. Kinabalu S to G. Lunjut, 1,350–3,700m. Races: *H. v. oreophilus* on G. Kinabalu, *H. v. banksi* elsewhere. **HABITS AND HABITAT** Undergrowth of primary and secondary montane forests, roadside scrub. Usually seen singly, this shy skulker creeps about inside dense undergrowth, gleaning for insects and small invertebrates. Often heard calling from bushes along mountain trails.

Mountain Leaftoiler ▪ *Phyllergates cucullatus* 10–12cm
(Malay: Perenjak-gunung Biasa. Indonesian: Cinenen Gunung)

DESCRIPTION Adult has orange forehead and crown, dark lores; narrow supercilium is yellow in front of eye and white behind. Nape, mantle, face and side of neck dark grey. Rest of upperparts olive yellow. Throat and upper breast pale grey, side of breast darker grey. Belly, vent and flanks olive-yellow. Iris reddish brown; bill dark grey, paler at base. Legs and feet dull orange.

DISTRIBUTION Southeast Asia, Greater and Lesser Sundas, Philippines, Malukus. Locally common Bornean montane resident, 1,000–2,650m. Race: *P. c. cinereicollis*. **HABITS AND HABITAT** Lower and upper montane primary and secondary forests and their edges, thickets, bamboo, undergrowth. Foliage-gleaning insectivore, often joining mixed feeding flocks. Favours lower and middle storeys, secondary growth and dense vegetation.

Striated Grassbird ■ *Megalurus palustris* 22–28cm
(Malay: Cekup Ekor-besar Biasa. Indonesian: Cica-koreng Jawa)

DESCRIPTION A largish warbler with a long tail. Adult has buff-brown forehead to nape, finely streaked dark brown; buff supercilium bordered below by indistinct dark brown eye-stripe; faint streaking at ear-coverts. Mantle and upper back buff-brown, broadly streaked black; lower back and rump plain buff-brown. Wings and tail feathers blackish, broadly fringed buff. Underparts buff with fine dark brown streaks on breast and flanks. Iris brown, bill grey, legs and feet pinkish to dark grey. **DISTRIBUTION** India to S China, Java, Philippines, Southeast Asia excluding Peninsular Malaysia and Sumatra. Locally common Bornean lowland immigrant resident that probably first arrived in the 1980s. Race: M. p. forbesi. **HABITS AND HABITAT** Grassland, scrub, paddy fields, cultivated areas, coastal vegetation, marshes, swamps. Often seen singly, perched on an overhead power cable, fence, stump or low bush. Forages in tall reeds and bushes for insects and small invertebrates.

Dark-necked Tailorbird
■ *Orthotomus atrogularis* 10–12cm
(Malay: Perenjak-pisang Leher Hitam.
Indonesian: Cinenen Belukar)

DESCRIPTION Adult male O. a. humphreysi has deep chestnut cap and nape, rest of upperparts olive-green. Ear-coverts grey. Chin, throat and upper breast black, variably streaked white; rest of underparts olive-yellow. Iris orange-brown; bill, legs and feet pinkish buff. Adult female is similar but lacks black on throat. Adult male O. a. atrogularis has less black on throat, lower breast streaked grey and white, whitish belly and flanks, yellow vent; adult female has duller chestnut cap and paler yellow on vent. **DISTRIBUTION** E India to SW China, Southeast Asia, Sumatra. Common lowland resident throughout Borneo, up to c. 1,000m. Races: O. a. humphreysi in Sabah (shown), O. a. atrogularis elsewhere. **HABITS AND HABITAT** Lowland and hill dipterocarp forests, kerangas, peat-swamp and secondary forests, forest edges, mangroves, scrub and thickets, plantation forests. Often seen singly or in pairs. A vocal bird and active skulker, hopping about from twig to twig as it forages for insects in dense foliage.

ABOVE: *Female*. BELOW: *Male*

Ashy Tailorbird ■ *Orthotomus ruficeps* 10–12cm
(Malay: Perenjak-pisang Kelabu Biasa. Indonesian: Cinenen Kelabu)

DESCRIPTION Adult male has deep rufous forehead, forecrown, face and chin. Hind-crown and mantle to rump dark ashy grey, wings and tail brownish grey. Throat and breast ashy grey, rest of underparts paler grey. Iris orange-yellow, bill pinkish buff with darker culmen, legs and feet pinkish buff. Adult female is similar but has paler underparts overall with white chin and throat. **DISTRIBUTION** Thai–Malay Peninsula, far S Vietnam, Sumatra, Java, Mapun. Common lowland resident throughout Borneo, including islands off Sabah, up to 1,500m. Race: *O. r. borneoensis*. **HABITS AND HABITAT** Secondary forests, kerangas, forest edges, scrub, coastal vegetation, gardens, cultivated areas, plantation forests. Often seen singly. A very vocal little bird, skulking in dense growth, and hopping from twig to twig foraging for insects.

LEFT: *Female*. RIGHT: *Male*

Rufous-tailed Tailorbird ■ *Orthotomus sericeus* 11–12cm
(Malay: Perenjak-pisang Ekor Merah. Indonesian: Cinenen Merah)

DESCRIPTION Adult male has rufous cap and nape. Mantle to rump dark grey, graduating to rufous tail. Chin and throat white, breast white with grey wash, belly and flanks white with buff-yellow wash. Indistinct grey patches on side of neck become black when neck is extended during singing. Iris orange-brown, bill pinkish with grey culmen, legs and feet pinkish buff. Adult female is similar but has olive wash on wings and dark sub-terminal spot on tail. **DISTRIBUTION** Thai–Malay Peninsula, Sumatra, Philippines. Common lowland resident throughout Borneo, up to 1,200m. Race: *O. s. sericeus*. **HABITS AND HABITAT** Secondary forests, forest edges, kerangas, mangroves, coastal vegetation, bamboo, scrub, grassland, gardens, plantation forests. Favours forests. Often seen singly. A very vocal little bird, skulking in dense growth, active and hopping from twig to twig as it forages for insects.

Yellow-bellied Prinia ▪ *Prinia flaviventris* 12–14cm
(Malay: Perenjak-padi Biasa. Indonesian: Perenjak Rawa)

DESCRIPTION The only prinia in Borneo. Adult has grey crown, nape, face and side of neck; dark lores and short white supercilium. Mantle, back and rump brownish green; wings and long tail browner. Underparts buff-whitish, with yellow wash on belly and stronger yellow on flanks. Iris orange-brown, bill black, legs and feet dull pinkish orange. Plumage can be quite variable, upperparts almost entirely grey with minimal traces of olive, and underparts in various intensities of yellow. **DISTRIBUTION** Pakistan to S China, Taiwan, Southeast Asia, Greater Sundas. Widespread and common lowland Bornean resident, up to 1,530m. Race: *P. f. latrunculus.* **HABITS AND HABITAT** Scrub, grassland, paddy fields, freshwater wetlands, gardens, cultivated areas. Foliage-gleaning insectivore, commonly heard singing from low bushes and scrub, or perched singly on a tall grass stem.

Velvet-fronted Nuthatch ▪ *Sitta frontalis* 12–12.5cm
(Malay: Pepatuk Biasa. Indonesian: Munguk Beledu)

DESCRIPTION Adult male has black lores and forehead; crown and rest of upperparts true blue, with black primaries and secondaries. Incomplete reddish eye-ring on upper orbital area, thin black stripe from behind eye-ring to nape. Face and ear-coverts blue, washed

pinkish. Underparts pinkish buff. Iris yellow; bill, legs and feet bright red. Adult female is similar but lacks black stripe behind eye. **DISTRIBUTION** Indian sub-continent, Southeast Asia, SW China, Greater Sundas, Philippines. Locally common lowland and montane resident throughout Borneo, 0–2,100m. Race: *S. f. corallipes.* **HABITS AND HABITAT** Lowland and hill dipterocarp forests, kerangas, peat-swamp and secondary forests, montane forests, coastal vegetation, plantation forests. Usually seen in small parties, foraging for invertebrates on the bark of tree trunks. Can climb vertically up and down the trunk.

LEFT: *Male.* RIGHT: *Female*

Common Hill Myna ■ *Gracula religiosa* 28–30cm
(Malay: Tiong-Emas Biasa. Indonesian: Tiong Emas)

DESCRIPTION A large myna with a stocky bill. Adult has entirely black body plumage with bluish iridescence and white wing-patch on primaries. Has a bright yellow bare skin patch below eye; another yellow skin patch runs from just behind eye across nape to form a yellow band, to which 2 roundish lappets are attached, 1 on each side of nape. Iris dark, bill reddish orange with yellow tip, legs and feet yellow. **DISTRIBUTION** India, S China, Southeast Asia, Greater and Lesser Sundas, Palawan. Common lowland resident throughout Borneo, up to 1,200m. Race: *G. r. religiosa*. **HABITS AND HABITAT** Lowland and hill dipterocarp forests, peat-swamp and secondary forests, mangroves, plantation forests. Usually seen in pairs or small parties. Feeds on fruits and insects, and perches on the top level of tall trees. Can mimic sounds.

Javan Myna ■ *Acridotheres javanicus* 25–26cm
(Malay: Gembala-kerbau Sawah Jawa. Indonesian: Kerak Kerbau)

DESCRIPTION Adult is overall deep greyish black, with a short, bristly tuft on forehead; darker on head, wings and white-tipped tail. White wing-patch on base of primaries, white under-tail coverts. Iris, bill, legs and feet yellow. **DISTRIBUTION** Java, Bali, S Sulawesi; introduced to Malay Peninsula, Sumatra, Singapore, Taiwan, Japan. Around Kuching since the 1980s, with a few records from Banjarmasin, Kalimantan Selatan. Established in Sepilok, near Sandakan in Sabah, since 2004, and now common there; its range is constantly expanding, with birds now sighted as far south as Tawau. Monotypic. **HABITS AND HABITAT** Roadsides, gardens, cultivated areas, open fields, villages, towns. Usually seen in pairs or small groups. Forages terrestrially for invertebrates; also settles near domestic animals to feed on insects disturbed by their movements.

Everett's Thrush ■ *Zoothera everetti* 19–20cm
(Malay: Murai-tanah Borneo. Indonesian: Anis Kinabalu)

DESCRIPTION A bird that blends well in dark montane forest floors, making it hard to spot. Adult has deep olive-grey head and upperparts, face and ear-coverts speckled white,

dark malar stripe, white throat. Breast, flanks and vent orange-chestnut, centre of belly white. Underwing shows two white stripes in flight, thinner leading stripe on lesser coverts, broader one on base of primaries. Iris dark brown, bill dark grey, legs and feet pink/flesh-coloured. **DISTRIBUTION** Scarce endemic in montane forest on G. Kinabalu to Dulit Range and Kelabit Highlands. Not recorded in Kalimantan. 1,200–2,200m. Monotypic. **HABITS AND HABITAT** Shy and inconspicuous; forages on montane forest floor for grubs, insects, worms and snails. Singly or in pairs.

Chestnut-capped Thrush ■ *Geokichla interpres* 16–18cm
(Malay: Murai-tanah Melayu. Indonesian: Anis Kembang)

DESCRIPTION A secretive bird of the lowland forest floor. Adult has chestnut crown and nape, pale lores, white ear patch. Face, throat and rest of upperparts black. Broad

white shoulder and wing bars. Breast black grading to white belly with bold black spots, flanks white spotted black, vent white. Iris black, bill dark grey, legs and feet pink/flesh-coloured. **DISTRIBUTION** Sundaland region, through to Flores and S Philippines. Uncommon to rare resident in forests up to 1,000m. Monotypic. **HABITS AND HABITAT** Mainly a bird of the forest floor and lower storey, occasionally found in fruiting trees, also recorded in forest plantation; feeds on insects, worms, earthworms as well as fruits.

Orange-headed Thrush ■ *Geokichla citrina* 20–23cm
(Malay: Murai-tanah Jingga Asia. Indonesian: Anis Merah)

DESCRIPTION Adult male has orange head and nape, with narrow buffish eye-ring and lores. Mantle to tail and wings blue-grey; white bar on wing coverts. Chin, throat, breast and flanks orange; belly paler orange; vent white. Iris black, bill dark grey, legs and feet pinkish. Adult female is similar but blue-grey on upperparts is replaced by olive-grey. **DISTRIBUTION** Himalayas to S China, Sri Lanka, Southeast Asia, Sumatra, Java, Bali. Rare sub-montane and montane resident in Crocker Range of Sabah, 750–1,800m. Race: *G. c. aurata* (shown); other races may migrate to Borneo. **HABITS AND HABITAT** Sub-montane and montane primary and secondary forests. Usually seen singly. A shy bird, gleaning leaf litter on the ground for insects; occasionally takes fruits from trees.

Male

Fruit-hunter ■ *Chlamydochaera jefferyi* 21–23cm ⓔ
(Malay: Murai-buah. Indonesian: Tawau Dada-hitam)

DESCRIPTION Adult male has buff forehead, grey crown; broad black eye-stripe runs from lores across eyes all the way to nape, bordered below by buffish ear-coverts and side of neck. Mantle, rest of upperparts and uppertail grey; primaries black. Tail tipped white with black sub-terminal band. Chin and throat buff, bold black patch on breast. Rest of underparts paler grey, under-tail feathers white. Iris reddish brown, bill black, legs and feet pinkish. Adult female is similar but grey is entirely replaced by brown, with a grey wash on crown and mantle, and a rufous forehead and throat. **DISTRIBUTION** Local, uncommon endemic montane resident, in N-central and SW mountain ranges, 700–3,200m. Monotypic. **HABITS AND HABITAT** Sub-montane and montane primary and secondary forests. Almost exclusively feeds on fruits. Quiet and unobtrusive, usually seen in pairs or small parties. May congregate at fruiting trees, sometimes joining mixed feeding flocks.

LEFT: *Male*. RIGHT: *Female*

ABOVE: *Female*. BELOW: *Male*

Oriental Magpie-robin ▪ *Copsychus saularis* 20cm
(Malay: Murai-kampung Biasa. Indonesian: Kucica Kampung)

DESCRIPTION Adult male *C. s. adamsi* has glossy black upperparts, broad white wing-stripe, black underparts with white under-tail feathers. Adult female is similar but has greyer underparts. *C. s. pluto* is like *C. s. adamsi* but tail is entirely black. *C. s. musicus* is also similar but belly to under-tail is white. Interbreeding has resulted in profusion of hybrids, these having varying amounts of white on belly (a *musicus* feature) and/or varying amounts of white in tail (an *adamsi* feature).

DISTRIBUTION Indian sub-continent, S China, Southeast Asia, Greater Sundas. Widespread and common lowland resident throughout Borneo and its offshore islands, 0–1,530m. Races: *C. s. musicus* in W and S Borneo, *C. s. adamsi* (shown) in N Borneo, *C. s. pluto* in E Borneo.

HABITS AND HABITAT Secondary forests, gardens, plantations, forest edges, mangroves coastal vegetation. Usually seen in pairs, perching conspicuously on low branches to sing and display. Pounces on insects and small invertebrates on the ground from a perch.

Rufous-tailed Shama ▪ *Copsychus pyrropygus* 20–21cm
(Malay: Murai-hutan Ekor Jingga. Indonesian: Kucica Ekor-kuning)

DESCRIPTION Adult male has dark grey upperparts, short white supercilium, paler-fringed primaries and secondaries; rufous rump and tail, the latter broadly tipped black. Chin to upper breast deep grey, graduating into yellow-rufous lower breast, flanks and belly. Vent and under-tail deeper rufous. Iris grey, bill black, legs and feet pinkish. Adult female similar but dark grey is replaced by greyish brown, and has rufous eye-ring instead of white supercilium. **DISTRIBUTION** Thai–Malay Peninsula, Sumatra. Scarce lowland resident throughout Borneo, up to 900m. Monotypic. **HABITS AND HABITAT** Lowland and hill dipterocarp

forests, kerangas, forests on ultra-basic soils, peat-swamp and secondary forests, plantation forests, forest edges. A shy bird, more often heard than seen, calling from a low perch. Usually solitary. Feeds on insects and, occasionally, fruits.

LEFT: *Male*. RIGHT: *Female*

White-crowned Shama ■ *Copsychus stricklandii* 25–27cm
(Malay: Murai-hutan Ubun Putih. Indonesian: Kucica Kalimantan)

DESCRIPTION Adult has black head with conspicuous white patch on crown that tapers off towards nape, black mantle and wings, white back and rump, black uppertail. Black chin and throat are cleanly demarcated from rufous-orange breast, belly and vent. Undertail feathers white. Iris and bill black, legs and feet pinkish buff. **Maratua Shama** C. *barbouri* is larger and has an all-black tail. **White-rumped Shama** C. *malabaricus*, resident elsewhere in Borneo, is similar but lacks white crown-patch. **DISTRIBUTION** Widespread and common endemic lowland resident throughout N Borneo and islands, including Kalimantan Timur, up to 1,220m. Monotypic. **HABITS AND HABITAT** Lowland and hill dipterocarp forests, kerangas, peat-swamp and secondary forests, lower montane forests, plantation forests. A great songster, more often heard than seen as it is quite shy and seldom perches conspicuously. Usually solitary. Feeds on insects and, occasionally, fruits.

Grey-chested Jungle-flycatcher ■ *Cyornis umbratilis* 15cm
(Malay: Sambar-hutan Melayu. Indonesian: Sikatan-rimba Dada-kelabu)

DESCRIPTION A nondescript brown jungle flycatcher with strong bill. Adult has entire upperparts dark-brown. Lores and area in front of eye grey; grey-tinged patch behind eye. Distinct bold, dark malar line demarcates bright white chin and throat from face. Breast grey clearly defined from white throat; lower breast, belly, flanks and vent much paler grey. Undertail feathers dark-brown. Iris brown, bill black, legs and feet pink/flesh. Similar to **Fulvous-chested Jungle-flycatcher** C. *olivaceus* a much rarer lowland resident, which lacks distinct, dark, malar line and has tawny-brown breast not clearly defined from throat. **DISTRIBUTION** Thai-Malay Peninsula and Sumatra. Common and widespread lowland and sub-montane resident from sea level to 500m. Monotypic. **HABITS AND HABITAT** Lowland and hill dipterocarp, peat-swamp, kerangas, secondary forests. Usually seen singly, gleaning and hawking for insects in middle and lower storey. Not a shy bird, occasionally forages at eye-level near observer.

Sunda Jungle-flycatcher ■ *Cyornis caerulatus* 14cm
(Malay: Sambar-biru Paruh Besar. Indonesian: Sikatan-rimba Biru-langit)

DESCRIPTION One of the similar-looking blue jungle-flycatchers in lowland Borneo.
Adult male very similar to Mangrove Jungle-flycatcher (p. 135), but has pale legs and more
extensive black chin; forehead, back and rump also brighter blue.
Adult female has orangish-brown upperparts, with blue wash on wing-
coverts and tail feathers; breast brown, paler at throat and belly. Iris
dark, bill black. Legs and feet pale flesh. *C. c. rufifrons* male has more
orange-rufous underparts, while female has more blue on wing-coverts.

DISTRIBUTION Sumatra and
Borneo. Fairly common in primary
lowland mixed dipterocarp forest,
up to 500m. Races: *C. c. caerulatus*
(shown) in N and E Borneo, *C. c.
rufifrons* in W Borneo. **HABITS
AND HABITAT** Usually single or
in pairs, perching prominently in
the open, and sallying for insects in
lower storey. Not particularly shy.

LEFT: *Male.* RIGHT: *Female*

Bornean Jungle-flycatcher ■ *Cyornis superbus* 15cm ⓔ
(Malay: Sambar-biru Borneo. Indonesian: Sikatan-rimba Kalimantan)

DESCRIPTION Adult male has black lores and cheeks; azure blue forehead, supercillium,
lower back and rump. Crown to mantle, upper back, scapulars and wing coverts dark
blue. Chin, throat and breast orange, gradually fading to orangish-white at belly, vent
orange. Bill black, iris brown, legs and feet flesh-grey. Adult female has pale eye ring, has
orange-brown instead of blue in upperparts, wings and flight feathers brown. The similar
male of Sunda Jungle-flycatcher (above) has extensive black chin, male of Mangrove
Jungle-flycatcher (p. 135) is duller blue without azure blue rump, female of **Malaysian
Jungle-flycatcher** *C. turcosus* is
lighter blue overall and lacks dark
flight feathers. **DISTRIBUTION**
Uncommon endemic sparsely
distributed throughout mainland
Borneo, from sea level to 1,530m.
Monotypic. **HABITS AND
HABITAT** Primary lowland and hill
dipterocarp, logged and secondary
forests. Usually near water, often
seen singly, feeds in mid-storey,
hawks for insects from a perch and
returns to the same perch.

LEFT: *Male.* RIGHT: *Female*

Mangrove Jungle-flycatcher ■ *Cyornis rufigastra* 14cm
(Malay: Sambar Biru Bakau. Indonesian: Sikatan Bakau)

DESCRIPTION Adult male has upperparts dull dark blue, paler at forehead, supercilium and rump; lores and face black. Chin black; throat to breast orange yellow, getting paler towards belly and flanks, graduating to yellowish-tinged white at belly and vent. Bill black, iris brown, legs and feet pinkish grey. Adult female is similar but has distinctive white lores; whitish chin and lower cheeks. **DISTRIBUTION** Greater Sundas and Philippines. Widespread sometimes common lowland resident chiefly in coastal areas and islands, also occurs inland far away from coast. Race: *C. r. rufigastra* on mainland Borneo. **HABITS AND HABITAT** Mangroves, peat-swamp, riverine, coastal scrub and secondary forests. It has been recorded a number of times in oil-palm plantation not near the coast, indicating this species is one of the few that could adapt to living in oil-palm estates. Feeds in lower storey, sallying for insects, usually seen in pairs. Not shy and will stay at perch when observed.

LEFT: *Female*. RIGHT: *Male*

Pale Blue Jungle-flycatcher ■ *Cyornis unicolor* 17cm
(Malay: Sambar-biru Muda. Indonesian: Sikatan-rimba Biru-muda)

DESCRIPTION Head, and back to uppertail of adult male cobalt blue; paler on forehead. Lores and face darker blue. Flight feathers greyish-brown. Chin to lower breast cobalt blue graduating into grey belly, flanks and vent. Adult female has grey-brown upperparts, with rufous rump and uppertail feathers; grey-beige underparts. Iris and bill black, legs and feet dark brownish-grey. Adult male similar to male Verditer Warbling-flycatcher (p. 136), which lacks grey on belly and has pale-tipped feathers in under-tail coverts. **DISTRIBUTION** Himalayas to SE Asia, Hainan, Greater Sundas. Scarce resident of lowland to submontane primary forests, at 200–1,500m. Race: *C. u. cyanopolia*. **HABITS AND HABITAT** Canopy species, occasionally perched prominently, and sallying for insects. Usually seen in pairs. Habit of taking bath in shallow water flowing over bedrock in forest streams, where it can be seen at close quarters.

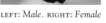

LEFT: *Male*. RIGHT: *Female*

Indigo Warbling-flycatcher ■ *Eumyias indigo* 14cm
(Malay: Sambar-ranting Sunda. Indonesian: Sikatan-kicau Ninon)

DESCRIPTION Adult has light sky-blue forecrown, deep indigo-blue hind-crown to back. Primaries, secondaries, rump and uppertail feathers dark blue. Lores, chin and areas around eyes black. Throat and breast deep indigo-blue, graduating into buffish-white belly and lower flanks; under-tail coverts pale orange. Iris, bill, legs and feet black. **DISTRIBUTION** Sumatra, Java. Common montane resident in N-central mountain ranges of Borneo, 825–2,650m. Race: *E. i. cerviniventris.* **HABITS AND HABITAT** Hill dipterocarp forests, montane forests, highland scrub. Usually seen singly, perched conspicuously in the open in middle and lower storeys. Tame and not wary of humans. Feeds on insects by catching them on sallying flights or gleaning foliage.

Verditer Warbling-flycatcher ■ *Eumyias thalassinus* 15–17cm
(Malay: Sambar-ranting Biasa. Indonesian: Sikatan-kicau Hijau-laut)

DESCRIPTION Adult male has forehead, lores and chin black, rest of plumage verditer blue, paler at belly and lower flanks. Under-tail coverts fringed paler. Bill black, legs and feet dark grey. Adult female is overall duller, with black in the male replaced by grey. Male of Pale Blue Jungle-flycatcher (p. 135) is similar to the female of this species but has belly grey and no pale-fringed feathers at undertail. **DISTRIBUTION** Himalayas to S China, Indochina, Sumatra and Borneo. Scarce lowland to sub-montane resident throughout, from sea level to 1,200m. Race: *E. t. thalassoides.* **HABITS AND HABITAT** Primary lowland, hill and sub-montane forests, logged and secondary forests. Insectivore and partial frugivore, often on open perches in upper and middle-storey, sallying for insects and returning to same perch.

LEFT: *Male.* RIGHT: *Female*

Bornean Shade-dweller ▪ *Vauriella gularis* 15cm ⓔ
(Malay: Sambar-hutan Bercelak Borneo. Indonesian: Decu-lembah Kalimantan)

DESCRIPTION Adult has greyish-brown forehead to crown, bordered below by broad buffish-white lores and supercilium that extends well behind eye. Nape, ear-coverts and rest of upperparts pale brown with brown-edged blackish primaries. Chin and throat buffish white, cleanly demarcated from dark greyish-brown upper breast; lower breast and rest of underparts paler grey. Iris pale brown,
bill black, legs and feet bluish grey.
DISTRIBUTION Locally common montane endemic resident, commoner in N-central mountain ranges, chiefly 1,500–2,150m. Races: *V. g. gularis* (shown) in Sabah, *V. g. kamlae* elsewhere. **HABITS AND HABITAT** Montane primary and secondary forests. Often seen singly or, occasionally, in small parties, on the ground or a low perch. Feeds on insects. Locally common and quite tame at forests near Kinabalu National Park headquarters.

Chestnut-naped Forktail ▪ *Enicurus ruficapillus* 20cm
(Malay: Cegar Tengkuk Merah. Indonesian: Meninting Cegar)

DESCRIPTION Adult male has white forehead, with narrow black frontal band; crown and nape chestnut, mantle black; back, rump and uppertail-coverts white. Wing black with feathers on secondaries broadly tipped white. Tail forked, graduated upper tail feathers black with broad white tip, creating bar-tailed effect. Chin and throat black. Breast and belly white with extensive bold black scales on breast. Vent and undertail feathers white. Iris dark-brown, bill black, legs and feet pale flesh colour. Adult female is similar except chestnut extends from nape covering mantle to back. **DISTRIBUTION** Thai-Malay Peninsula and Sumatra. Very local resident throughout lowlands, patchily distributed, sea level to 1,250m. Monotypic. **HABITS AND HABITAT** Along clear water streams running through undisturbed and logged dipterocarp forests. Usually in pairs or small family groups, making its high-pitched, monotone whistle-like calls while foraging for insects along streams, on rocks on or near streams and grounds at water's edge.

LEFT: *Female*. RIGHT: *Male*

Bornean Forktail ▪ *Enicurus borneensis* 25–28cm
(Malay: Cegar Raya Borneo. Indonesian: Meninting Kalimantan)

DESCRIPTION Adult has white feathers on forehead to forecrown, which can be lifted in erect position. Nape to mantle black, cleanly demarcated from white back and rump. Wing black with white-tipped secondaries, broad white bar across wing coverts. Black tail is deeply forked, with feathers of progressive length that are broadly tipped white, appearing bar-like on closed tail. Chin to breast black, belly to under-tail feathers white. Iris and bill black, legs and feet pinkish buff. **Malayan Forktail** *E. frontalis* is similar but occurs on

lowlands and has a more extensive white crown. **DISTRIBUTION** Locally common endemic montane resident of Sabah, and on mountains of Kelabit Highlands and Kayan Mentarang National Park, 900–2,000m. Monotypic. **HABITS AND HABITAT** Pristine rocky streams in sub-montane and montane primary forests. An active bird, hopping and running from rock to rock in flowing streams as it forages for invertebrates. Birds in Kinabalu National Park are not very wary of people.

Bornean Whistling-thrush ▪ *Myophonus borneensis* 24–26cm
(Malay: Tiong-belacan Bukit Borneo. Indonesian: Ciung-batu Kalimantan)

DESCRIPTION Adult male has overall dark blue-black plumage; more bluish tinge on body, less on wings and tail, which are more brownish black. Iris dark brown; bill, legs and

feet black. Adult female is similar but lacks bluish tinge, and instead has dark greyish-brown body plumage and browner wings. **DISTRIBUTION** Locally common montane and sub-montane endemic throughout Borneo; up to 2,750m, although some Sarawak records are close to sea-level. Monotypic. **HABITS AND HABITAT** Rocky mountain streams, around limestone caves. Commonly seen foraging on the ground along the road from Kinabalu National Park headquarters to the power station; also common at Masilau. Usually solitary, gleaning leaf litter for insects, frogs and small invertebrates. Frequently fans out tail.

Male

Little Pied Flycatcher ■ *Ficedula westermanni* 10–11cm
(Malay: Sambar Gunung Biasa. Indonesian: Sikatan Belang)

DESCRIPTION Adult male has glossy black upperparts with a broad white wing-stripe and broad white supercilium running from lores to nape. Chin and throat plain white; rest of underparts white, washed blackish, with black under-tail feathers. Iris, bill, legs and feet black. Adult female has dark grey upperparts, with brown-washed wings, rump and uppertail. Underparts are like male's but with brown under-tail feathers.

DISTRIBUTION Nepal and E India to SW China, Southeast Asia, Greater and Lesser Sundas, Philippines. Common Bornean montane resident, 850–3,100m. Race: *F. w. westermanni*.

HABITS AND HABITAT Sub-montane and montane primary and secondary forests and forest edges. Usually seen singly or in pairs. Tame, perching conspicuously in the open in middle and upper storeys. Sallies for insects on the wing.

LEFT: *Female*. RIGHT: *Male*

Snowy-browed Flycatcher ■ *Ficedula hyperythra* 11–13cm
(Malay: Sambar Gunung Dahi Putih. Indonesian: Sikatan Bodoh)

DESCRIPTION Tiny flycatcher of understorey of montane forests. Adult male has dark greyish-blue upperparts, and prominent white eyebrows above lores. Flight feathers tinged brown. Cheek and front part of chin dark greyish-blue. Throat and breast orange-yellow, graduating into much paler belly, flanks and vent. Female has no eyebrow, and greyish-olive replaces greyish-blue of male; entire underparts buff. Bill black, legs and feet pale horn. **DISTRIBUTION** Himalayas, India to SE Asia, Greater and Lesser Sundas, Philippines. Common montane resident along the spinal chain from G. Kinabalu to Tama Abu range and G. Mulu; also isolated pocket on G. Pueh and G. Nyiut, at 1,200–3,300m. Races: *F. h. mjobergi* on G. Pueh and G. Nyiut, *F. h. sumatrana* (shown) elsewhere. **HABITS AND HABITAT** Always seen in pairs. Very tame and inquisitive. Often perches on mossy tree roots and moist trunks near the ground to forage for insects and grubs; also feeds on berries.

ABOVE: *Female*. BELOW: *Male*

Asian Fairy-bluebird ■ *Irene puella* 24–26cm
(Malay: Murai-gajah Biasa. Indonesian: Kecembang Gadung)

DESCRIPTION Adult male has deep sky-blue forecrown to nape, wing coverts and rest of upperparts. Primaries, secondaries and tail black. Forehead, face, chin, neck side, throat to belly and flanks black, under-tail coverts deep sky-blue as in upperparts. Adult female has overall dark cobalt-blue plumage, blackish at wings and tail. Iris red; bill, legs and feet black. **DISTRIBUTION** Indian sub-continent, Southeast Asia, SW China, Greater Sundas. Common lowland resident throughout Borneo, up to 1,900m. Race: *I. p. crinigera.* **HABITS AND HABITAT** Lowland and hill dipterocarp forests, peat-swamp and secondary forests, kerangas, plantation forests, oil-palm plantations, lower montane forests. Usually seen in pairs, feeding at fruiting trees with bulbuls, barbets, hornbills and pigeons. May snatch at fruits in hovering flight.

LEFT: *Male.* RIGHT: *Female*

Lesser Green Leafbird ■ *Chloropsis cyanopogon* 16–19cm
(Malay: Burung-daun Kecil. Indonesian: Cica-daun Kecil)

DESCRIPTION Adults resemble respective sexes of Greater Green Leafbird (p. 141), but are smaller and have a weaker, shorter bill; female also has a less prominent yellow eye-ring and lacks yellow at throat. **DISTRIBUTION** Thai–Malay Peninsula, Sumatra. Common lowland resident throughout Borneo, up to 950m. Race: *C. c. cyanopogon.* **HABITS AND HABITAT** Lowland and hill dipterocarp forests, peat-swamp and secondary forests, kerangas, coastal vegetation, plantation forests. Usually seen singly or in pairs. Feeds on nectar, fruits and insects, often in the upper storey, sometimes in mixed feeding flocks. Calls are rather loud and can be quite melodious.

LEFT: *Male.* RIGHT: *Female*

Greater Green Leafbird

◼ *Chloropsis sonnerati* 20.5–22.5cm
(Malay: Burung-daun Besar. Indonesian: Cica-daun Besar)

DESCRIPTION Adult male has distinctive black lores, cheek, chin and upper throat, with glossy blue malar stripe. Rest of upperparts green, with dark grey on inner web of primaries and secondaries. Entire underparts paler green, with dark grey under-tail feathers. Iris dark grey, bill black, legs and feet greyish blue. Adult female is similar but lacks black, and has prominent yellow eye-ring and yellow throat with faint blue malar stripe. Lesser Green Leafbird (p. 140) is similar. **DISTRIBUTION** Thai–Malay Peninsula, Greater Sundas. Common lowland resident throughout Borneo, up to 1,300m. Race: *C. s. zosterops*. **HABITS AND HABITAT** Lowland and hill dipterocarp forests, kerangas, riverine forests, peat-swamp and secondary forests, plantation forests. Usually seen singly or in pairs. Feeds on nectar, fruits and insects, often in the upper storey, sometimes in mixed feeding flocks.

Female

Bornean Leafbird ◼ *Chloropsis kinabaluensis* 16–18cm ⓔ
(Malay: Burung-daun Kinabalu. Indonesian: Cica-daun Kalimantan)

DESCRIPTION Adult male has black patch that covers lores and cheeks to upper throat, bordered by bright yellow. Blue malar stripe visible only in good light. Rest of upperparts green, with cobalt-blue on wing coverts and on outer webs of primaries and secondaries; tip of tail washed blue. Inner web of primaries and secondaries dark grey. Lower throat and rest of underparts yellowish green, under-tail feathers blue. Iris brown, bill black, legs and feet greenish grey. Adult female is similar but lacks malar stripe, and has bluish green instead of yellow surrounding black face-patch. **Blue-winged Leafbird** *C. moluccensis* is similar but adult female has no black in plumage; occurs in Borneo lowlands, records from Sabah are from Maliau Basin only. **DISTRIBUTION** Locally common sub-montane and montane endemic in N-central mountain ranges, 500–2,200m. Monotypic. **HABITS AND HABITAT** Primary and secondary sub-montane and montane forests. Usually seen singly or in pairs. Feeds on nectar, fruits and insects, often in the upper storey, sometimes in mixed feeding flocks.

Male

Scarlet-breasted Flowerpecker ■ *Prionochilus thoracicus* 10cm
(Malay: Sepah-puteri Belakang Kuning. Indonesian: Pentis Kumbang)

DESCRIPTION Fondly called 'Superman' for its breast patch that resembles a comic superhero. Adult male has black hood, with a scarlet patch at centre of crown, another large scarlet patch at middle of breast broadly bordered black. Back and rump yellow, belly to vent paler yellow. Wings and tail black. Bill dark grey, legs and feet black. Female has olive-grey head and face, rest of upperparts olive-green, throat pale grey, underparts pale yellow with orange wash on breast. **DISTRIBUTION** Thai-Malay peninsula, Sumatra, Belitung and Borneo. Locally common resident of primary and secondary forests, up to 1,300m. **HABITS AND HABITAT** Usually in pairs or small parties foraging in canopy for mistletoes, will come lower down in stunted forest for suitable wild fruits.

LEFT: *Male*. RIGHT: *Female*

Yellow-rumped Flowerpecker ⓔ
■ *Prionochilus xanthopygius* 9–10cm
(Malay: Sepah-puteri Pelangi Borneo. Indonesian: Pentis Kalimantan)

DESCRIPTION Adult male has a narrow red crown-patch, blue-black head and rest of upperparts, and bright yellow rump. Visible white pectoral tufts. Chin, throat and breast yellow with red patch at middle of breast. Belly, flanks and vent whitish, washed yellow. Iris brown, upper mandible black, lower mandible grey, legs and feet black. Adult female is similar, but blue-black in upperparts is replaced by greyish olive, crown and breast-patch are yellow, and underparts are duller yellow. The rare resident **Crimson-breasted Flowerpecker** *P. percussus*, patchily distributed throughout, is similar but has white malar stripe and lacks yellow rump. **DISTRIBUTION** Widespread and common endemic lowland resident throughout, up to 1,700m. Monotypic. **HABITS AND HABITAT** Lowland and hill dipterocarp forests, peat-swamp and secondary forests, kerangas, scrub, forest edges, plantation forests. Usually seen singly or in pairs. Forages for fruits, especially those of Straits Rhododendron *Melastoma malabathricum*, and insects in lower storey of forests and scrubby vegetation.

ABOVE: *Male*. BELOW: *Female*

Yellow-vented Flowerpecker ■ *Pachyglossa chrysorrhea* 9–9.5cm
(Malay: Sepah-puteri Tongkeng Kuning. Indonesian: Cabai Rimba)

DESCRIPTION Adult has olive-green upperparts, black primaries and tail. Whitish lores; chin and throat white with prominent bold black malar stripe. Bold black streaks on breast, more diffused streaks on flanks and belly. Diagnostic bright yellow vent. Iris reddish orange, upper mandible black, lower mandible grey, legs and feet black. **DISTRIBUTION** N Indian subcontinent to SW China, Southeast Asia, Sumatra, Java. Scarce lowland resident throughout Borneo, up to 1,700m. Race: *P. c. chrysorrhea*. **HABITS AND HABITAT** Lowland and hill dipterocarp forests, lower montane, peat-swamp and secondary forests, kerangas, plantation forests, forest edges. Active bird that dashes about among dense foliage of hanging mistletoes, foraging for insects and fruits; favours *Scurrula ferruginea*.

Orange-bellied Flowerpecker ■ *Dicaeum trigonostigma* 8cm
(Malay: Sepah-puteri Perut Jingga. Indonesian: Cabai Bunga-api)

DESCRIPTION Adult male has dark steel-blue face, forehead to mantle, and tail; back to rump bright orange, pectoral tuft white. Chin and throat dark grey, cleanly demarcated from bright orange breast and rest of underparts. Iris reddish brown; bill, legs and feet black. Adult female has olive-green upperparts with orange wash on rump and uppertail coverts. Primaries dark grey, edged olive. Chin and throat grey, washed yellow; rest of underparts pale yellow. **DISTRIBUTION** E India, Southeast Asia, Greater Sundas, Philippines. Common lowland resident throughout Borneo and islands, up to 1,700m. Race: *D. t. dayakanum* on main island. **HABITS AND HABITAT** Lowland and hill dipterocarp forests, kerangas, lower montane forests, mangroves, scrub jungle, secondary forests, plantations, gardens. Usually seen in pairs. Feeds on fruits, especially those of Straits Rhododendron *Melastoma malabathricum*, and nectar, plus insects.

LEFT: *Female*. RIGHT: *Male*

Plain Flowerpecker ■ *Dicaeum minullum* 8cm
(Malay: Sepah-puteri Kecil Biasa. Indonesian: Cabai Polos)

DESCRIPTION Adult has greyish upperparts washed with olive, and olive wings with dark grey primaries. Secondaries and tail feathers dark grey, fringed olive. Chin to upper breast greyish, washed olive; rest of underparts buffish white, vent yellower. Iris black, upper mandible black, base of lower mandible grey, legs and feet black. **DISTRIBUTION** Nepal, S China, Taiwan, Southeast Asia, Greater Sundas. Scarce, mainly sub-montane resident in the hills of Borneo, 0–1,200m. Race: *D. m. borneanum*. **HABITS AND HABITAT** Secondary forests, plantation forests, scrub jungle, forest edges. One of the smallest birds in Borneo, usually seen singly. Active, dashing about among dense foliage of hanging mistletoes, foraging for insects and fruits; favours *Scurrula ferruginea*.

Bornean Flowerpecker ■ *Dicaeum monticolum* 8cm ℯ
(Malay: Sepah-puteri Gunung Borneo. Indonesian: Cabai Panggul-hitam)

DESCRIPTION Adult male has black lores, face and side of neck; rest of upperparts dark blackish blue, darker at wings and with white pectoral tufts. Chin white; throat and upper breast scarlet, cleanly demarcated from dark grey lower breast. Belly, flanks and vent grey, washed yellowish. Iris, bill, legs and feet black. Adult female has plain olive-green upperparts with dark grey primaries and secondaries; rump washed yellow. Chin, throat and rest of underparts pale grey with yellow-washed belly, flanks and vent. **DISTRIBUTION** Locally common sub-montane and montane endemic in the N-central mountain ranges, 460–2,540m. Monotypic. **HABITS AND HABITAT** Primary and secondary sub-montane and montane forests, kerangas, forest edges, gardens. Usually seen singly. Active at lower storey, foraging for fruits and insects. At Kinabalu National Park, usually seen feeding on fruits of *Medinilla* sp.

LEFT: *Male*. RIGHT: *Female*

Scarlet-backed Flowerpecker ■ *Dicaeum cruentatum* 8–9cm
(Malay: Sepah-puteri Belakang Merah. Indonesian: Cabai Merah)

DESCRIPTION Adult male has scarlet forehead and crown to rump; rest of upperparts black, with white pectoral tufts. Chin, throat, breast sides and flanks black; broad white centre of breast connects to white belly and vent. Iris dark brown; bill, legs and feet black. Adult female has olive-green upperparts with scarlet rump; wings darker olive, with white pectoral tufts. Underparts greyish olive; buff centre of breast connects to buff belly and vent. Where they overlap in S Borneo, adult female is similar to adult female **Scarlet-headed Flowerpecker** *D. trochileum*, but that has reddish wash on head and mantle. **DISTRIBUTION** Nepal, N India, S China, Southeast Asia, Sumatra. Common resident throughout Borneo, 0–1,750m. Race: *D. c. nigrimentum*. **HABITS AND HABITAT** Mangroves, kerangas, forest edges, gardens, lower montane forests, peat swamps, scrub jungle. Usually seen in pairs or family groups, commonly in gardens. Feeds on fruits and insects.

ABOVE *Female*. BELOW: *Male*

Ornate Sunbird ■ *Cinnyris ornatus* 10cm
(Malay: Kelicap Biasa. Indonesian: Burung-madu Sriganti)

DESCRIPTION Adult male has metallic bluish-green forehead, olive-green crown and rest of upperparts; uppertail feathers black, wings darker olive with orange pectoral tufts. Lores, chin, throat and breast metallic bluish green/purple; rest of underparts bright yellow with white under-tail feathers. Iris reddish brown; bill, legs and feet black. Adult female is similar but lacks all metallic bluish green/purple and has a fine yellow supercilium. In eclipse male metallic bluish-green/purple feathers are confined to centre of throat and breast. **DISTRIBUTION** SE China, Southeast Asia, Greater Sundas, Lesser Sundas. Common lowland resident throughout Borneo, including islands, up to 1,565m. Race: *C. o. ornatus*. **HABITS AND HABITAT** Kerangas, mangroves, scrub, gardens, secondary vegetation, riverine forests, cultivated areas. Usually seen singly or in pairs. Forages in lower storey for nectar and insects, and often seen at ornamental flowering shrubs.

ABOVE: *Eclipse male*. LEFT: *Male*. RIGHT: *Female*

Van Hasselt's Sunbird ■ *Leptocoma brasiliana* 9–10cm
(Malay: Kelicap Belacan Biasa. Indonesian: Burung-madu Pengantin)

DESCRIPTION Adult male has forehead to crown metallic green, face, nape and wings black, rump metallic green. Throat metallic purple, breast metallic scarlet, belly to vent

Male

dark grey. However, these metallic colours only become obvious with the right lighting, otherwise bird appears to be black. Female has green-olive upperparts, yellow-olive underparts. Iris, bill, legs and feet black. **DISTRIBUTION** Burma to S Vietnam, Thai-Malay Peninsula, Sumatra, Belitung, Java, Philippines, Borneo. Locally common lowland resident up to 1,200m. **HABITS AND HABITAT** Disturbed forest, forest edges, open country, tree plantations, mangroves; usually in canopy, singly or in pairs, actively foraging for insects, worms, nectars, fruits, seeds.

Brown-throated Sunbird ■ *Anthreptes malacensis* 12.5–13cm
(Malay: Kelicap Mayang Kelapa. Indonesian: Burung-madu Kelapa)

DESCRIPTION Adult male has deep metallic blue upperparts, reddish-brown patch on scapulars, brown on greater coverts, blackish brown on wings. Lores and cheek to ear-coverts dark brown, bordered below by bright metallic blue/purple malar stripe. Chin and throat brown, cleanly demarcated from bright yellow breast and rest of underparts. Iris reddish brown, bill black, legs and feet greenish yellow. Adult female has olive-green upperparts, pale yellow around eye, dark grey on inner web of wing feathers, and yellow underparts. **Red-throated Sunbird** *A. rhodolaemus* is similar but adult male has reddish throat and cheeks with more red on wing coverts. **DISTRIBUTION** Southeast Asia, Greater Sundas, Philippines, Sulawesi. Common lowland resident throughout Borneo, including islands, up to 1,220m. Races: *A. m. bornensis* (shown) in Sabah, *A. m. malacensis*

LEFT: *Male*. RIGHT: *Female*

in Kalimantan; Sarawak birds are an intermediate form. **HABITS AND HABITAT** Mangroves, peat swamps, coastal scrub, kerangas, forest edges, gardens, plantation forests, open areas. Usually seen in pairs, favouring flowering shrubs, wild ginger, cultivated heliconias, etc., whose nectar it feeds on. Also feeds on insects and overripe tree fruits.

Plain Sunbird ■ *Anthreptes simplex* 12–12.5cm
(Malay: Kelicap Kelabu Melayu. Indonesian: Burung-madu Polos)

DESCRIPTION Adult male has diagnostic metallic green forehead patch; rest of upperparts plain olive. Chin, throat and rest of underparts greyish white, with yellow wash on belly, flanks and vent. Iris brown, bill black, legs and feet greenish yellow. Adult female is similar but lacks green forehead patch. **DISTRIBUTION** Thai–Malay Peninsula, Sumatra. Common lowland resident throughout Borneo, up to 1,220m. Monotypic. **HABITS AND HABITAT** Lowland and hill dipterocarp forests, kerangas, peat-swamp and secondary forests, plantation forests, gardens. Usually seen singly, dashing among dense foliage, flowers or fruiting branches. Feeds on nectar, insects and fruits.

LEFT: *Female*. RIGHT: *Male*

Crimson Sunbird
■ *Aethopyga siparaja* 9–11cm
(Malay: Kelicap Merah Biasa. Indonesian: Burung-madu Sepah-raja)

DESCRIPTION Adult male has dark blue forehead and forecrown, crimson on rest of head to back, and yellow rump (grey in eclipse plumage); wings dark grey with olive fringes on primaries and secondaries, uppertail feathers dark metallic blue. Lores black, chin to upper breast crimson with metallic blue malar stripe, rest of underparts dark grey. Iris brown; bill, legs and feet dark grey. Adult female has green-olive upperparts, and yellow-olive underparts with a greyish wash; under-tail feathers tipped white. **DISTRIBUTION** India, S China, Southeast Asia, Greater Sundas, Sulawesi. Common lowland resident throughout Borneo, and on islands, generally up to 600m. Race: *A. s. siparaja*. **HABITS AND HABITAT** Scrub, kerangas, mangroves, riverine and peat-swamp forests, gardens, forest edges, cultivated areas. Usually seen singly or in pairs. Feeds on nectar and insects, foraging in middle and lower storeys; will also hover to take nectar from flowers.

Male

Temminck's Sunbird ■ *Aethopyga temminckii* 11cm
(Malay: Kelicap Merah Ekor Api. Indonesian: Burung-madu Ekor-merah)

DESCRIPTION Adult male has crimson head to back with metallic violet lateral crown-stripes that connect at nape. Wings brown, rump yellow, uppertail coverts violet, uppertail feathers scarlet. Lores black; face and chin to upper breast scarlet with metallic violet malar stripes. Grey lower breast is cleanly demarcated from scarlet upper breast; belly,

flanks and vent yellowish grey. Iris dark brown; bill, legs and feet black. Adult female has grey head, rest of upperparts olive-green, wings and tail feathers washed with orange, underparts olive-grey; tail is much shorter. **DISTRIBUTION** Thai–Malay Peninsula, Sumatra. Common sub-montane and montane resident throughout Borneo, 120–1,680m. Monotypic. **HABITS AND HABITAT** Primary and secondary lower montane and montane forests, forest edges, plantation forests, cultivated areas. Feeds on nectar and insects, foraging at all levels of the forest but mainly in middle storey; occasionally joins mixed feeding flocks.

Male

Ruby-cheeked Sunbird
■ *Chalcoparia singalensis* 10–11cm
(Malay: Kelicap Pipi Merah.
Indonesian: Burung-madu Belukar)

DESCRIPTION Adult male has metallic green forehead to tail; primaries, secondaries and greater covert feathers black. Lores black, cheek and ear-coverts dark brown; metallic purple moustachial patch. Chin to breast cinnamon; belly, flanks and vent bright yellow. Iris reddish, bill black, legs and feet olive. Adult female is similar but has plain olive face and ear-coverts, olive-green upperparts washed with grey. Primaries, secondaries, greater coverts and tail feathers yellow-olive. **DISTRIBUTION** NE Indian sub-continent to SW China, Southeast Asia, Sumatra, Java. Locally common lowland resident throughout Borneo, including islands, up to 1,200m. Race: *C. s. borneana.* **HABITS AND HABITAT** Lowland and hill dipterocarp forests, peat-swamp and secondary forests, kerangas, scrub, coastal vegetation, plantation forests, gardens. The only sunbird that is found in family parties. Feeds on insects, fruits and nectar in middle and upper storeys.

ABOVE: *Male.* BELOW: *Female*

Bornean Spiderhunter ■ *Arachnothera everetti* 18cm ⓔ
(Malay: Kelicap-jantung Kelabu Besar. Indonesian: Pijantung Kalimantan)

DESCRIPTION Adult has olive-green upperparts, with crown appearing spotty from dark-centred feathers. Inner web of primaries blackish, dark sub-terminal band at tail. Underparts yellowish grey with neatly arranged, dark grey spots on chin and throat; indistinct broad, dark grey streaks on breast to belly. Under-tail feathers dark grey. Iris brown, decurved bill black, legs and feet pink. **Grey-breasted Spiderhunter** *A. modesta* is similar, but is absent from Sabah, is smaller in size and has a shorter bill. **DISTRIBUTION** Locally common endemic of lowland and montane areas in Sabah, and sub-montane and montane areas elsewhere in Borneo. Monotypic. **HABITS AND HABITAT** Primary and secondary lowland and montane forests, forest edges, gardens, plantation forests. Usually seen singly. Feeds on nectar and insects, often in thickets of wild banana and ginger.

Whitehead's Spiderhunter
■ *Arachnothera juliae* 18cm ⓔ
(Malay: Kelicap-jantung Gunung Borneo. Indonesian: Pijantung Whitehead)

DESCRIPTION Adult has chocolate-brown upperparts finely streaked buff and white; wings and tail plain blackish brown, rump bright yellow. Underparts dark greyish brown, densely covered with white streaks, finer at throat and broader at belly and flanks. Vent bright yellow, under-tail plain blackish brown. Iris brown; bill, legs and feet black. **DISTRIBUTION** Locally common endemic montane resident in N-central mountain ranges, 945–2,100m. Monotypic. **HABITS AND HABITAT** Primary and secondary lower and upper montane forests, forest edges, scrub. Feeds on nectar, insects and fruits; often seen foraging for nectar from *Wightia borneensis*, epiphytic rhododendrons and other flowering plants growing high in upper storey of montane forests.

Spectacled Spiderhunter ■ *Arachnothera flavigaster* 22cm
(Malay: Kelicap-jantung Besar. Indonesian: Pijantung Tasmak)

DESCRIPTION Adult has diagnostic broad yellow eye-ring and ear-patch; forehead to rump dark olive-green, wings and tail browner. Underpart colour varies with individuals, from dark olive-green to yellow, but always with faint white/pale grey streaks on throat and breast. Iris dark brown; decurved bill black, pinkish at base; legs and feet orange-yellow. Similar to Yellow-eared Spiderhunter (below) but that is smaller, with a thinner eye-ring and finer, longer bill. **DISTRIBUTION** Thai–Malay Peninsula, Sumatra. Scarce lowland resident throughout Borneo, up to 1,680m. Monotypic. **HABITS AND HABITAT** Lowland and hill dipterocarp forests, peat-swamp and secondary forests, kerangas, forest edges, plantation forests. Usually seen singly, feeding on nectar and insects; often seen in thickets of wild banana and ginger. Also forages at canopy.

Yellow-eared Spiderhunter ■ *Arachnothera chrysogenys* 18cm
(Malay: Kelicap-jantung Telinga Berus. Indonesian: Pijantung Telinga-kuning)

DESCRIPTION Adult has diagnostic yellow ear-patch, which is made up of a tuft of long yellow feathers; upperparts dark olive-green, browner at wings and tail. Thin yellow eye-ring, with bottom part barely visible. Pinkish skin below gape line; rest of underparts olive-yellow with faint greyish blotches, breast feathers with fine, dark shaft streaks. Iris dark brown; long, slender, decurved bill black, edged yellow at mid-section; legs and feet pinkish brown. Spectacled Spiderhunter (above) is similar. **DISTRIBUTION** Thai–Malay Peninsula, Greater Sundas. Scarce lowland resident throughout Borneo, up to 1,220m. Races: *A. c. harrissoni* (shown) in E Borneo, *A. c. chrysogenys* in W Borneo. **HABITS AND HABITAT** Lowland and hill dipterocarp forests, peat-swamp and secondary forests, mangroves, kerangas, forest edges, gardens, plantation forests. Usually seen singly. Feeds on nectar, fruits and insects, often foraging in thickets of flowering shrubs.

Little Spiderhunter ■ *Arachnothera longirostra* 15.5–16.5cm
(Malay: Kelicap-jantung Kecil Biasa. Indonesian: Pijantung Kecil)

DESCRIPTION Adult has dark olive-green upperparts; feathers on forehead and crown pale-fringed, creating a scaly appearance. Greyish-brown mask across eye, with short, pale supercilium above and pale grey loral stripe below. Dark greyish-brown moustachial stripe contrasts with whitish-grey chin and throat. Breast and rest of underparts yellow, with white-tipped under-tail feathers. Iris brown; long, decurved bill black with pale grey at base of lower mandible; legs and feet black.

Thick-billed Spiderhunter (below) is similar.
DISTRIBUTION India, Nepal, SW China, Southeast Asia, Greater Sundas. Abundant lowland resident throughout Borneo, up to 1,500m. Race: *A. l. buettikoferi*.
HABITS AND HABITAT Lowland and hill dipterocarp forests, kerangas, peat-swamp and secondary forests, forest edges, coastal vegetation, gardens, plantation forests. Usually seen singly, dashing in and out of low-growing scrubs, foraging for nectar and insects; often seen feeding in thickets of wild banana and ginger flowers.

Thick-billed Spiderhunter ■ *Arachnothera crassirostris* 15–16cm
(Malay: Kelicap-jantung Paruh Tebal. Indonesian: Pijantung Kampung)

DESCRIPTION Adult has dark olive-green upperparts, indistinct broken yellowish eye-ring, yellow fringes on wings and tail feathers, orange pectoral tufts. Chin to breast plain, dark olive-green, graduating into bright yellow belly, flanks and vent. Iris pale brown; bill, legs and feet black. Similar to Little Spiderhunter (above) but that has a whitish-grey chin and throat.

DISTRIBUTION Thai–Malay Peninsula, Sumatra. Uncommon lowland resident throughout Borneo, up to 1,200m. Monotypic.
HABITS AND HABITAT Lowland and hill dipterocarp forests, peat-swamp and secondary forests, kerangas, forest edges, plantation forests. Usually seen singly, feeding on nectar and insects; often seen feeding in thickets of wild banana and ginger.

Purple-naped Spiderhunter ■ *Arachnothera hypogrammica* 14–15cm
(Malay: Kelicap Rimba. Indonesian: Pijantung Rimba)

DESCRIPTION Adult male has olive-green upperparts with diagnostic purple patch across nape. Lower back and rump metallic bluish purple, with tips of wings and uppertail feathers blackish olive. Underparts buff yellow with broad, dark olive streaks; under-tail feathers tipped white. Iris reddish brown, bill black, legs and feet dark olive. Adult female is similar but lacks purple patch on nape and bluish purple on lower back and rump.
DISTRIBUTION Southeast Asia, Sumatra. Common lowland resident throughout Borneo, up to 1,000m. Race: *A. h. hypogrammica*

HABITS AND HABITAT Lowland and hill dipterocarp forests, peat-swamp and secondary forests, kerangas, plantation forests. Usually seen singly or in pairs. Active in the lower storey. Feeds on nectar of wild banana and ginger, also on insects and fruits.

LEFT: *Male*. RIGHT: *Female*

ABOVE: *Males*. BELOW: *Female*

Red Avadavat ■ *Amandava amandava* 10cm
(Malay: Ciak Merah. Indonesian: Pipit Benggala)

DESCRIPTION Breeding male has dark red forehead, face and ear-coverts; dark red crown and nape mottled brown; brown mantle and back; blackish-brown wings sparsely spotted white; dark red rump; black tail. Underparts dark red, with breast side, belly and flanks covered in white spots; vent blackish, mottled white. Iris red-brown, bill red with dark culmen, legs and feet pink. Adult female has dark lores and eye-patch, greyish-brown upperparts, darker wings with few white spots, plain dark red rump and black tail; underparts plain buffish brown with grey wash at breast sides and flanks. Non-breeding male is like adult female but has more white spots on rump. **DISTRIBUTION** Indian sub-continent to SW China, Southeast Asia, Java, Lesser Sundas. Rare introduced resident in Borneo's coastal lowlands, recorded in Sabah, Brunei and S Kalimantan. Race: uncertain. **HABITS AND HABITAT** Dry sandy and gritty grassland, paddy fields. Often seen in small family parties, foraging among pebbles and grit on dry ground.

Scaly-breasted Munia ▪ *Lonchura punctulata* 10–11cm
(Malay: Ciak-padi Pinang. Indonesian: Bondol Peking)

DESCRIPTION Adult *L. p. cabanisi* has mid-brown upperparts with buff streaks, buff-fringed feathers on lower back and rump. Lores, face, chin and throat darker brown; breast and flanks buffish white with brown scallops; belly and vent buffish white with brown mottling on vent. Iris reddish brown; bill dark grey, paler at lower mandible; legs and feet dark bluish grey. Adult *L. p. nisoria* has dark reddish-brown face; whitish underparts with clear blackish single scallops; grey rump and spotted uppertail coverts. **DISTRIBUTION** Indian sub-continent, S China, Taiwan, Southeast Asia, Greater and Lesser Sundas, Philippines. Locally common lowland resident throughout Borneo; first recorded in S Kalimantan in 1974, later recorded in Sabah in 1993; has since spread remarkably well and is now increasingly common. Races: *L. p. cabanisi* (shown) in Sabah, possibly Brunei and Sarawak; *L. p. nisoria* in Kalimantan. **HABITS AND HABITAT** Paddy fields, grassland, cultivated areas. Usually seen in flocks, and not as shy as Dusky Munia (p. 154). Forages in standing tall grass, often with other munias, feeding on rice and grass seeds.

White-bellied Munia ▪ *Lonchura leucogastra* 9.5–11.5cm
(Malay: Ciak-padi Rimba. Indonesian: Bondol Perut-putih)

DESCRIPTION Adult *L. l. palawana* has dark chocolate-brown upperparts with buff shaft streaks from crown to back and wing coverts. Uppertail buff with dark brown edges. Chin to breast dark chocolate-brown, central belly and lower flanks white. Thigh, vent and under-tail feathers dark brown. Iris reddish brown, upper mandible black, lower mandible bluish grey, legs and feet black. Adult *L. l. castanonota* has deep rufous-chestnut upperparts, with face, rump and under-tail coverts black. Adult *L. l. smythiesi* has greyer-brown upperparts and no black rump. **DISTRIBUTION** Thai–Malay Peninsula, Sumatra, Philippines. Uncommon lowland resident throughout Borneo, up to 200m. Races: *L. l. castanonota* in Kalimantan, *L. l. smythiesi* in SW Sarawak, *L. l. palawana* (shown) elsewhere; however, geographic boundaries between races and local movements are unclear. **HABITS AND HABITAT** Peat-swamp and secondary forests, plantation forests, forest edges, open areas with tall grass around villages and towns. Usually seen singly or in flocks. Extremely shy, skulking in tall grass, often with other munias, and feeding on rice and grass seeds.

Dusky Munia ■ *Lonchura fuscans* 10cm ⓔ
(Malay: Ciak-padi Kelam. Indonesian: Bondol Kalimantan)

DESCRIPTION A small, dark brown munia. Adult has blackish-brown plumage with darker fringes, making them appear blotchy. Wing and tail feathers plain blackish brown. Iris black; upper mandible black, lower mandible pale bluish; legs and feet greyish blue. **DISTRIBUTION** Common lowland endemic resident throughout Borneo, including offshore islands (small population recorded on Mapun, Philippines), up to 1,600m. Monotypic. **HABITS AND HABITAT** Paddy fields, grassland, forest edges, plantation forests, secondary forests, gardens. Feeds on rice and grass seeds, often in flocks, which can be damaging to rice crops. Also forages on ground for seeds. More wary of humans and more furtive than Black-headed Munia (below).

Black-headed Munia ■ *Lonchura atricapilla* 11–12.5cm
(Malay: Ciak-padi Rawa Biasa. Indonesian: Bondol Rawa)

DESCRIPTION Adult has black forehead to nape, face, and chin to upper breast, resembling a black hood; rest of upperparts chestnut. Chestnut band across breast joins to chestnut belly sides and flanks; massive black patch covers centre of breast to central

belly and vent; under-tail feathers chestnut. Iris brown, bill silvery grey, legs and feet bluish grey. **DISTRIBUTION** S China, South and Southeast Asia, Taiwan, Greater Sundas, Philippines, Sulawesi, Malukus, Micronesia. Abundant and widespread lowland resident throughout Borneo, up to 1,680m. Race: *L. a. jagori*. **HABITS AND HABITAT** Grassland, swamps, paddy fields, gardens, cultivated areas, parks. Commonest munia in Borneo, usually seen in flocks. Builds nest in flowering plants in gardens, and feeds on rice and grass seeds.

Java Sparrow ▪ *Lonchura oryzivora* 16–17cm
(Malay: Jelatik Jawa. Indonesian: Gelatik Jawa)

DESCRIPTION Adult is unmistakable, with an attractive colour scheme. Head black, with extensive white face-patch covering cheek to ear-coverts, like a black hood with white on face. Mantle and back greyish blue, rump and uppertail black. Chin and upper throat black, breast greyish blue, belly and flanks pink, vent and under-tail coverts white. Iris red with pinkish-red eye-ring, bill pink with paler tip, legs pink. **DISTRIBUTION** Java, Kangean, Bali; introduced to many areas in Asia and elsewhere. Introduced resident in lowlands of Borneo, patchily distributed, but well established in certain areas. Monotypic. **HABITS AND HABITAT** Open grassland, gardens, paddy fields, plantations. Usually seen in flocks. Feeds on grass seeds and paddy, sometimes foraging with other munias.

Paddyfield Pipit ▪ *Anthus rufulus* 15–16cm
(Malay: Apit-apit Biasa. Indonesian: Apung Tanah)

DESCRIPTION Adult has brown forehead to crown finely streaked dark brown; rest of upperparts heavily streaked dark brown; wings and greater covert feathers blackish grey, fringed buff; tail blackish with pale outer feathers. Long buffish supercilium, dark lores across eye to ear-coverts; buffish-white sub-moustachial stripe with narrow brown malar stripe. Underparts whitish buff with variable amount of streaking on breast. Iris brown, bill pinkish yellow with dark grey culmen, legs and feet pinkish brown. Very similar to **Richard's Pipit** *A. richardi*, but that is larger and has pale lores, and is a rare winter visitor. **DISTRIBUTION** South Asia to S China, Southeast Asia, Greater and Lesser Sundas, Philippines. Locally common Bornean lowland resident, commoner in the N and scarcer in the S. Race: *A. r. malayensis*. **HABITS AND HABITAT** Grassy areas, open fields, gardens, roadsides, golf courses, airfields. Forages on the ground, moving agilely on grassland as it runs and darts after insects.

Symbols

E	Endemic resident
R	Known to have bred; typically but not necessarily resident all year
M	Migrant, passage migrant or non-breeding visitor
V	Accidental visitor, typically less than 10 records
?	Insufficient data to determine status
-	Does not occur

Global status according to IUCN Red List 2022

LC	Least Concern
NT	Near Threatened
VU	Vulnerable
EN	Endangered
CR	Critically Endangered
DD	Data Deficient
NE	Not Evaluated

Common Name	Scientific Name	Sabah	Sarawak	Brunei	Kalimantan	Global Sataus
Anatidae (Ducks, Geese & Swans)						
Wandering Whistling-duck	*Dendrocygna arcuata*	R	-	R	R	LC
Lesser Whistling-duck	*Dendrocygna javanica*	R	R	R	R	LC
Cotton Pygmy-goose	*Nettapus coromandelianus*	V	V	V	V	LC
Eurasian Wigeon	*Anas penelope*	M	M	M	-	LC
Chinese Spot-billed Duck	*Anas zonorhyncha*	V	-	-	-	LC
Mallard	*Anas platyrhynchos*	V	V	V	-	LC
Pacific Black Duck	*Anas superciliosa*	-	-	-	V	LC
Northern Pintail	*Anas acuta*	M	M	M	-	LC
EurasianTeal	*Anas crecca*	V	-	V	-	LC
Sunda Teal	*Anas gibberifrons*	R	-	-	R	NT
Garganey	*Spatula querquedula*	M	M	M	M	LC
Northern Shoveler	*Spatula clypeata*	M	M	M	-	LC
Tufted Duck	*Aythya fuligula*	M	M	M	-	LC
Megapodiidae (Megapodes)						
Tabon Scrubfowl	*Megapodius cumingii*	R	-	-	R	LC
Phasianidae (Pheasants & Allies)						
Long-billed Partridge	*Rhizothera longirostris*	R	R	-	R	NT
Dulit Partridge	*Rhizothera dulitensis*	E	E	-	-	VU
Roulroul	*Rollulus rouloul*	R	R	R	R	VU
Ferruginous Partridge	*Caloperdix oculeus*	R	R	-	R	NT
Black Partridge	*Melanoperdix niger*	R	R	R	R	VU
Bornean Partridge	*Arborophila hyperythra*	E	E		E	LC
Sabah Partridge	*Tropicoperdix graydoni*	E	-	-	-	NT
Great Argus	*Argusianus argus*	R	R	R	R	VU

Common Name	Scientific Name	Sabah	Sarawak	Brunei	Kalimantan	Global Sataus
Bornean Peacock Pheasant	*Polyplectron schleiermacheri*	E	E	-	E	EN
Bloodhead	*Haematortyx sanguiniceps*	E	E	-	E	LC
Blue-breasted Quail	*Synoicus chinensis*	R	R	R	R	LC
Red Junglefowl	*Gallus gallus*	R	-	-	-	LC
Bornean Crestless Fireback	*Lophura pyronota*	R	R	R	R	EN
Bornean Crested Fireback	*Lophura ignita*	R	R	R	R	VU
Bulwer's Pheasant	*Lophura bulweri*	E	E	E	E	VU
Podicipedidae (Grebes)						
Little Grebe	*Tachybaptus ruficollis*	R	-	V	V	LC
Columbidae (Pigeons & Doves)						
Domestic Pigeon	*Columba livia*	R	R	R	R	LC
Silvery Wood-pigeon	*Columba argentina*	-	R	-	R	CR
Metallic Pigeon	*Columba vitiensis*	R	R	-	R	LC
Philippine Collared Dove	*Streptopelia dusumieri*	V	V	-	-	VU
Red Collared Dove	*Streptopelia tranquebarica*	?R				LC
Eastern Spotted Dove	*Spilopelia chinensis*	R	R	R	R	LC
Zebra Dove	*Geopelia striata*	R	R	R	R	LC
Philippine Cuckoo Dove	*Macropygia tenuirostris*	R	R	R	R	LC
Little Cuckoo Dove	*Macropygia ruficeps*	R	R	R	R	LC
Nicobar Pigeon	*Caloenas nicobarica*	R	-	R	R	NT
Asian Emerald Dove	*Chalcophaps indica*	R	R	R	R	LC
Cinnamon-headed Green Pigeon	*Treron fulvicollis*	R	R	R	R	NT
Little Green Pigeon	*Treron olax*	R	R	R	R	LC
Pink-necked Green-pigeon	*Treron vernans*	R	R	R	R	LC
Thick-billed Green-pigeon	*Treron curvirostra*	R	R	R	R	LC
Large Green-pigeon	*Treron capellei*	R	R	R	R	VU
Jambu Fruit Dove	*Ptilinopus jambu*	R	R	R	R	NT
Black-naped Fruit Dove	*Ptilinopus melanospilus*	R	-	-	R	LC
Grey Imperial Pigeon	*Ducula pickeringii*	R	R	R	R	VU
Green Imperial Pigeon	*Ducula aenea*	R	R	R	R	NT
Mountain Imperial Pigeon	*Ducula badia*	R	R	R	R	LC
Pied Imperial Pigeon	*Ducula bicolor*	R	R	R	R	LC
Cuculidae (Cuckoos)						
Rhinortha	*Rhinortha chlorophaea*	R	R	R	R	LC
Red-billed Malkoha	*Phaenicophaeus javanicus*	R	R	R	R	LC
Chestnut-bellied Malkoha	*Phaenicophaeus sumatranus*	R	R	R	R	NT
Black-bellied Malkoha	*Phaenicophaeus diardi*	R	R	R	R	NT
Chestnut-breasted Malkoha	*Phaenicophaeus curvirostris*	R	R	R	R	LC
Chestnut-winged Cuckoo	*Clamator coromandus*	M	M	M	M	LC
Drongo-cuckoo	*Surniculus lugubris*	R	R	R	R	LC
Indian Cuckoo	*Cuculus micropterus*	R	R	R	R	LC
Sunda Cuckoo	*Cuculus lepidus*	R	R	-	R	LC
Common Cuckoo	*Cuculus canorus*	V	-	-	-	LC
Himalayan Cuckoo	*Cuculus saturatus*	M	M	-	-	LC
Oriental Cuckoo	*Cuculus optatus*	M	M	-	M	LC
Moustached Hawk-cuckoo	*Hierococcyx vagans*	R	R	R	R	NT
Northern Hawk-cuckoo	*Hierococcyx hyperythrus*	M	M	-	M	LC
Malaysian Hawk-cuckoo	*Hierococcyx fugax*	R	R	R	R	LC
Whistling Hawk-cuckoo	*Hierococcyx nisicolor*	M	M	-	-	LC
Large Hawk-cuckoo	*Hierococcyx sparverioides*	V	V	-	-	LC

Common Name	Scientific Name	Sabah	Sarawak	Brunei	Kalimantan	Global Sataus
Bock's Hawk-cuckoo	*Hierococcyx bocki*	R	R	-	R	LC
Banded Bay Cuckoo	*Cacomantis sonneratii*	R	R	R	R	LC
Plaintive Cuckoo	*Cacomantis merulinus*	R	R	R	R	LC
Sunda Brush Cuckoo	*Cacomantis sepulcralis*	R	R	R	R	LC
Horsfield's Bronze Cuckoo	*Chrysococcyx basalis*	-	M	M	M	LC
Little Bronze Cuckoo	*Chrysococcyx minutillus*	R	R	R	R	LC
Violet Cuckoo	*Chrysococcyx xanthorhynchus*	R	R	R	R	LC
Asian Koel	*Eudynamys scolopaceus*	R	R	R	R	LC
Short-toed Coucal	*Centropus rectunguis*	R	R	R	R	VU
Greater Coucal	*Centropus sinensis*	R	R	R	R	LC
Lesser Coucal	*Centropus bengalensis*	R	R	R	R	LC
Bornean Ground-cuckoo	*Carpococcyx radiceus*	E	E	E	E	VU
Hemiprocnidae (Treeswifts)						
Whiskered Treeswift	*Hemiprocne comata*	R	R	R	R	LC
Grey-rumped Treeswift	*Hemiprocne longipennis*	R	R	R	R	LC
Apodidae (Swifts)						
Silver-rumped Spinetail	*Rhaphidura leucopygialis*	R	R	R	R	LC
House Swift	*Apus nipalensis*	R	R	R	R	LC
Pacific Swift	*Apus pacificus*	M	M	M	M	LC
Asian Palm Swift	*Cypsiurus balasiensis*	R	R	R	R	LC
Giant Swiftlet	*Hydrochrous gigas*	R	R	R	R	NT
Uniform Swiftlet	*Aerodramus vanikorensis*	R	R	R	R	LC
Black-nest Swiftlet	*Aerodramus maximus*	R	R	R	R	LC
Edible-nest Swiftlet	*Aerodramus fuciphagus*	R	R	R	R	LC
Bornean Swiftlet	*Collocalia dodgei*	E	E	-	-	NE
Plume-toed Swiftlet	*Collocalia affinis*	R	R	R	R	NE
White-throated Needletail	*Hirundapus caudacutus*	M	M	M	-	LC
Brown-backed Needletail	*Hirundapus giganteus*	R	R	R	R	LC
Podargidae (Frogmouths)						
Gould's Frogmouth	*Batrachostomus stellatus*	R	R	R	R	NT
Bornean Frogmouth	*Batrachostomus mixtus*	E	E	-	E	NT
Blyth's Frogmouth	*Batrachostomus affinis*	R	R	R	R	LC
Sunda Frogmouth	*Batrachostomus cornutus*	R	R	R	R	LC
Large Frogmouth	*Batrachostomus auritus*	R	R	R	R	NT
Dulit Frogmouth	*Batrachostomus harterti*	E	E	-	E	NT
Caprimulgidae (Nightjars)						
Malaysian Eared-nightjar	*Lyncornis temminckii*	R	R	R	R	LC
Grey Nightjar	*Caprimulgus jotaka*	M	M	M	-	LC
Large-tailed Nightjar	*Caprimulgus macrurus*	R	R	R	R	LC
Savanna Nightjar	*Caprimulgus affinis*	R	R	-	R	LC
Bonaparte's Nightjar	*Caprimulgus concretus*	R	R	R	R	VU
Rallidae (Rails, Crakes & Coots)						
Barred Rail	*Gallirallus torquatus*	R	-	-	-	LC
Buff-banded Rail	*Gallirallus philippensis*	R	R	R	R	LC
Slaty-breasted Rail	*Lewinia striata*	R	R	R	R	LC
Eastern Water Rail	*Rallus indicus*	-	V	V	-	LC
Red-legged Crake	*Rallina fasciata*	R	R	R	R	LC
Slaty-legged Crake	*Rallina eurizonoides*	V	-	-	-	LC
Baillon's Crake	*Zapornia pusilla*	M	M	M	M	LC

Common Name	Scientific Name	Sabah	Sarawak	Brunei	Kalimantan	Global Sataus
Ruddy-breasted Crake	*Zapornia fusca*	M	M	-	M	LC
Band-bellied Crake	*Zapornia paykulli*	-	M	M	M	NT
White-browed Crake	*Poliolimnas cinereus*	R	R	R	R	LC
Watercock	*Gallicrex cinerea*	RM	M	M	M	LC
White-breasted Waterhen	*Amaurornis phoenicurus*	R	R	R	R	LC
Purple Swamphen	*Porphyrio porphyrio*	R	-	R	R	LC
Common Moorhen	*Gallinula chloropus*	RM	RM	RM	RM	LC
Common Coot	*Fulica atra*	V	-	V	-	LC
Heliornithidae (Finfoots)						
Masked Finfoot	*Heliopais personatus*	-	V	-	-	CR
Burhinidae (Thick-knees)						
Beach Thick-knee	*Esacus magnirostris*	R	R	R	-	NT
Recurvirostridae (Stilts & Avocets)						
Pied Stilt	*Himantopus leucocephalus*	V	V	V	V	LC
Black-winged Stilt	*Himantopus himantopus*	M	M	M	M	LC
Pied Avocet	*Recurvirostra avosetta*	V	V	-	-	LC
Haematopodidae (Oystercatchers)						
Far Eastern Oystercatcher	*Haematopus osculans*	-	V	-	-	NT
Charadriidae (Lapwings & Plovers)						
Pacific Golden Plover	*Pluvialis fulva*	M	M	M	M	LC
Grey Plover	*Pluvialis squatarola*	M	M	M	M	LC
Grey-headed Lapwing	*Vanellus cinereus*	-	V	V	-	LC
Red-wattled Lapwing	*Vanellus indicus*	-	V	-	-	LC
Northern Lapwing	*Vanellus vanellus*	-	-	V	-	NT
Oriental Plover	*Anarhynchus veredus*	V	V	V	V	LC
Tibetan Plover	*Anarhynchus atrifrons*	M	M	M	M	LC
Siberian Plover	*Anarhynchus mongolus*	M	M	M	M	LC
Greater Sand Plover	*Anarhynchus leschenaultii*	M	M	M	M	LC
Malaysian Plover	*Anarhynchus peronii*	R	R	R	R	NT
Kentish Plover	*Anarhynchus alexandrinus*	M	M	M	M	LC
White-faced Plover	*Anarhynchus dealbatus*	-	M	M	-	DD
Little Ringed Plover	*Charadrius dubius*	M	M	M	M	LC
Common Ringed Plover	*Charadrius hiaticula*	V	-	V	-	LC
Long-billed Plover	*Charadrius placidus*	V	-	V	-	LC
Rostratulidae (Painted-snipes)						
Greater Painted-snipe	*Rostratula benghalensis*	RM	M	M	M	LC
Jacanidae (Jacanas)						
Pheasant-tailed Jacana	*Hydrophasianus chirurgus*	V	-	-	V	LC
Comb-crested Jacana	*Irediparra gallinacea*	-	-	-	R	LC
Scolopacidae (Sandpipers & Snipes)						
Red-necked Phalarope	*Phalaropus lobatus*	M	M	M	M	LC
Red Phalarope	*Phalaropus fulicarius*	-	V	-	-	LC
Terek Sandpiper	*Xenus cinereus*	M	M	M	M	LC
Common Sandpiper	*Actitis hypoleucos*	M	M	M	M	LC
Green Sandpiper	*Tringa ochropus*	M	M	M	M	LC
Grey-tailed Tattler	*Tringa brevipes*	M	M	M	M	NT
Spotted Redshank	*Tringa erythropus*	V	V	V	-	LC
Common Greenshank	*Tringa nebularia*	M	M	M	M	LC
Nordmann's Greenshank	*Tringa guttifer*	M	M	M	M	EN
Marsh Sandpiper	*Tringa stagnatilis*	M	M	M	M	LC

Common Name	Scientific Name	Sabah	Sarawak	Brunei	Kalimantan	Global Sataus
Wood Sandpiper	Tringa glareola	M	M	M	M	LC
Common Redshank	Tringa totanus	M	M	M	M	LC
Ruddy Turnstone	Arenaria interpres	M	M	M	M	LC
Sanderling	Calidris alba	M	M	M	M	LC
Little Stint	Calidris minuta	V	V	V	V	LC
Red-necked Stint	Calidris ruficollis	M	M	M	M	NT
Temminck's Stint	Calidris temminckii	M	M	M	M	LC
Long-toed Stint	Calidris subminuta	M	M	M	M	LC
Spoon-billed Sandpiper	Calidris pygmaea	-	V	-	-	CR
Curlew Sandpiper	Calidris ferruginea	M	M	M	V	NT
Dunlin	Calidris alpina	V	V	V	V	LC
Broad-billed Sandpiper	Limicola falcinellus	M	M	M	M	LC
Sharp-tailed Sandpiper	Calidris acuminata	V	V	V	-	VU
Ruff	Calidris pugnax	M	M	M	M	LC
Great Knot	Calidris tenuirostris	M	M	M	M	EN
Red Knot	Calidris canutus	M	M	M	M	NT
Common Snipe	Gallinago gallinago	M	M	M	M	LC
Pintail Snipe	Gallinago stenura	M	M	M	M	LC
Swinhoe's Snipe	Gallinago megala	M	M	M	M	LC
Eurasian Woodcock	Scolopax rusticola	V	-	V	-	LC
Long-billed Dowitcher	Limnodromus scolopaceus	V	V	-	-	LC
Asian Dowitcher	Limnodromus semipalmatus	M	M	M	M	NT
Black-tailed Godwit	Limosa limosa	M	M	M	M	NT
Bar-tailed Godwit	Limosa lapponica	M	M	M	M	NT
Little Curlew	Numenius minutus	V	V	V	-	LC
Eurasian Whimbrel	Numenius phaeopus	M	M	M	M	LC
Far Eastern Curlew	Numenius madagascariensis	M	M	M	M	EN
Eurasian Curlew	Numenius arquata	M	M	M	M	NT
Glareolidae (Pratincoles)						
Australian Pratincole	Stiltia isabella	V	V	-	V	LC
Oriental Pratincole	Glareola maldivarum	M	RM	RM	M	LC
Laridae (Gulls & Terns)						
Brown Noddy	Anous stolidus	V	V	V	V	LC
Black Noddy	Anous minutus	V	V	-	-	LC
Heuglin's Gull	Larus heuglini	V	-	-	V	LC
Black-tailed Gull	Larus crassirostris	V	-	-	-	LC
Black-headed Gull	Larus ridibundus	M	M	M	-	LC
Sooty Tern	Onychoprion fuscatus	RM	M	M	RM	LC
Bridled Tern	Onychoprion anaethetus	R	R	R	R	LC
Aleutian Tern	Onychoprion aleuticus	M	M	M	M	VU
White-winged Tern	Chlidonias leucopterus	M	M	M	M	LC
Whiskered Tern	Chlidonias hybrida	M	M	M	M	LC
Little Tern	Sternula albifrons	RM	RM	RM	RM	LC
Roseate Tern	Sterna dougallii	M	M	RM	RM	LC
Black-naped Tern	Sterna sumatrana	RM	RM	RM	RM	LC
Common Tern	Sterna hirundo	M	M	M	M	LC
Gull-billed Tern	Gelochelidon nilotica	M	M	M	M	LC
Caspian Tern	Hydroprogne caspia	V	V	V	-	LC
Great Crested Tern	Thalasseus bergii	RM	M	M	RM	LC
Lesser Crested Tern	Thalasseus bengalensis	M	M	M	M	LC

Common Name	Scientific Name	Sabah	Sarawak	Brunei	Kalimantan	Global Sataus
Chinese Crested Tern	Thalasseus bernsteini	-	V	-	-	CR
Stercorariidae (Skuas)						
South Polar Skua	Stercorarius maccormicki	V	-	-	-	LC
Pomarine Skua	Stercorarius pomarinus	M	-	M	M	LC
Arctic Skua	Stercorarius parasiticus	V	V	-	-	LC
Long-tailed Skua	Stercorarius longicaudus	V	-	V	-	LC
Phaethontidae (Tropicbirds)						
White-tailed Tropicbird	Phaethon lepturus	V	-	-	V	LC
Procellariidae (Shearwaters & Petrels)						
Streaked Shearwater	Calonectris leucomelas	M	M	M	M	NT
Wedge-tailed Shearwater	Ardenna pacifica	V	V	-	-	LC
Bulwer's Petrel	Bulweria bulwerii	M	M	M	M	LC
Hydrobatidae (Storm-petrels)						
Swinhoe's Storm-petrel	Hydrobates monorhis	V	V	-	-	NT
Phalacrocoracidae (Cormorants & Shags)						
Little Black Cormorant	Phalacrocorax sulcirostris	-	-	-	V	LC
Great Cormorant	Phalacrocorax carbo	RM	-	M	M	LC
Little Pied Cormorant	Microcarbo melanoleucos	-	-	-	V	LC
Little Cormorant	Microcarbo niger	-	-	-	V	LC
Oriental Darter	Anhinga melanogaster	R	R	R	R	NT
Sulidae (Boobies & Gannets)						
Masked Booby	Sula dactylatra	RV	V	-	-	LC
Brown Booby	Sula leucogaster	RM	M	M	-	LC
Red-footed Booby	Sula sula	RV	V	V	-	LC
Fregatidae (Frigatebirds)						
Christmas Frigatebird	Fregata andrewsi	M	M	M	M	VU
Great Frigatebird	Fregata minor	M	M	M	M	LC
Lesser Frigatebird	Fregata ariel	M	M	M	M	LC
Threskiornithidae (Ibises & Spoonbills)						
Glossy Ibis	Plegadis falcinellus	V	-	V	V	LC
Black-headed Ibis	Threskiornis melanocephalus	V	V	-	-	NT
White-shouldered Ibis	Pseudibis davisoni	-	-	-	R	CR
Black-faced Spoonbill	Platalea minor	V	-	V	-	EN
Ciconiidae (Storks)						
Storm's Stork	Ciconia Stormi	R	R	R	R	EN
Lesser Adjutant	Leptoptilos javanicus	R	R	R	R	VU
Ardeidae (Herons, Egrets & Bitterns)						
Eurasian Bittern	Botaurus stellaris	V	-	V	-	LC
Yellow Bittern	Ixobrychus sinensis	RM	RM	RM	RM	LC
Schrenck's Bittern	Ixobrychus eurhythmus	M	M	M	M	LC
Cinnamon Bittern	Ixobrychus cinnamomeus	R	R	R	R	LC
Black Bittern	Ixobrychus flavicollis	M	M	M	M	LC
Striated Heron	Butorides striata	RM	RM	RM	RM	LC
Black-crowned Night Heron	Nycticorax nycticorax	RM	RM	RM	RM	LC
Rufous Night Heron	Nycticorax caledonicus	R	-	R	-	LC
Japanese Night Heron	Gorsachius goisagi	V	-	V	-	VU
Malayan Night Heron	Gorsachius melanolophus	M	M	M	M	LC
Chinese Pond Heron	Ardeola bacchus	M	M	M	-	LC
Javan Pond Heron	Ardeola speciosa	R	R	R	R	LC
Grey Heron	Ardea cinerea	M	M	M	M	LC

Common Name	Scientific Name	Sabah	Sarawak	Brunei	Kalimantan	Global Sataus
Purple Heron	*Ardea purpurea*	RM	RM	RM	RM	LC
Great-billed Heron	*Ardea sumatrana*	R	R	R	R	LC
Great Egret	*Ardea alba*	RM	M	M	RM	LC
Intermediate Egret	*Ardea intermedia*	RM	M	M	RM	LC
Cattle Egret	*Ardea ibis*	M	M	M	M	LC
Chinese Egret	*Egretta eulophotes*	M	M	M	M	VU
Little Egret	*Egretta garzetta*	M	M	M	RM	LC
Pacific Reef Egret	*Egretta sacra*	R	R	R	R	LC
Pandionidae (Ospreys)						
Osprey	*Pandion haliaetus*	RM	M	M	RM	LC
Accipitridae (Kites, Hawks & Eagles)						
Black-winged Kite	*Elanus caeruleus*	R	R	R	R	LC
Jerdon's Baza	*Aviceda jerdoni*	R	R	R	R	LC
Oriental Honeybuzzard	*Pernis ruficollis*	M	M	M	M	LC
Sunda Honeybuzzard	*Pernis ptilorhynchus*	R	R	R	R	NE
Crested Serpent-eagle	*Spilornis cheela*	R	R	R	R	LC
Mountain Serpent-eagle	*Spilornis kinabaluensis*	E	E	E	E	NT
Bat Hawk	*Macheiramphus alcinus*	R	R	R	R	LC
Rufous-bellied Eagle	*Lophotriorchis kienerii*	R	R	R	R	NT
Black Eagle	*Ictinaetus malaiensis*	R	R	R	R	LC
Changeable Hawk Eagle	*Nisaetus limnaeetus*	R	R	R	R	NE
Blyth's Hawk Eagle	*Nisaetus alboniger*	R	R	R	R	LC
Wallace's Hawk Eagle	*Nisaetus nanus*	R	R	R	R	VU
White-bellied Fish-eagle	*Icthyophaga leucogaster*	R	R	R	R	LC
Lesser Fish-eagle	*Icthyophaga humilis*	R	R	R	R	NT
Grey-headed Fish-eagle	*Icthyophaga ichthyaetus*	R	R	-	R	NT
Black Kite	*Milvus migrans*	V	V	V	V	LC
Brahminy Kite	*Haliastur indus*	R	R	R	R	LC
Grey-faced Buzzard	*Butastur indicus*	M	M	M	M	LC
Eurasian Buzzard	*Buteo buteo*	-	-	V	V	LC
Eastern Marsh Harrier	*Circus spilonotus*	M	M	M	M	LC
Pied Harrier	*Circus melanoleucos*	M	M	M	M	LC
Hen Harrier	*Circus cyaneus*	V	V	V	V	LC
Eurasian Sparrowhawk	*Accipiter nisus*	-	V	-	-	LC
Chinese Sparrowhawk	*Tachyspiza soloensis*	M	M	M	M	LC
Japanese Sparrowhawk	*Tachyspiza gularis*	M	M	M	M	LC
Besra	*Tachyspiza virgata*	R	R	R	R	LC
Crested Goshawk	*Lophospiza trivirgata*	R	R	R	R	LC
Tytonidae (Barn Owls)						
Eastern Barn Owl	*Tyto javanica*	R	-	R	-	NE
Grass Owl	*Tyto capensis*	R	-	-	R	LC
Oriental Bay Owl	*Phodilus badius*	R	R	R	R	LC
Strigidae (True Owls)						
Sunda Owlet	*Taenioptynx sylvatica*	E	E	E	E	LC
Mantanani Scops Owl	*Otus mantananensis*	R	-	-	-	NT
Collared Scops Owl	*Otus lempiji*	R	R	R	R	LC
Rajah Scops Owl	*Otus brookii*	R	R	-	-	LC
Reddish Scops Owl	*Otus rufescens*	R	R	R	R	NT
Mountain Scops Owl	*Otus spilocephalus*	R	R	-	R	LC
Barred Eagle Owl	*Bubo sumatranus*	R	R	R	R	NT

Common Name	Scientific Name	Sabah	Sarawak	Brunei	Kalimantan	Global Sataus
Buffy Fish Owl	*Bubo ketupu*	R	R	R	R	LC
Short-eared Owl	*Asio flammeus*	V	V	V	-	LC
Sunda Wood Owl	*Strix leptogrammica*	R	R	R	R	LC
Brown Boobook	*Ninox scutulata*	R	R	R	R	LC
Northern Boobook	*Ninox japonica*	M	M	M	M	LC
Trogonidae (Trogons)						
Red-naped Trogon	*Harpactes kasumba*	R	R	R	R	NT
Diard's Trogon	*Harpactes diardii*	R	R	R	R	NT
Cinnamon-rumped Trogon	*Harpactes orrhophaeus*	R	R	R	R	NT
Scarlet-rumped Trogon	*Harpactes duvaucelii*	R	R	R	R	NT
Orange-breasted Trogon	*Harpactes oreskios*	R	R	-	R	LC
Whitehead's Trogon	*Harpactes whiteheadi*	E	E	-	E	NT
Bucerotidae (Hornbills)						
Wreathed Hornbill	*Rhyticeros undulatus*	R	R	R	R	VU
Rhinoceros Hornbill	*Buceros rhinoceros*	R	R	R	R	VU
Helmeted Hornbill	*Rhinoplax vigil*	R	R	R	R	CR
Wrinkled Hornbill	*Rhabdotorrhinus corrugatus*	R	R	R	R	EN
White-crowned Hornbill	*Berenicornis comatus*	R	R	R	R	EN
Bushy-crested Hornbill	*Anorrhinus galeritus*	R	R	R	R	NT
Oriental Pied Hornbill	*Anthracoceros albirostris*	R	R	R	R	LC
Black Hornbill	*Anthracoceros malayanus*	R	R	R	R	VU
Megalaimidae (Asian Barbets)						
Blue-eared Barbet	*Psilopogon australis*	R	R	R	R	LC
Bornean Barbet	*Psilopogon eximius*	E	E	-	E	LC
Gold-whiskered Barbet	*Psilopogon chrysopogon*	R	R	R	R	LC
Red-crowned Barbet	*Psilopogon rafflesii*	R	R	R	R	NT
Red-throated Barbet	*Psilopogon mystacophanos*	R	R	R	R	NT
Mountain Barbet	*Psilopogon monticola*	E	E	-	E	LC
Yellow-crowned Barbet	*Psilopogon henricii*	R	R	R	R	NT
Golden-naped Barbet	*Psilopogon pulcherrimus*	E	E	-	E	LC
Bornean Brown Barbet	*Caloramphus fuliginosus*	E	E	E	E	LC
Indicatoridae (Honeyguides)						
Sunda Honeyguide	*Indicator archipelagicus*	R	R	R	R	NT
Picidae (Woodpeckers)						
Speckled Piculet	*Picumnus innominatus*	R	-	-	R	LC
Rufous Piculet	*Sasia abnormis*	R	R	R	R	LC
Grey-and-buff Woodpecker	*Hemicircus concretus*	R	R	R	R	LC
Buff-rumped Woodpecker	*Meiglyptes tristis*	R	R	R	R	EN
Buff-necked Woodpecker	*Meiglyptes tukki*	R	R	R	R	NT
Orange-backed Woodpecker	*Chrysocolaptes validus*	R	R	R	R	LC
Greater Flameback	*Chrysocolaptes guttacristatus*	R	-	-	R	LC
Olive-backed Woodpecker	*Chloropicoides rafflesii*	R	R	R	R	NT
Common Flameback	*Dinopium javanense*	R	R	R	R	LC
Rufous Woodpecker	*Micropternus brachyurus*	R	R	R	R	LC
Banded Yellownape	*Chrysophlegma miniaceum*	R	R	R	R	LC
Checker-throated Yellownape	*Chrysophlegma mentale*	R	R	R	R	NT
Crimson-winged Woodpecker	*Picus puniceus*	R	R	R	R	LC
Maroon Woodpecker	*Blythipicus rubiginosus*	R	R	R	R	LC
Great Slaty Woodpecker	*Dryocopus pulverulentus*	R	R	R	R	VU
White-bellied Woodpecker	*Dryocopus javensis*	R	R	R	R	LC

Common Name	Scientific Name	Sabah	Sarawak	Brunei	Kalimantan	Global Sataus
Sunda Pygmy-woodpecker	*Picoides moluccensis*	R	R	R	R	LC
Grey-capped Pygmy-woodpecker	*Picoides canicapillus*	R	R	R	R	LC
Alcedinidae (Kingfishers)						
Rufous-collared Kingfisher	*Actenoides concretus*	R	R	R	R	NT
Banded Kingfisher	*Lacedo pulchella*	R	R	R	R	LC
Stork-billed Kingfisher	*Pelargopsis capensis*	R	R	R	R	LC
Ruddy Kingfisher	*Halcyon coromanda*	R	R	R	R	LC
White-breasted Kingfisher	*Halcyon smyrnensis*	-	-	-	V	LC
Black-capped Kingfisher	*Halcyon pileata*	M	M	M	M	VU
Collared Kingfisher	*Todiramphus chloris*	R	R	R	R	LC
Sacred Kingfisher	*Todiramphus sanctus*	M	M	M	M	LC
Rufous-backed Dwarf-kingfisher	*Ceyx rufidorsa*	R	R	R	R	LC
Blue-banded Kingfisher	*Alcedo euryzona*	R	R	R	R	CR
Blue-eared Kingfisher	*Alcedo meninting*	R	R	R	R	LC
Common Kingfisher	*Alcedo atthis*	M	M	M	M	LC
Meropidae (Bee-eaters)						
Red-bearded Bee-eater	*Nyctyornis amictus*	R	R	R	R	LC
Blue-tailed Bee-eater	*Merops philippinus*	M	M	-	M	LC
Rainbow Bee-eater	*Merops ornatus*	M	-	V	V	LC
Blue-throated Bee-eater	*Merops viridis*	R	R	R	R	LC
Coraciidae (Rollers)						
Common Dollarbird	*Eurystomus orientalis*	R	R	R	R	LC
Upupidae (Hoopoes)						
Hoopoe	*Upupa epops*	V	V	V	-	LC
Falconidae (Falcons)						
Eurasian Kestrel	*Falco tinnunculus*	V	V	V	V	LC
Indonesian Kestrel	*Falco moluccensis*	-	-	-	V	LC
Oriental Hobby	*Falco severus*	V	-	V	V	LC
Eurasian Hobby	*Falco subbuteo*	-	-	V	V	LC
Peregrine Falcon	*Falco peregrinus*	RM	RM	M	M	LC
Black-thighed Falconet	*Microhierax fringillarius*	R	R	R	R	LC
White-fronted Falconet	*Microhierax latifrons*	E	E	E	E	NT
Psittacidae (Parrots)						
Blue-rumped Parrot	*Psittinus cyanurus*	R	R	R	R	NT
Blue-naped Parrot	*Tanygnathus lucionensis*	R	R	-	R	NT
Red-breasted Parakeet	*Psittacula alexandri*	-	-	-	R	NT
Long-tailed Parakeet	*Psittacula longicauda*	R	R	R	R	VU
Blue-crowned Hanging Parrot	*Loriculus galgulus*	R	R	R	R	LC
Calyptomenidae (African & Green Broadbills)						
Green Broadbill	*Calyptomena viridis*	R	R	R	R	NT
Hose's Broadbill	*Calyptomena hosii*	E	E	-	E	NT
Whitehead's Broadbill	*Calyptomena whiteheadi*	E	E	-	E	LC
Eurylaimidae (Asian Broadbills)						
Black-and-red Broadbill	*Cymbirhynchus macrorhynchos*	R	R	R	R	LC
Long-tailed Broadbill	*Psarisomus dalhousiae*	R	R	-	R	LC
Banded Broadbill	*Eurylaimus javanicus*	R	R	R	R	NT
Black-and-yellow Broadbill	*Eurylaimus ochromalus*	R	R	R	R	NT
Dusky Broadbill	*Corydon sumatranus*	R	R	R	R	LC
Pittidae (Pittas)						
Giant Pitta	*Hydrornis caeruleus*	R	R	R	R	NT

Common Name	Scientific Name	Sabah	Sarawak	Brunei	Kalimantan	Global Sataus
Bornean Banded Pitta	*Hydrornis schwaneri*	E	E	E	E	LC
Blue-headed Pitta	*Hydrornis baudii*	E	E	E	E	VU
Blue-banded Pitta	*Erythropitta arquata*	E	E	-	E	LC
Garnet Pitta	*Erythropitta granatina*	-	R	R	R	NT
Black-crowned Pitta	*Erythropitta ussheri*	E	-	-	-	LC
Blue-winged Pitta	*Pitta moluccensis*	M	M	M	M	LC
Fairy Pitta	*Pitta nympha*	M	M	M	M	VU
Asian Hooded Pitta	*Pitta sordida*	R	R	R	R	LC
Pardalotidae (Parladotes)						
Golden-bellied Gerygone	*Gerygone sulphurea*	R	R	R	R	LC
Vireonidae (Vireos)						
Blyth's Shrike-vireo	*Pteruthius aeralatus*	R	R	-	R	LC
Erpornis	*Erpornis zantholeuca*	R	R	R	R	LC
Oriolidae (Orioles)						
Black-naped Oriole	*Oriolus chinensis*	?R	?R	?R	?R	LC
Black-hooded Oriole	*Oriolus xanthornus*	R	-	-	R	LC
Black Oriole	*Oriolus hosii*	-	E	-	E	NT
Black-and-crimson Oriole	*Oriolus cruentus*	R	R	-	R	DD
Dark-throated Oriole	*Oriolus xanthonotus*	R	R	R	R	NT
Pachycephalidae (Whistlers & Allies)						
Mangrove Whistler	*Pachycephala cinerea*	R	R	R	R	LC
White-vented Whistler	*Pachycephala homeyeri*	R	-	-	-	LC
Bornean Whistler	*Pachycephala hypoxantha*	E	E	-	E	LC
Vangidae (Vangas & Allies)						
Bar-winged Flycatcher-shrike	*Hemipus picatus*	R	R	R	R	LC
Black-winged Flycatcher-shrike	*Hemipus hirundinaceus*	R	R	R	R	LC
Large Woodshrike	*Tephrodornis virgatus*	R	R	R	R	LC
Rufous-winged Philentoma	*Philentoma pyrhoptera*	R	R	R	R	LC
Maroon-breasted Philentoma	*Philentoma velata*	R	R	R	R	NT
Pityriaseidae (Bristleheads)						
Bristlehead	*Pityriasis gymnocephala*	E	E	E	E	VU
Aegithinidae (Ioras)						
Common Iora	*Aegithina tiphia*	R	R	R	R	LC
Green Iora	*Aegithina viridissima*	R	R	R	R	NT
Artamidae (Woodswallows & Butcherbirds)						
White-breasted Woodswallow	*Artamus leucorynchus*	R	R	R	R	LC
Campephagidae (Cuckooshrikes & Allies)						
Roving Cuckooshrike	*Coracina sumatrensis*	R	R	R	R	NE
Sunda Cuckooshrike	*Coracina larvata*	R	R	-	R	LC
Lesser Cicadabird	*Lalage fimbriata*	R	R	R	R	LC
Pied Triller	*Lalage nigra*	R	R	R	R	LC
Ashy Minivet	*Pericrocotus divaricatus*	M	M	-	M	LC
Scarlet Minivet	*Pericrocotus flammeus*	R	R	R	R	LC
Grey-chinned Minivet	*Pericrocotus solaris*	R	R	R	R	LC
Small Minivet	*Pericrocotus cinnamomeus*	-	-	-	V	LC
Fiery Minivet	*Pericrocotus igneus*	R	R	R	R	NT
Rhipiduridae (Fantails & Allies)						
Spotted Fantail	*Rhipidura perlata*	R	R	R	R	LC
White-throated Fantail	*Rhipidura albicollis*	R	R	R	R	LC
Sunda Pied Fantail	*Rhipidura javanica*	R	R	R	R	LC

Common Name	Scientific Name	Sabah	Sarawak	Brunei	Kalimantan	Global Sataus
Dicruridae (Drongos)						
Black Drongo	*Dicrurus macrocercus*	V	-	-	-	LC
Bronzed Drongo	*Dicrurus aeneus*	R	R	R	R	LC
Crow-billed Drongo	*Dicrurus annectans*	M	M	M	M	LC
Greater Racket-tailed Drongo	*Dicrurus paradiseus*	R	R	R	R	LC
Ashy Drongo	*Dicrurus leucophaeus*	R	R	-	R	LC
Bornean Spangled Drongo	*Dicrurus borneensis*	E	E	E	E	NE
Monarchidae (Monarchs)						
Black-naped Monarch	*Hypothymis azurea*	R	R	R	R	LC
Blyth's Paradise-flycatcher	*Terpsiphone affinis*	R	R	R	R	LC
Japanese Paradise-flycatcher	*Terpsiphone atrocaudata*	V	-	-	-	NT
Laniidae (Shrikes)						
Tiger Shrike	*Lanius tigrinus*	M	M	M	M	LC
Brown Shrike	*Lanius cristatus*	M	M	M	M	LC
Long-tailed Shrike	*Lanius schach*	R	R	-	R	LC
Great Grey Shrike	*Lanius excubitor*	-	-	V	-	LC
Jay Shrike	*Platylophus galericulatus*	R	R	R	R	NT
Corvidae (Crows)						
Bornean Treepie	*Dendrocitta cinerascens*	E	E	E	E	LC
Racquet-tailed Treepie	*Crypsirina temia*	-	-	-	?R	LC
Bornean Black Magpie	*Platysmurus aterrimus*	E	E	E	E	LC
Common Green Magpie	*Cissa chinensis*	R	R	-	R	LC
Bornean Green Magpie	*Cissa jefferyi*	E	E	-	-	LC
House Crow	*Corvus splendens*	R	-	-	-	LC
Large-billed Crow	*Corvus macrorhynchos*	?M, ?R	?M, ?R	-	?M, ?R	LC
Sunda Crow	*Corvus enca*	R	R	R	R	LC
Eupetidae (Rail-babblers)						
Rail-babbler	*Eupetes macrocerus*	R	R	-	R	NT
Stenostiridae (Fairy Flycatchers)						
Grey-headed Canary-flycatcher	*Culicicapa ceylonensis*	R	R	R	R	LC
Paridae (Tits & Chickadees)						
Cinereous Tit	*Parus cinereus*	R	R	-	R	NE
Alaudidae (Larks)						
Australasian Bushlark	*Mirafra javanica*	-	-	-	?R	LC
Eurasian Skylark	*Alauda arvensis*	V	V	-	-	LC
Hirundinidae (Swallows & Martins)						
Sand Martin	*Riparia riparia*	M	M	M	M	LC
Barn Swallow	*Hirundo rustica*	M	M	M	M	LC
Pacific Swallow	*Hirundo javanica*	R	R	R	R	LC
Daurian Swallow	*Cecropis daurica*	M	-	M	M	LC
Asian House-martin	*Delichon dasypus*	V	V	V	V	LC
Pycnonotidae (Bulbuls)						
Sooty-headed Bulbul	*Pycnonotus aurigaster*	-	-	-	?R	LC
Sunda Yellow-vented Bulbul	*Pycnonotus analis*	R	R	R	R	NE
Pale-faced Bulbul	*Pycnonotus leucops*	E	E	-	E	LC
Straw-headed Bulbul	*Pycnonotus zeylanicus*	R	R	R	R	CR
Bornean Bulbul	*Pycnonotus montis*	E	E	E	E	LC
Scaly-breasted Bulbul	*Pycnonotus squamatus*	R	R	R	R	NT
Grey-bellied Bulbul	*Pycnonotus cyaniventris*	R	R	R	R	NT
Olive-winged Bulbul	*Pycnonotus plumosus*	R	R	R	R	LC

Common Name	Scientific Name	Sabah	Sarawak	Brunei	Kalimantan	Global Sataus
Cream-vented Bulbul	*Pycnonotus simplex*	R	R	R	R	LC
Cream-eyed Bulbul	*Pycnonotus pseudosimplex*	E	E	E	E	LC
Asian Red-eyed Bulbul	*Pycnonotus brunneus*	R	R	R	R	LC
Spectacled Bulbul	*Pycnonotus erythropthalmos*	R	R	R	R	LC
Yellow-bellied Bulbul	*Alophoixus phaeocephalus*	R	R	R	R	LC
Grey-cheeked Bulbul	*Alophoixus tephrogenys*	R	R	R	R	VU
Penan Bulbul	*Alophoixus ruficrissus*	E	E	E	E	LC
Black-headed Bulbul	*Microtarsus melanocephalos*	R	R	R	R	NE
Black-and-white Bulbul	*Microtarsus melanoleucos*	R	R	R	R	NT
Puff-backed Bulbul	*Microtarsus eutilotus*	R	R	R	R	NT
Hook-billed Bulbul	*Setornis criniger*	R	R	R	R	VU
Finsch's Bulbul	*Iole finschii*	R	R	R	R	NT
Charlotte's Bulbul	*Iole charlottae*	E	E	E	E	NT
Hairy-backed Bulbul	*Tricholestes criniger*	R	R	R	R	LC
Cinereous Bulbul	*Hemixos cinereus*	R	R	R	R	LC
Streaked Bulbul	*Ixos malaccensis*	R	R	R	R	NT
Timaliidae (Old World Babblers)						
Bold-striped Tit-babbler	*Mixornis bornensis*	R	R	R	R	LC
Fluffy-backed Babbler	*Macronous ptilosus*	R	R	R	R	NT
Rufous-fronted Babbler	*Cyanoderma rufifrons*	R	R	R	R	LC
Bicoloured Babbler	*Cyanoderma bicolor*	E	E	E	E	LC
Sunda Scimitar Babbler	*Pomatorhinus bornensis*	R	R	R	R	NE
Bare-headed Scimitar Babbler	*Melanocichla calva*	E	E	E	-	LC
White-necked Babbler	*Stachyris leucotis*	R	R	R	R	NT
Grey-headed Babbler	*Stachyris poliocephala*	R	R	R	R	LC
Grey-throated Babbler	*Stachyris nigriceps*	R	R	R	R	LC
Chestnut-rumped Babbler	*Stachyris maculata*	R	R	R	R	NT
Black-throated Babbler	*Stachyris nigricollis*	R	R	R	R	NT
Pellorneidae (Ground Babblers)						
Moustached Babbler	*Malacopteron magnirostre*	R	R	R	R	LC
Rufous-crowned Babbler	*Malacopteron magnum*	R	R	R	R	NT
Scaly-crowned Babbler	*Malacopteron cinereum*	R	R	R	R	LC
Grey-breasted Babbler	*Malacopteron albogulare*	R	R	R	R	NT
Sooty-capped Babbler	*Malacopteron affine*	R	R	R	R	NT
Temminck's Babbler	*Pellorneum pyrrogenys*	R	R	-	R	LC
Bornean Swamp Babbler	*Pellorneum macropterum*	E	E	E	E	NE
Ferruginous Babbler	*Pellorneum bicolor*	R	R	R	R	LC
Glissando Babbler	*Pellorneum saturatum*		R	R	R	NE
Leaflitter Babbler	*Pellorneum poliogene*	E	E	E	E	NE
Bornean Black-capped Babbler	*Pellorneum capistratoides*	E	E	E	E	NE
Black-browed Babbler	*Malacocincla perspicillata*	-	-	-	E	DD
Abbott's Babbler	*Malacocincla abbotti*	R	R	-	R	LC
Horsfield's Babbler	*Malacocincla sepiaria*	R	R	R	R	LC
Mountain Wren Babbler	*Malacocincla crassa*	E	E	-	E	LC
Eye-browed Wren Babbler	*Napothera epilepidota*	R	R	R	R	LC
Striped Wren Babbler	*Kenopia striata*	R	R	R	R	NT
Bornean Ground Babbler	*Ptilocichla leucogrammica*	E	E	E	E	VU
Black-throated Wren Babbler	*Turdinus atrigularis*	E	E	E	E	NT
Alcippeidae (Fulvettas)						
Sunda Fulvetta	*Alcippe brunneicauda*	R	R	R	R	NT

Common Name	Scientific Name	Sabah	Sarawak	Brunei	Kalimantan	Global Sataus
Leiothrichidae (Laughingthrushes)						
Sunda Laughingthrush	Garrulax palliatus	R	R	R	R	NT
Chestnut-hooded Laughingthrush	Garrulax treacheri	E	E	E	E	LC
Zosteropidae (White-eyes)						
Chestnut-crested Yuhina	Staphida everetti	E	E	E	E	LC
Pygmy Heleia	Apalopteron squamifrons	E	E	-	E	LC
Mountain Black-eye	Zosterops emiliae	E	E	-	E	LC
Swinhoe's White-eye	Zosterops simplex	R	R	R	R	LC
Hume's White-eye	Zosterops auriventer	R	R	R	R	LC
Black-capped White-eye	Zosterops atricapilla	R	R	R	R	LC
Meratus White-eye	Zosperops sp.	-	-	-	E	NE
Lemon-bellied White-eye	Zosterops chloris	-	-	R	R	LC
Javan White-eye	Zosterops flavus	-	R	-	R	EN
Phylloscopidae (Leaf Warblers & Allies)						
Yellow-browed Warbler	Phylloscopus inornatus	-	V	-	-	LC
Two-barred Warbler	Phylloscopus plumbeitarsus	V	-	-	-	LC
Arctic Warbler	Phylloscopus borealis	M	M	M	M	LC
Japanese Leaf Warbler	Seicercus xanthodryas	M	M	M	M	LC
Kamchatka Leaf Warbler	Seicercus examinandus	V	-	-	-	LC
Dusky Warbler	Phylloscopus fuscatus	V	-	-	-	LC
Willow warbler	Phylloscopus trochilus	V	-	-	-	LC
Mountain Leaf Warbler	Phylloscopus trivirgatus	R	R	-	R	LC
Sunda Warbler	Phylloscopus grammiceps	R	R	-	R	LC
Cettidae (Bush Warblers)						
Bornean Stubtail	Urosphena whiteheadi	E	E	-	E	LC
Yellow-bellied Warbler	Abroscopus superciliaris	R	R	R	R	LC
Sunda Bush Warbler	Horornis vulcanius	R	R	-	R	NE
Manchurian Bush Warbler	Horornis canturians	V	-	-	-	LC
Mountain Leaftoiler	Phyllergates cucullatus	R	R	R	R	LC
Acrocephalidae (Reed Warblers)						
Oriental Reed Warbler	Acrocephalus orientalis	M	M	M	M	LC
Australasian Reed Warbler	Acrocephalus australis	-	-	R	R	LC
Black-browed Reed Warbler	Acrocephalus bistrigiceps	V	-	-	-	
Locustellidae (Grassbirds)						
Striated Grassbird	Megalurus palustris	R	R	R	R	LC
Lanceolated Warbler	Locustella lanceolata	M	M	-	-	LC
Pallas's Grasshopper Warbler	Locustella certhiola	M	M	M	M	LC
Middendorf's Grasshopper Warbler	Locustella ochotensis	M	M	M	M	LC
Friendly Grasshopper Warbler	Locustella accentor	E	-	-	-	LC
Cisticolidae (Cisticolas & Allies)						
Dark-necked Tailorbird	Orthotomus atrogularis	R	R	R	R	LC
Ashy Tailorbird	Orthotomus ruficeps	R	R	R	R	LC
Rufous-tailed Tailorbird	Orthotomus sericeus	R	R	R	R	LC
Bar-winged Prinia	Prinia familiaris	-	-	-	R	NT
Yellow-bellied Prinia	Prinia flaviventris	R	R	R	R	LC
Golden-headed Cisticola	Cisticola exilis	-	-	-	?R	LC
Sittidae (Nuthatches)						
Velvet-fronted Nuthatch	Sitta frontalis	R	R	R	R	LC
Sturnidae (Starlings)						
Asian Glossy Starling	Aplonis panayensis	R	R	R	R	LC

Common Name	Scientific Name	Sabah	Sarawak	Brunei	Kalimantan	Global Sataus
Grosbeak Myna	Scissirostrum dubium	-	-	-	R	LC
Common Hill Myna	Gracula religiosa	R	R	R	R	LC
Common Myna	Acridotheres tristis	R	R	R	R	LC
Crested Myna	Acridotheres cristatellus	R	-	R	R	LC
Javan Myna	Acridotheres javanicus	R	R	R	R	VU
Makassar Myna	Acridotheres cinereus	R	-	-	-	VU
Red-billed Starling	Spodiopsar sericeus	V	-	-	-	LC
White-shouldered Starling	Sturnia sinensis	V	V	V	V	LC
Daurian Starling	Agropsar sturninus	V	V	V	-	LC
Chestnut-cheeked Starling	Agropsar philippensis	M	M	M	M	LC
Rosy Starling	Pastor roseus	V	-	-	-	LC
Eurasian Starling	Sturnus vulgaris	V	-	V	-	LC
Turdidae (Thrushes)						
Everett's Thrush	Zoothera everetti	E	E	-	-	NT
White's Thrush	Zoothera aurea	V	-	-	-	LC
Chestnut-capped Thrush	Geokichla interpres	R	R	R	R	EN
Orange-headed Thrush	Geokichla citrina	R	-	-	R	LC
Siberian Thrush	Geokichla sibirica	V	V	V	-	LC
Eyebrowed Thrush	Turdus obscurus	M	M	M	-	LC
Japanese Thrush	Turdus cardis	V	-	-	-	LC
Island Thrush	Turdus poliocephalus	R	-	-	-	LC
Fruit-hunter	Chlamydochaera jefferyi	E	E	-	E	LC
Muscicapidae (Old World Flycatchers)						
Oriental Magpie-robin	Copsychus saularis	R	R	R	R	LC
Rufous-tailed Shama	Copsychus pyrropygus	R	R	R	R	NT
White-crowned Shama	Copsychus stricklandii	E	-	-	E	NE
Maratua Shama	Copsychus barbouri	-	-	-	E	NE
White-rumped Shama	Copsychus malabaricus	R	R	R	R	LC
Ferruginous Flycatcher	Muscicapa ferruginea	M	M	-	-	LC
Asian Brown Flycatcher	Muscicapa dauurica	M	M	M	M	LC
Umber Flycatcher	Muscicapa umbrosa	R	R	R	R	NE
Grey-streaked Flycatcher	Muscicapa griseisticta	V	V	-	V	LC
Dark-sided Flycatcher	Muscicapa sibirica	M	M	M	M	LC
Fulvous-chested Jungle-flycatcher	Cyornis olivaceus	R	-	R	R	LC
Grey-chested Jungle-flycatcher	Cyornis umbratilis	R	R	R	R	NT
Brown-chested Jungle-flycatcher	Cyornis brunneatus	-	-	V	-	VU
Crocker Jungle-flycatcher	Cyornis ruficrissa	E	E	E	E	NE
Dayak Jungle-flycatcher	Cyornis montanus	E	E	E	E	NE
Meratus Jungle-flycatcher	Cyornis sp.	-	-	-	E	NE
Sunda Jungle-flycatcher	Cyornis caerulatus	R	R	R	R	VU
Malaysian Jungle-flycatcher	Cyornis turcosus	R	R	R	R	NT
Bornean Jungle-flycatcher	Cyornis superbus	E	E	E	E	LC
Mangrove Jungle-flycatcher	Cyornis rufigastra	R	R	R	R	LC
Pale Blue Jungle-flycatcher	Cyornis unicolor	R	R	R	R	LC
White-tailed Flycatcher	Cyornis concretus	R	R	R	R	LC
Blue-and-white Flycatcher	Cyanoptila cyanomelana	M	M	M	M	LC
Zappey's Flycatcher	Cyanoptila cumatilis	M	-	-	M	NT
Indigo Warbling-flycatcher	Eumyias indigo	R	R	R	R	LC
Verditer Warbling-flycatcher	Eumyias thalassinus	R	R	R	R	LC
Bornean Shade-dweller	Vauriella gularis	E	E	-	E	LC

Common Name	Scientific Name	Sabah	Sarawak	Brunei	Kalimantan	Global Status
Bornean Shortwing	Brachypteryx erythrogyna	E	E	-	E	LC
Siberian Blue Robin	Larvivora cyane	M	M	M	M	LC
Siberian Rubythroat	Calliope calliope	V	-	V	-	LC
Siberian Bluetail	Tarsiger cyanurus	V	-	-	-	LC
Chestnut-naped Forktail	Enicurus ruficapillus	R	R	R	R	NT
Bornean Forktail	Enicurus borneensis	E	E	-	E	NE
Malayan Forktail	Enicurus frontalis	R	R	-	R	NE
Bornean Whistling-thrush	Myophonus borneensis	E	E	E	E	LC
Blue Rock-thrush	Monticola solitarius	M	M	-	M	LC
White-throated Rock-thrush	Monticola gularis	-	V	-	-	LC
Northern Wheatear	Oenanthe oenanthe	V	V	-	-	LC
Stejneger's Stonechat	Saxicola stejnegeri	V	V	V	-	NE
Pied Bushchat	Saxicola caprata	V	-	V	-	LC
Taiga Flycatcher	Ficedula albicilla	M	M	M	-	LC
Yellow-rumped Flycatcher	Ficedula zanthopygia	V	-	V	V	LC
Narcissus Flycatcher	Ficedula narcissina	M	M	M	M	LC
Green-backed Flycatcher	Ficedula elisae	V	-	-	-	LC
Mugimaki Flycatcher	Ficedula mugimaki	M	M	M	M	LC
Little Pied Flycatcher	Ficedula westermanni	R	R	-	R	LC
Snowy-browed Flycatcher	Ficedula hyperythra	R	R	-	R	LC
Rufous-chested Flycatcher	Ficedula dumetoria	R	R	R	R	LC
Pygmy Flycatcher	Ficedula hodgsoni	R	R	-	R	LC
Irenidae (Fairy-bluebirds)						
Asian Fairy-bluebird	Irena puella	R	R	R	R	LC
Chloropseidae (Leafbirds)						
Lesser Green Leafbird	Chloropsis cyanopogon	R	R	R	R	NT
Greater Green Leafbird	Chloropsis sonnerati	R	R	R	R	EN
Blue-winged Leafbird	Chloropsis moluccensis	R	R	R	R	LC
Bornean Leafbird	Chloropsis kinabaluensis	E	E	E	E	LC
Dicaeidae (Flowerpeckers)						
Yellow-breasted Flowerpecker	Prionochilus maculatus	R	R	R	R	LC
Scarlet-breasted Flowerpecker	Prionochilus thoracicus	R	R	R	R	NT
Crimson-breasted Flowerpecker	Prionochilus percussus	R	R	R	R	LC
Yellow-rumped Flowerpecker	Prionochilus xanthopygius	E	E	E	E	LC
Yellow-vented Flowerpecker	Pachyglossa chrysorrhea	R	R	R	R	LC
Brown-backed Flowerpecker	Pachyglossa everetti	R	R	R	R	NT
Modest Flowerpecker	Pachyglossa modesta	R	R	-	R	NT
Spectacled Flowerpecker	Dicaeum dayakorum	E	E	E	E	DD
Orange-bellied Flowerpecker	Dicaeum trigonostigma	R	R	R	R	LC
Plain Flowerpecker	Dicaeum minullum	R	R	R	R	LC
Bornean Flowerpecker	Dicaeum monticolum	E	E	-	E	LC
Scarlet-backed Flowerpecker	Dicaeum cruentatum	R	R	R	R	LC
Scarlet-headed Flowerpecker	Dicaeum trochileum	-	-	-	R	LC
Nectariniidae (Sunbirds & Spiderhunters)						
Ornate Sunbird	Cinnyris ornatus	R	R	R	R	LC
Copper-throated Sunbird	Leptocoma calcostetha	R	R	R	R	LC
Van Hasselt's Sunbird	Leptocoma brasiliana	R	R	R	R	LC
Purple-throated Sunbird	Leptocoma sperata	-	-	-	R	LC
Brown-throated Sunbird	Anthreptes malacensis	R	R	R	R	LC
Red-throated Sunbird	Anthreptes rhodolaemus	R	R	R	R	NT

Common Name	Scientific Name	Sabah	Sarawak	Brunei	Kalimantan	Global Status
Plain Sunbird	*Anthreptes simplex*	R	R	R	R	LC
Crimson Sunbird	*Aethopyga siparaja*	R	R	R	R	LC
Temminck's Sunbird	*Aethopyga temminckii*	R	R	R	R	LC
Ruby-cheeked Sunbird	*Chalcoparia singalensis*	R	R	R	R	LC
Bornean Spiderhunter	*Arachnothera everetti*	E	E	E	E	NE
Grey-breasted Spiderhunter	*Arachnothera modesta*	-	R	R	R	LC
Whitehead's Spiderhunter	*Arachnothera juliae*	E	E	-	E	LC
Spectacled Spiderhunter	*Arachnothera flavigaster*	R	R	R	R	LC
Yellow-eared Spiderhunter	*Arachnothera chrysogenys*	R	R	R	R	LC
Little Spiderhunter	*Arachnothera longirostra*	R	R	R	R	LC
Thick-billed Spiderhunter	*Arachnothera crassirostris*	R	R	R	R	LC
Long-billed Spiderhunter	*Arachnothera robusta*	R	R	R	R	LC
Purple-naped Spiderhunter	*Arachnothera hypogrammica*	R	R	R	R	LC
Ploceidae (Weaverbirds)						
Streaked Weaver	*Ploceus manyar*	-	-	-	R	LC
Baya Weaver	*Ploceus philippinus*	R	R	-	-	LC
Estrildidae (Estrildid Finches)						
Red Avadavat	*Amandava amandava*	R	-	R	R	LC
Pin-tailed Parrotfinch	*Erythrura prasina*	R	R	R	R	LC
Tawny-breasted Parrotfinch	*Erythrura hyperythra*	R	R	-	R	LC
Scaly-breasted Munia	*Lonchura punctulata*	R	R	R	R	LC
Javan Munia	*Lonchura leucogastroides*	-	-	-	R	LC
White-bellied Munia	*Lonchura leucogastra*	R	R	R	R	LC
Dusky Munia	*Lonchura fuscans*	E	E	E	E	LC
Black-headed Munia	*Lonchura atricapilla*	R	R	R	R	LC
Java Sparrow	*Lonchura oryzivora*	R	R	R	R	EN
Passeridae (Sparrows)						
Eurasian Tree Sparrow	*Passer montanus*	R	R	R	R	LC
Motacillidae (Wagtails & Pipits)						
Forest Wagtail	*Dendronanthus indicus*	M	M	M	-	LC
Grey Wagtail	*Motacilla cinerea*	M	M	M	M	LC
Eastern Yellow Wagtail	*Motacilla tschutschensis*	M	M	M	M	LC
White Wagtail	*Motacilla alba*	M	M	M	-	LC
Olive-backed Pipit	*Anthus hodgsoni*	M	M	M	-	LC
Red-throated Pipit	*Anthus cervinus*	M	M	M	M	LC
Pechora Pipit	*Anthus gustavi*	M	M	M	-	LC
Paddyfield Pipit	*Anthus rufulus*	R	R	R	R	LC
Richard's Pipit	*Anthus richardi*	M	?M	?M	?M	LC
Emberizidae (Buntings)						
Little Bunting	*Emberiza pusilla*	V	V	-	-	LC
Yellow-breasted Bunting	*Emberiza aureola*	V	V	V	-	CR
Black-headed Bunting	*Emberiza melanocephala*	V	-	V	-	LC

FURTHER READING

Davison, G.W.H. and Yeap, C.A. (2018). *A Naturalist's Guide to the Birds of Malaysia including Sabah and Sarawak.* 3rd edn. John Beaufoy Publishing Ltd.

Eaton, J.A., van Balen, B., Brickle, N.W. & Rheindt, F.E. (2021). *Birds of the Indonesian Archipelago.* Greater Sundas and Wallacea. Lynx Edicions. Barcelona.

Lim, K. S., Yong, D. L., Lim, K. C. & Gardner, (2020). *A Field Guide to the Birds of Malaysia & Singapore.* John Beaufoy Publishing Ltd.

D. MacKinnon, J. and Phillipps, K. (1993). *A Field Guide to the Birds of Borneo, Sumatra, Java and Bali.* Oxford University Press Inc.

Mann, C.F. (2008). *The Birds of Borneo: an Annotated Checklist.* British Ornithologists' Union.

Message, S. and Taylor, D. (2005). *Waders of Europe, Asia, and North America.* Christopher Helm.

Myers, S. (2016) *Birds of Borneo, Sabah, Sarawak, Brunei and Kalimantan.* Christopher Helm.

Phillipps, Q. and Phillipps, K. (2016). *Phillipps' Field Guide to the Birds of Borneo.* 3rd edn. John Beaufoy Publishing Ltd.

Sheldon, F.H., Moyle, R.G. and Kennard, J. (2001). *Ornithology of Sabah: History, Gazetteer, Annotated Checklist, and Bibliography.* American Ornithologists' Union.

Smythies, B.E. (1999). *The Birds of Borneo.* 4th edn. Natural History Publications (Borneo) Sdn. Bhd. and the Sabah Society.

USEFUL RESOURCES

Borneo Bird Images
http://www.borneobirdimages.com

Sandakan Borneo Bird Club
http://borneobirdclub.blogspot.com

Malaysian Nature Society – Kuching Branch
http://mnskuching.blogspot.com

Birds-Indonesia (Burung Nusantara)
http://burung-nusantara.org

Indonesian Ornithologists' Union
http://kukila2004.wordpress.com/kukila

Oriental Bird Images
https://www.macaulaylibrary.org/oriental-bird-images

Oriental Bird Club
www.orientalbirdclub.org

eBird
https://ebird.org/home

■ INDEX ■